THE HANDY BOOK
To
ENGLISH GENEALOGY

Third Edition

By Rachael Melle

D1563310

HERITAGE BOOKS, INC.

Third Edition – revised and expanded

Formerly entitled
A Practical Guide for the Genealogist in England

Published 1990 By

Heritage Books, Inc.
1540-E Pointer Ridge Place, Bowie, MD 20716

ISBN 1-55613-359-6

This book is dedicated to the memory
of my mother, Betty Butler, 1916–1984

ACKNOWLEDGEMENTS

I am indebted to many kind-hearted and patient people for their help and encouragement in the writing and research for this new edition, not least to my editor, Karen Ackermann, and the staff at Heritage Books. My husband, Robert, has been very patient and helpful, as have my sisters, Ruth Dipple and Tess Shirley, who have done much legwork for me on the other side of the Atlantic. I would like to thank E. Joan Miller for her encouragement and willingness to listen to my problems.

Among the many people and institutions who answered questions for me were Colin Johnson of the Bath Record Office, Peter Durrant of the Berkshire Record Office, H.A. Hanley of the Buckinghamshire Record Office, Michael Farrar of the Cambridgeshire Record Office, R.G. Burley of the Bristol City Record Office, D.H. Tyrrell of the Cleveland Record Office, H.M. Bidwell of the Cheshire Record Office, Colin Edwards of the Cornwall Record Office, D.M. Bowcock of the Cumbria Record Office, J.G. Evans of the Derbyshire Record Office, Elizabeth A. Stuart of the West Devon Record Office, M.M. Rowe of the Devon Record Office (Exeter). Miss M.S. McCollum of the Department of Paleography and Diplomatic, University of Durham; J. Butler of the Durham County Record Office, Janet Smith of the Essex Record Office, David Smith of the Gloucestershire Record Office, Rosemary Dunhill of the Hampshire Record Office, Sue Hubbard of the Hereford branch of the Hereford and Worcester Record Office, Peter Walne of the Hertfordshire Record Office, S. Woolgar of the Southampton City Record Office, V. Quarl of the Portsmouth City Record Office, J. Wilson of the South Humberside Area Record Office, K.W. Holt of the Humberside Record Office, J. Sanders of the Huntingdon County Record Office, Anne Whateley of the Canterbury Cathedral Archives and Library, K. Hall and Jacqui Crosby of the Lancashire Record Office, Janet Smith of the Liverpool City Record Office, J. Broughton of the Leicestershire Record Office, G.A. Knight of the Lincolnshire Record Office, C.M. Clubb of the City of London Record Office James Sewell of the Corporation of London Record Office, Rachel Watson of the Northamptonshire Record Office, Paul Rutledge of the Norfolk Record Office, Annette M. Burton of the Northumberland Record Office, John Plumb of the Nottinghamshire Archives Office, Linda Shaw of the Department of Manuscripts and Special Collections at the University of Nottingham, Marion T. Halford of the Shropshire Record Office, B.D. Bush of the Somerset Record Office, Josephine Parker of the Suffolk Record Office (Bury branch), David Jones of the Ipswich branch of the same Record Office, Dr. R. B. Robinson of the

Surrey Record Office, Shirley Cooke of the Guildford Muniment Room, Judith A. Brent of the East Sussex Record Office, Patricia Gill of the West Sussex Record Office, B. Jackson of the Tyne and Wear Archives Service, Christine Woodland of the Warwickshire Record Office, J. Hampartumian of the Lichfield Joint Record Office, K. Rogers of the Wiltshire Record Office, Michael Bottomley of the West Yorkshire Record Office, Christopher Neff of the Borthwick Institute, W. J. Conner of the Leeds District Archives, and Mr. A.M. Wherry of the Worcester branch of the Hereford and Worcester Record Office.

In addition, I would like to thank the staffs of the following Record Offices: Bedfordshire, Dorset, the Isle of Wight, Kent, Greater Manchester, Greater London, Oxfordshire, Staffordshire, Kingston-upon-Hull, Sheffield, and North Yorkshire.

ILLUSTRATIONS

Many thanks to Alan Crosby for the beautiful maps in Chapters 3 and 7, and to Mr. A.M. Wherry and Miss Jean Kennedy of the Hereford and Worcester and Norfolk Record Offices for granting permission to reproduce documents in their jurisdiction. In addition, Mr. Wherry generously gave permission to reproduce the maps of Saton Fields, Bromsgrove, found in Chapter 9.

vi

TABLE OF CONTENTS

INTRODUCTION

1980. A cool July day in a remote village in County Durham. My nephew and I spent the morning combing the parish cemetery for Bonds and Turners, ancestors of my husband, with some success on the Bond side. An inquiry in the local grocery shop sent us on a visit to the retired school teacher, the authority on local history. She happened to be living on property once owned by my husband's ancestors and she took us to the gentleman who now owned the Bond Foundry. Interesting, to be sure, but not sensational!

I decided to head for the parish church to ask about examing the burial records. It was a Saturday and a little old lady, Miss Gill, was arranging flowers for a wedding. I asked her about reading the registers and discovered that the priest was in Durham all morning, much to my disappointment. (Moral: Never ask to search registers on a Saturday.)

The lady asked me why I was interested in the parish registers; I told her I was searching for the burial of Abraham Turner. Her face lit up: "Old Abraham Turner! Why yes, when I was a little girl I saw a painting of him in his guards' uniform."

Eureka!

Miss Gill was only too eager to explain that she had regularly, as a young girl, visited Abraham Turner's widow, who was born a Bond. She remembered Mrs. Turner as a china doll lady dressed in black, with white hair and a lace cap. As we came out of the church, Miss Gill showed my nephew and me the house where Mrs. Turner had died. Miss Gill, the daughter of a foreman in the Bond foundry, filled me in on many little details of the family and local history. Even though this was only 'hearsay' evidence, it confirmed other evidence and stimulated my desire to find out more. To see and be there - that is the stuff of living family history.

Two years later, I re-visited Miss Gill with my American husband, great-great-great grandson of Mrs. Turner, so that he could hear Miss Gill's stories himself. We had tea in her drawing room overlooking the Pennines and the family returned to its origins.

Not everyone who visits England in search of their ancestry will be thus rewarded but the prospects of a rich harvest are great. With proper preparation and realistic objectives, you can locate valuable docmentary evidence, acquire a true appreciation of your ancestors' homeland, perhaps contact distant relatives, and certainly make new friends. This manual will attempt to aid you in your preparations and guide you in your searches.

CHAPTER 1

THE BASICS OF ENGLISH GENEALOGY

Genealogy is an increasingly popular hobby, particularly since the Bicentennial celebrations and the publication of *Roots* by Alex Haley. Haley's book has given encouragement to many to trace their family's history even though they may have come from a very humble background. Genealogy now has a mass appeal.

So where do you begin? How will you organize your findings? What do you need to know about English history and geography? In this chapter, I will answer these questions sequentially.

Where To Begin

Genealogical research always goes from the known to the unknown. Your first task is to collect data on yourself: weed out your birth and marriage certificates, and any diaries, letters, or journals you may have kept. Get your children's certificates, too. You are now ready to fill in a Family Group Sheet. See Fig. 1A.

The Family Group Sheet outlines three generations. It is a very important tool as it summarizes at a glance the status of your research. There are spaces for all the basic facts about one couple, including vital statistics on their parents and their children. Note the space for sources at the bottom; this will remind you where your information came from and allows you to double-check at a later time and avoid repetitious research. When you are certain your facts are correct, use ink; if in doubt, use pencil.

Branching Out

Having collected as much about yourself as possible, the next step is to interview (in person or by letter), all your older relatives. This can be difficult if the relative is in ill-health or if some family feud is still smoldering, but you will probably be surprised at how pleased many old folks are in the interest you express in their parents and grandparents.

Take along a tape-recorder if possible; you can then have a fairly natural conversation without seeming like a news reporter. Jot down a list of questions about the subject's family beforehand, but don't feel compelled to stick religiously to the list. Rambling diversions can sometimes lead to important clues. Be aware that there may be a 'skeleton in the closet', which, even after many years, a person is still anxious to hide. Respect their right to privacy. It will make your research more challenging, but it pays to be tactful.

Sometimes the subject may not be aware of the 'skeleton': I could never garner any information from my grandmother about her father-in-law except that he died accidentally in 1911. Later research revealed he was illegitimate – a fact he probably tried to 'forget'.

Family Documents

By the time you have interviewed all possible relatives, you may have also acquired photographs; letters; diaries; certificates of birth, baptism, marriage, and death; plus family bibles, passports, and other family documents. These are important in confirming the oral facts you have heard and can be divided into two categories:

a) Primary sources: written by the people involved or someone who was there. In this category come wills, letters, diaries, birth/marriage certificates, school reports, etc. These documents have greater reliability and credibility than secondary sources because they are first-hand evidence.

b) Secondary sources: written by people who were not eyewitnesses to events referred to in the documents. In this category come obituaries (which often describe events that took place before the informant's own birth), death certificates, family bible records (to some extent), oral history, and newspaper reports. These sources may not be totally reliable and must, if possible, be backed up by a primary source. It is for this reason that genealogists become so involved in searching for birth and marriage certificates and, in an earlier period, church records of baptisms, weddings, and burials.

Documenting Your Findings

Now begin to build a framework of the solid evidence which you have unearthed about your family members. The Pedigree Chart is a map of the family, the sign posts being your direct ancestors. (See Figure 1B.) Begin on the left with #1 (yourself) and work across to the right, filling in as much data as you can. Use pencil if you are not sure of your facts.

Names should always be written thus: John SMITH. If the person was better known by a nickname, write this in parentheses: John (Kipper) SMITH. Dates are always written with the number first, then month abbreviated in capitals, and the year in full. For example, 10 APR 1852.

Pedigree charts are standard amongst genealogists. Later you may find yourself exchanging charts with hitherto unknown relatives, so make sure you follow the standard formula.

After the chart is filled in, your next step is to recheck the information on each generation by gathering the necessary birth, marriage, and death certificates. In the U.S.A., vital statistic registration is a recent innovation; in Illinois, for example, it was not compulsory until 1916. To find out when your state began registration, call the county clerk's office or write to the U.S. Government

Printing Office, Superintendent of Documents, Washington D.C. 20402 and ask for the pamphlet *Where to Write for Birth, Marriage, and Death Certificates.* This lists addresses for each state, record dates, and certificate costs.

Due to the relatively late arrival of vital statistic registration in the United States, you may find it necessary to visit and/or write to churches in the towns in which your ancestors lived. Many churches have records dating from the early nineteenth century, some go back to the eighteenth century. But beware! The records may be written in Latin, German, Polish, Italian, or French, depending on the nationality of the immigrant group which they served. NOTE: Some churches do not allow record searching. In such a case, tact and patience are the researcher's main assets, but it may be necessary to rely on diaries, probate, or guardianship records. You cannot force an institution to show its records.

Wills are an important primary source. Leaving a will has been a much more common practice in the United States than in Britain, due to the fact that more people were property holders in the U.S. Wills and other probate documents can name a large proportion of the deceased's family and include such facts as the deceased's name, residence, date of death, list of property and heirs, testators and executors.

Since photostat copies are relatively inexpensive, a copy of a probate record would be a better 'buy' than a death certificate. (Death certificates usually contain the following facts: deceased's name, date and place of birth, cause and date of death, deceased's parents' names. However, these details vary between states and are likely to be less complete before the twentieth century.)

One major source of secondary information is the cemetery inscription. Although the amount of information varies enormously from stone to stone, the inscription can give you some unexpected leads and it is important to find out if a tombstone exists. Copy the inscription verbatim, even apparent misspellings, and, if possible, take a photograph. (See Chapter 8.) Vandalism and erosion may eliminate this source if you wait too long!

Finding Out Where Your Ancestors Came From

By now you have probably reached back to the nineteenth century or even earlier. From tombstones, letters, or oral tradition you may have a good idea whence your ancestors emigrated and when. How can you confirm this? There are three main sources:

a) Censuses, taken every ten years since 1790 (except 1940), have become more and more detailed. Before 1850, censuses listed only the head of household by name; the rest of the family and servants or slaves were categorized by sex and age, and were not named. The early censuses therefore have a more limited use, especially as country of origin was not noted. Since 1850, the censuses have shown the place of birth (usually given as a state or county); since 1880, the birthplace of parents has been given; on the 1900 and 1910 censuses immigrants had to state their year of arrival. (Unfortunately, the 1890 census was almost completely destroyed by fire.) If you do not know where your ancestors were residing in 1900 or 1910 there is a Soundex (index) on microfilm which can be consulted through interlibrary loan. Libraries can also obtain microfilm of the census this way.

b) Naturalization records were held at county courthouses until the formation of the Immigration and Naturalization Service in 1906. Prior to 1906 information obtained in records was so sketchy as to be worthless genealogically; after that date, however, much fuller statements were required. Thus, after 1906, naturalization papers gave the petitioner's name, address, last address in the country of origin, birthplace, parents' names (including mother's maiden name), port of entry into the U.S., and date of entry. Copies of declarations of intention and petitions for naturalization may be obtained by sending for form N-585 from the Immigration and Naturalization Service, 119 D Street NW, Washington D.C. 20536, and returning it with the appropriate fee.

c) Ships' passenger lists and customs records: provide the most complete information on the immigrant. After 1820, this included name, last residence, age, occupation, port of embarkation, and destination in the United States. Some ports have been fully indexed, 1820-1874. New York (the busiest!) is indexed only for 1820-1846 and 1883-1906. If your ancestor came between 1846 and 1883, you need to know the exact date and name of the vessel - or be prepared to search miles of microfilm! The passenger index microfilms can be consulted at branches of the National Archives, established regionally.

I was fortunate enough to find an ancestor on the New York index, so I filled out form 81 (11-84) for a copy of the complete record from the National Archives, only to be told that the original list had been lost. A great disappointment.

Help! Where In England Did My Ancestors Come From?

Perhaps you can only establish that your family is from England, or perhaps you are more fortunate and have a particular county of origin. How can you establish which town or parish was your ancestor's birthplace? This is another situation akin to searching for a needle in a haystack, but help is at hand, thanks in most part to the Church of Jesus Christ of the Latter Day Saints (the L.D.S. Church). They are microfilming as many parish registers of England as possible and extracting all the names onto a microfiche index known as the International Genealogical Index (IGI). (See Chapter 2.)

Keeping Your Records In Order

Everyone has his or her own system of filing research and it is important that you have one, too. Don't just throw your notes in a folder or box hoping one day to create order out of mayhem. Devise a plan and stick with it. Here is mine; I guarantee it works for me.

For each surname I have a large brown envelope into which go all my notes. Each book or record consulted on that name is recorded

4

on a piece of notepaper with the surname in the upper right-hand corner and the place/call number/date in the left margin. These are also recorded on a Research Index (see Figure 1C), *even if the search was fruitless* and the index pages are numbered. Any correspondence is also kept in order and recorded on a Correspondence Index.

All family group sheets and pedigree charts are in a blue folder, in alphabetical order by head of household. Spare forms are also kept in here. This is really the master index to your complete research. You should be able to quite easily look up details of any individual and the research which led you to him.

Geography Of England

It is my common experience that few Americans know the location of any English city except London - many seem to equate London and England as one and the same! Do not let this be you!

Firstly, familiarize yourself with the counties. In 1974, the boundaries were changed - some counties ceased to exist and new ones were created (see maps). You will need to know if the counties in which you are interested were affected, because each county has a record office (archives), and it would be wasteful of time and money to go to the wrong one.

You will need a detailed map for travel in England. A modern road atlas, such as the AA Road Atlas of Great Britain, available though the British Tourist Authority, is a good start. You may also want to acquire Frank Smith's *Genealogical Gazetteer of England* (1977), which gives information on extinct chapelries, villages, and parishes, as well as thriving ones.

Planning Research Objectives In England

A research trip will be costly and probably of a relatively short duration - there will not be time to waste on wild goose chases. Therefore, the key to a successful expedition is planning.

1) Organize your completed research. Read carefully through your completed work on your English lines, with a notepad at your elbow. As you read, ideas will occur for 'solutions' to the various research 'problems': when was X born?; were Y and Z his parents?; if so, how can it be proven or disproven? For each family, construct a list of ideas to follow up. If you have a particularly sticky or dead-end problem, try to discuss it with a more experienced colleague.

2) Examine your list of ideas and determine which can be followed through in the U.S. Keep in mind the tools available at L.D.S. branch libraries.

3) Exhaust all possibilities. This will pare down your list to research that *cannot* be done in the U.S., e.g.:

-parish registers not microfilmed by the Latter Day Saints program.

-parish registers searched on microfilm which you suspect may have missing pages.

-probate records.

-civil registration.

-miscellaneous records which may be in libraries or County Record Offices. (See Public Record Office Chapter 5.)

-graveyard inscriptions.

-oral interviews.

4) Lay out your research objectives in a logical order. If you need to confirm a suspicion before embarking on a second idea, plan your itinerary accordingly. (It is not always possible to do this, in which case all potentially pertinent data at the second location will have to be noted and then left to a process of elimination by subsequent findings.)

Example: At St. Peter's, Totting, you find the baptism of three John Halls, any of which might be your man. List them all, plus any other Halls, in your notes. At Binghan All Souls you discover a marriage entry that lists "John Hall, labourer of Totting, married Anne Bone, spinster, of this parish" with the groom's father, Zebedee, witnessing with his mark. You can now single out the correct John from your notes at Totting.

5) Write to all the locations (churches, libraries, and record offices) which you plan to visit and make an appointment. Try to describe, as exactly as possible, the records you wish to consult. The purpose of this is two-fold: firstly, to find out if that source actually holds the records you believe it to; secondly, to warn the custodian well in advance so he can have the records ready for you. In writing to parishes, give two alternate dates and enclose two International Reply Coupons (available at all U.S. Post Offices) for reply. (See sample letter below.) Names and addresses of Church of England priests can be found in Crockford's *Clerical Directory*. Most L.D.S. branch libraries hold a copy. A sample letter follows:

1234 Washington Street
Lincoln, Ohio 12345
U.S.A.

Rev. O. B. Smith
The Rectory
Middle Snoring
Gloucestershire, GL3 7NX
England   1 January 1985

Dear Rev. Smith,
        I am conducting research into my family's ancestry and would

like an appointment to read the baptismal registers of Middle Snoring from 1752 to 1812, and the burials from 1806 to 1857. Two possible dates for my visit are July 16th and 17th. Which is most convenient for you? I am enclosing two International Reply Coupons for your use.

Yours, etc.

Record offices only need one date option when you write for an appointment, but many have limited amounts of seating and you may need to have a table or microfilm reader reserved. In addition, the archivist may be able to suggest alternative records to consult, so a brief outline of your research goals would not come amiss. (Don't be too verbose, however, as archivists are already overburdened.) Addresses of County Record Offices can be found in Chapter 6.

Send letters air-mail. Surface mail takes six to eight weeks.

General Preparations For The Visit

Your first major decision is whether to engage a travel agent to plan and book your itinerary for you, or to do it yourself. If you have never travelled abroad before, you may feel strongly tempted to visit a travel agent, discuss your hopes and plans, and sit back, confident that your vacation is in the lap of a professional. There are, however, several considerations to be made.

Make sure that the travel agent you engage is a reputable professional. Personal recommendation by close acquaintances is probably your strongest guide, though an agent's membership in a travel agency association such as the American Society of Travel Agents, or the Association of Retail Travel Agents, is also a good plus. I hope you never experience the same frustration I had when booked on a nonexistent flight to London. The travel agent had failed to relay to me a change of date, causing a 24-hour delay and the necessity of changing flights. Needless to say, I have never since engaged that particular agency!

Be aware, too, that if an agent plans and books a complete itinerary for you (as opposed to merely booking a flight), you will be charged for their professional services, including such items as cablegrams to hotels. You are paying for the agent's expertise and knowledge of the travel scene of the country you are visiting.

Additionally, most smaller European hotels, unlike large American hotel chains, do not pay travel agents a commission and, of course, do not have sales representatives in the United States. Travel agents, quite naturally, will book you into the more expensive 'name' hotels - comfortable, to be sure, but tiringly monotonous the world over. If you do not want this type of vacation, plan your own itinerary.

Self-planning will mean doing a lot of homework, especially in booking your own accommodation. Air fares can be quite a jungle, too. (Even agents cannot keep up with the daily round of gimmicks being meted out by airlines!) A self-planner can feel a sense of achievement and control of his or her time, while saving money on an agent's commission and hotel bills. The following section is therefore dedicated to the self-planner.

1) Airline Reservations. When planning the season for your vacation, bear in mind these points:

-cheapest months on scheduled carriers are October through March (except Christmas) but you are less likely to find a charter flight at that time of year.

-charter flights are usually considerably cheaper than regular or discount coach tickets. Companies will offer a discount incentive to book early, for example, before mid-April.

-regular carriers have hit back with APEX fares; seats must be purchased at least twenty-one days in advance and you must stay at least seven days.

-airline coupons: You may have seen notices in the classified ad sections of *The Wall Street Journal* and other national newspapers advertising airline awards, or airline coupons' for sale at up to seventy percent off the regular first class or economy fare. These programs are based on transferal of frequent-flier awards from their original earner to you via an agency. Though not strictly illegal, airline regulations do forbid transfer of awards and frown upon the activities of these agencies. However, they are almost powerless to trace the transfers and there is definitely a growing trade in coupons. If you have no compunction about using them, you can save a great deal. Booking takes several weeks.

-standbys are offered by the major airlines to compete with the 'no-frills' brigade. Standbys are cheaper than APEX and the voucher can be purchased in advance, but you cannot be sure of a reservation until the day of the flight. Summer season is therefore a less likely time to have standby seats left, as are Christmas and to a lesser extent Easter. To find out if there are seats available you may call the airline you have selected on their toll-free number, rather than camp out at the airport. It is really an efficient system and quite painless as long as your schedule has some flexibility.

2) Booking Accommodations. The prospective traveler can be dazzled by the variety of alternatives available. Go over this section carefully before deciding what you want to do.

-'name' hotels exist in Britain and can be booked through the regular reservations system here in the U.S. Several disadvantages must be mentioned, however. Firstly, to be profitable the large chain hotels are usually situated in a metropolitan area such as London, Birmingham or Glasgow; okay for the conventional tourist but not for the genealogist who wishes to investigate the wilds of Norfolk! Secondly, chain hotels are impersonal and do not reflect local color to such a degree as you night want. Thirdly, they are expensive.

-go-as-you-please tours, are arranged by companies such as Thompson's or British Airways. You select the category of hotel you want and are supplied with vouchers good for a range of hotels up and down the country (usually British 'chains' such as Embassy or Trust House Forte). These are usually less expensive than 'name' hotels, and just as comfortable with private bath and TV in each room. Many are converted from older mansions or homes and have great charm. You are unlikely to find one in an out-of-the-way spot but perhaps you might compromise a little and rent a car out, an option which will be discussed in a later section.

-private hotels and guest houses range in size from a manor house down to a terraced city dwelling. Some have private baths, many do not. Smaller guest houses are usually private homes which offer 'bed and breakfast' in the tourist season. Locally they are known as b & b's.

How can you, a foreigner, distinguish the good from the bad? Write to the regional tourist board of the area in which you are planning to stay (see Appendix C) and ask for a list of approved hotels and guesthouses (establishments which are inspected regularly and meet official guidelines). The list also grades the type of accommodation from deluxe down to good, and will give the price-range and any facilities such as a bar, TV lounge, or baby-sitting service.

You will also find on the list an intriguing variety of places offering b & b - from farmhouses to castles. One of my most enjoyable visits was to Durham, where I had a room in the castle's keep: walls fifteen feet thick, breakfast and a gourmet evening meal in the medieval great hall, and all a stone's throw from the cathedral and city center.

3) How to book accommodations in advance:

-select several places in the same area, in case your first choice is booked.

-write to the proprietor, specifying your dates, the number of people in your party, and how many rooms you will need. Enclose a deposit to the value of the first night's accommodation. This should be a cashier's check for the correct number of dollars plus three extra to cover bank conversion in England.

Summary

At least one year prior to your trip:

-check over your research to date. Plan out carefully the research that needs to be done and follow through as much as possible in the United States. An outline of the genealogical research process follows on the next page:

Collect oral evidence
↓
Collect family documents
↓
Evaluate contents
↙   ↘
File in surname   Seek supporting
folder   primary evidence
↖   ↙
Evaluate contents
↓
Place conclusions on pedigree charts and
family group sheets
↓
Establish new goals

-make an outline of your research plans in England and plan an itinerary around this.

-write for appointments with record offices and clergy.

-write to Regional Tourists Boards for hotel lists and make reservations.

-keep a close check on the airfare situation. Decide which type of fare best suits your needs and book accordingly.

Further Reading

The Genealogical Helper. Logan, Utah: Everton. (Bimonthly magazine.)

Greenwood, Val D. *The Researcher's Guide To American Genealogy*, Baltimore, MD; Genealogical Publishing Co., 1973.

Smith, Frank and David Gardner. *Genealogical Research in England and Wales* (3 vols.) Salt Lake City, Utah: Bookcraft, 1959, 1964, 1976.

Westin, Jean Eddy. *Finding Your Roots*, New York: Ballantine, 1977.

Wright, Norman Edgar. *Building An American Pedigree: a study in genealogy* Provo, Utah; Brigham Young University Press, 1974.

Fig. 1A FAMILY GROUP SHEET

Name and address of researcher:

Husband's name:	Wife's name:
Born - place & date:	Born - place & date:
Married - place & date:	Died - place & date:
Died - place & date:	
Husband's father:	Wife's father:
Born - place & date:	Born - place & date:
Married - place & date:	Married - place & date:
Died - place & date:	Died - place & date:
Husband's mother:	Wife's mother:
Born - place & date:	Born - place & date:
Died - place & date:	Died - place & date:

Other date about husband: religion _____ occupation _____ names of other wives _____

Children

Name	Sex	Date of birth of baptism	Place	Spouse's name & date of marriage	Date of death or burial	Place
1.						
2.						
3.						
4.						
5.						
6.						
7.						
8.						
9.						
10.						
11.						
12.						
13.						

Sources:

Fig. 1B PEDIGREE CHART

Name and address of compiler:

Chart #___

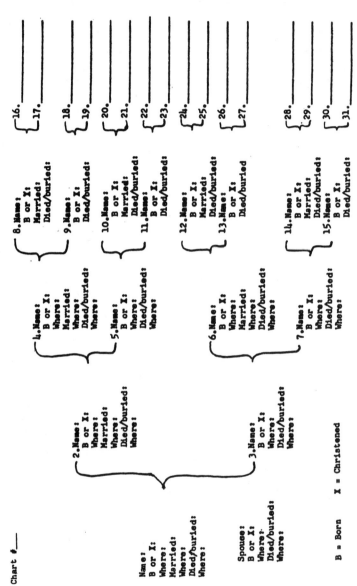

Name:
B or X:
Where:
Married:
Where:
Died/buried:
Where:

Spouse:
B or X:
Where:
Died/buried:
Where:

2. Name:
B or X:
Where:
Married:
Where:
Died/buried:
Where:

3. Name:
B or X:
Where:
Died/buried:
Where:

4. Name:
B or X:
Where:
Married:
Where:
Died/buried:
Where:

5. Name:
B or X:
Where:
Died/buried:
Where:

6. Name:
B or X:
Where:
Married:
Where:
Died/buried:
Where:

7. Name:
B or X:
Where:
Died/buried:
Where:

8. Name:
B or X:
Married:
Died/buried:

9. Name:
B or X:
Died/buried:

10. Name:
B or X:
Married:
Died/buried:

11. Name:
B or X:
Died/buried:

12. Name:
B or X:
Married:
Died/buried:

13. Name:
B or X:
Died/buried:

14. Name:
B or X:
Married:
Died/buried:

15. Name:
B or X:
Died/buried:

16._____
17._____
18._____
19._____
20._____
21._____
22._____
23._____
24._____
25._____
26._____
27._____
28._____
29._____
30._____
31._____

B = Born   X = Christened

Fig. 1C RESEARCH INDEX

Surname of interest: Page:
Name and address of researcher:

Record repository	Call #	Description of source	Results	File #

THE ENGLISH COUNTIES
PRIOR TO 1974

THE ENGLISH COUNTIES
SINCE 1974

CHAPTER 2

ENGLISH GENEALOGICAL RESOURCES IN U.S. LIBRARIES

Perhaps because so many Americans are descendants of English emigrants, English genealogical materials are very well represented in American library collections. In this chapter I shall outline the main collections and indicate how they can be accessed. The largest and best-known collection is that of the L.D.S. Church in Salt Lake City and I shall begin by describing their English materials.

Genealogical Library of the Church of Jesus Christ of the Latter Day Saints

35 North West Temple Street
Salt Lake City, Utah 84150
HOURS: Monday: 7.30 a.m.-6 p.m.; Tuesday-Friday: 7.30 a.m.-10 p.m.; Saturday: 7.30. a.m.-5 p.m.

There are over 1.4 million rolls of microfilmed records available in this library, a good proportion of them relating to England. In addition, there are over 165,000 books: county histories, family histories, printed parish registers, and so on. Trained staff members are on hand to help with research problems and with use of the records. The L.D.S. Church has published a series of research papers dealing with English records in general and probate records county-by-county.

Using the Catalogue
A microfiche catalogue of the Library's holdings is available on each floor of the Library.

Copy services
Only materials that are not under copyright may be photocopied. The current cost is 5 cents from books and 10 cents from microform for each page. Copies can also be obtained by mail for 15 cents and 25 cents respectively. There are copy centers on each of the Library's floors.

Rules of the Library
No food or drink is permitted in the Library. Smoking is not permitted and children under 12 should be kept under control.
Five rolls of microfilm and five books may be used at any one time. The Library has an open-stack system and books should be

returned to the red shelves at the end of the stack where they were found. You should refile microfilm yourself.

You must keep personal belongings with you at all times and if you expect to be away from a microfilm reader for more than 20 minutes, remove your belongings so others can use the machine.

The English Collection
    The L.D.S. Church has had, and continues to have, an extensive program on microfilming English genealogical materials, in cooperation with the British government and the Church of England. Many diocesan records have been filmed, but this depends on the cooperation of the local bishop and priests, and in some areas this has not been forthcoming. Among the main items of interest that have been filmed are:

1) Parish registers: baptismal, marriage, and burial. 'Parish' refers only to the Church of England, but even non-conformists often were married and buried in the Church of England parish.

2) Index to births, marriages, and deaths at the General Registry Office (St. Catherine's House, London) from July 1, 1837. After the appropriate reference has been obtained, the researcher can then apply to St. Catherine's for a copy of the certificate. (See Chapter 7.)

3) Census returns for the whole country, 1841-1881. (The returns for 1891 should be available in 1991).

4) Boyd's Marriage Index, which covers many counties though not all, from 1538 to 1812 or 1837. There are also separate indexes for the following counties: Gloucestershire, Hertfordshire, Oxfordshire, and Rutland (now part of Cambridgeshire).

5) Commercial directories, mainly post-1800.

6) Marriage licenses and bonds, issued by the Church of England since the sixteenth century. About forty-five percent of the estimated total in existence have been filmed.

7) Probate records: A publication of the L.D.S. Church states that "almost all of the pre-1858 probates of England are on microfilm at the Genealogical Library in Salt Lake City."(1)   Indexes to wills, 1857-1957, now at Somerset House in London, are also on microfilm.

8) Non-conformist registers: All registers prior to 1837 were supposed to have been deposited by the minister in charge of them at the Public Record Office in London in 1837. These have been microfilmed.

(1) *Genealogical Research Guide for England*, Genealogical Department of the Church of Jesus Christ of the Latter Day Saints, Series A No. 59, 1983, p. 38.

9) Printed parish registers: Transcribed mainly by county historical, record, and archaeological societies during the nineteenth and early twentieth centuries. Some stand as independent volumes, others figure as part of the journal series of a particular society.

10) Bishop's transcripts: annual copies of the parish registers sent to the local bishop.

According to 1983 figures released by the L.D.S. Church, the Anglican records for each county have been microfilmed in the following proportions:

Bedfordshire: 88%	Lincolnshire: 95%
Berkshire: 73%	London: 95%
Buckinghamshire: 91%	Middlesex: 18%
Cambridgeshire: 74%	Norfolk: 48%
Cheshire: 15%	Northamptonshire: 3%
Cornwall: 87%	Northumberland: 94%
Cumberland: 85%	Nottinghamshire: 85%
Derbyshire: 95%	Oxfordshire: 60%
Devon: 66%	Rutland: 2%
Dorset: 8%	Shropshire: 94%
Durham: 85%	Somerset: 3%
Essex: 33%	Staffordshire: 95%
Gloucestershire: 89%	Suffolk: 90%
Hampshire: 48%	Surrey: 64%
Herefordshire: 90%	Sussex: 49%
Hertfordshire: 81%	Warwickshire: 95%
Huntingdonshire: 60%	Westmoreland: 50%
Kent: 30%	Wiltshire: 18%
Lancashire: 48%	Worcestershire: 97%
Leicestershire: 90%	Yorkshire: 87%(2)

The International Genealogical Index (IGI)

I am constantly amazed, when giving presentations to genealogical societies, by the number of genealogists who have never used the IGI. It is probably the foremost reference tool for English genealogy available in the U.S. today, and it is difficult to imagine how it could be surpassed. Previously known as the Computer File Index (CFI), the IGI is a computerized list of names of individuals in the annals of the Genealogical Library in Salt Lake City. Some are names submitted by members of the L.D.S. Church in proving their ancestry; these pedigrees are properly documented and proven. Other names are extracted from microfilmed records such as civil and parish records. This program of extraction is ongoing and is performed in lieu of missionary service by young women of the church. The coverage of individual English counties is therefore dependent on the initial microfilming program; Worcestershire, for example, will be covered almost entirely, while other counties such as Somerset will not.

(2) Ibid. p. 26

All persons listed on the IGI are deceased. Some fifteenth century references may be found, but most begin with the institution of parish registers in the sixteenth century and really good coverage often begins around 1700. As a rule, names from the late nineteenth and twentieth centuries are not included.

The IGI is published in the form of microfiche, in several thousand sheets. It is divided firstly by country and then by county. The section for England is the largest part of the collection so you should have no trouble locating it! Within the county subdivision, names are arranged alphabetically by surname, Christian name and then chronologically. The following fictitious Example 1 will demonstrate the principle:

John HARBACH - Tom HARBACH/ - M C 17 Jun 1790 Bromsgrove
John HARBACH - Elizabeth Smith - M M 21 Dec 1810 Bromsgrove
John HARBACH - J. HARBACH/Ruth - M C 3 Mar 1812 Tardebigge
Lilah HARBACH - Martha HARBACH - F C 5 Jun 1611 Belbroughton
Martha HARBACH - John PRIDDY - F M 29 Jun 1611 Bromsgrove
Rich HARBECK - Matthew HARBECK - M W 11 Oct 1719 Bromsrove
Peter HARBRIDGE - M B 31 Dec 1660 Stoke Prior

In this example, the three John Harbaches are distinguished by putting the events in which they are mentioned in chronological order. Abbreviations used on the IGI in Column 4 are:

B   burial
C   christening
M   marriage
N   census
W   will

Looking further at the example, we see that variants of the name HARBACH such as HARBECK and HARBRIDGE are included with HARBACH. If you were to look under HARBECK, you would find a cross-reference to HARBACH. This is a very useful aspect of the IGI, as our ancestors were certainly not fussy as to how their surnames were spelled, but do be careful as the compilers of the IGI may not be aware of all the variants - there are real HARBACH family members in the Bromsgrove parish registers who do not show under HARBACH on the IGI because they were recorded under a different variant.

Returning to the above example, let us examine the contents of each column. Column 1 records the name of the ancestor; Column 2 the parents or spouse, depending on the event; Column 5, the date of the event; Column 3, the sex of the person (not always discernible by the Christian name!); Column 4 indicates the event that took place and the date it was recorded; Column 6 has the place of the event, usually a parish. On the actual IGI there are other columns to the right with batch and serial numbers. These can help put you in contact with the church member who originally submitted that name in their ancestry. This could be an important step in finding out what work has already been completed on a particular line.

It is sometimes possible to reconstruct an entire family using information first obtained from the IGI, even if the family moved several times, which poorer families often did. Consider Example 2 below, also fictitious:

James JARVIS - John JARVIS/Maria M C 9 Oct 1846 Cockthorpe
John JARVIS - John JARVIS/Maria BELL M C 1 Dec 1840 Cockthorpe
Mary Ann JARVIS - John JARVIS/Marie F C 10 Mar 1837 Burnham
Matilda JARVIS - John JARVIS F C 27 Jun 1850 Cockthorpe
Samuel JARVIS - John JARVIS/Maria M C 7 Nov 1848 Cockthorpe
William JARVIS - John JARVIS/Maria M C 4 Jun 1838 Burnham

A chronological rearrangement would show the migration pattern of the family and certain members, such as Mary Ann and William, show up who might otherwise be unsuspected. This is an especially pressing problem in a county such as Norfolk, which is composed of hundreds of minute parishes where the agricultural workforce moved frequently. The L.D.S. Church recently instituted a pilot program in which the entire 1988 edition of the IGI has been transferred to computer. Researchers at the Library can use terminals to extract all the children of a particular individual or couple or all references to one name. It does not take much imagination to foresee how this will cut short some complex research problems. In addition, the searcher can bring his own floppy discs, unload the information onto the disc, and take it home for use on his own personal computer!

Pitfalls in using the IGI
The main mistake the researcher tends to make is to use the IGI as a primary source. It is actually only an INDEX and an effort should always be made to locate the original record, be it a baptismal register, will, or census. There are several reasons: the IGI transcriber may have made a mistake or even omitted a reference; the original document may contain much fuller information than the IGI entry, giving details of witnesses, places of residence, and so on. In the case of a baptism, burial registers must be searched to ensure that the infant did not die before reaching maturity - sadly, the odds were stacked against the child until the twentieth century.

In Example 2 above, we see the children of a couple named John and Maria Jarvis. Are they all children of the same couple? Is Maria and Marie the same person? Only further research can tell the answers, but the IGI gives one a good start.

Further Reading
A complete and thorough guide to the L.D.S. Library in Salt Lake City has recently been published: *The Library: A Guide to the L.D.S. Family History Library* by Johni Cerny and Wendy Elliott (Ancestry Publishing Co., Salt Lake City, Utah, 1988). In addition, the L.D.S. Church has published a number of research papers, pamphlets of about fifty pages on specific aspects of genealogy with special reference to the L.D.S. collection. These include *A Genealogical Research Guide for England* (Series A, No. 59, 1983), and *Pre-1858 English Probate Jurisdictions* (Series A, Nos. 7-46), one for each county; and *Population Movements during the Industrial Revolution in*

England and Wales (Series A, No. 51). These are available for purchase at the Library.

Family History Centers: L.D.S. Church

You may have been excited to read of the resources of the L.D.S. Church but wonder when you'll ever have the time to visit Salt Lake City. Not to worry. The L.D.S. Church has established branches of the main library all over the United States, indeed all over the world. They used to be known as Stake Libraries, but have recently been re-designated as Family History Centers. I believe this reflects their function much more accurately to the general public, because they are open to all, regardless of religious affiliation.   There are over 220 Family History Centers in the U.S., each associated with a branch of the L.D.S. Church. They vary greatly in the scope of their facilities and in-house collection. Some will have opened only recently and cannot be expected to have built up much of a reference collection; their staff (who are all volunteer, by the way) may not have the depth of experience that others possess. Other Centers are large and well-established. They may have a fine reference collection, but concentrating on one ethnic group such as Germans or Poles or English. They may also have acquired their own copies of microfilmed records relating to that specific geographical area.

Family History Centers do differ from regular lending libraries, however. The bulk of their collection is in Salt Lake City. Required records can be borrowed from Salt Lake City for up to six months for an extremely reasonable fee which mainly covers postage and handling. The microfilms cannot be taken from the Centers but must be viewed in-house.

How to order a microfilmed record

Nothing could be simpler! Ask the librarian for the Locality Catalogue. This is a microfiche index of all places for which the L.D.S. Library has some type of record. Look under the heading ENGLAND then the name of the county and finally the town or parish in which you are interested. You will find a brief description of records relating to that area and a call number for each item. Fill in a request-slip carefully noting the call number and submit it to the librarian along with the appropriate payment. She will call you or send a postcard notifying you when the film is in. If you cannot make it to the Center during the initial lending period of two weeks, a small sum can be paid to extend the time to six months. Before sending in a request, the librarian will probably check for you that they do not already have that film either permanently or for another patron. Such a check can save you time and money!

Family History Registry

This is another useful tool which should be consulted early on in your research. It is a list, on microfiche, of names being researched by others, together with the names of the researchers and their addresses.

The IGI
Every Family History Center has its own copy of the entire IGI (the latest to date is 1988). Before using, ascertain whether the librarian wants you to re-file your own fiche or leave it in a box for the staff to do.

Micro-film and -fiche readers
Since the bulk of each Family History Center's resources are either on microfilm or microfiche, most of the space tends to be dominated by readers. Fiche readers are particularly easy to operate: switch on the bulb, pull the glass drawer towards you, and insert the fiche upside down; then push in the glass drawer and focus. Microfilm readers tend to come in all shapes and sizes, so if you are in doubt as to how to thread the film, do not hesitate to ask the staff. Much better to ask than to break a film or, worst still, a reader! Don't be intimidated by so much technology – it's there to help. Many readers are also printers, so you can obtain print-outs of the IGI or parish register or census for your records.

Addresses of Family History Centers
An updated list of all Centers is published quarterly giving both mailing address, location, and phone number. Write to the Library in Salt Lake City; see address above.

Newberry Library

60 W. Walton Street
Chicago, IL 60610
TEL: (312) 943-9090
HOURS: Tuesday-Thursday: 11 a.m.-7.30 p.m.; Friday: 11 a.m.-5 p.m.; Saturday: 9 a.m.-5 p.m.

Newberry Library was founded in 1887 from a bequest of Chicago entrepreneur Walter Loomis Newberry, to preserve and collect rare manuscripts, maps, and local and family histories. The library now houses nearly 1.5 million volumes, five million manuscript pages and 60,000 historic maps. It is a non-circulating, closed-stack library which is privately funded. This means that you cannot request Newberry books on inter-library loan nor will you be able to 'browse' through the collection as at most public and university libraries.
Security is a particularly urgent concern at Newberry, since so many rare documents have been spirited away over the years. Readers must complete a form for a registration card and sign in the daily log book at the reception desk. Cloakroom lockers are provided on the first floor west for coats, food, cameras, bags, and so forth. Cases and large handbags are not allowed past the security desk. On leaving the library, security staff inspect any books, portfolios, or smaller bags you are carrying, and your departure time is entered in the log book.

First Floor (Main Entrance)
This is the 'front door' of the library, where you will find the

security desk and cloakroom lockers. To the west there are also restrooms and a visitor's lounge where a sack lunch can be consumed and drinks purchased from a vending machine. A bookstore stands to the right of the main lobby which sells genealogical supplies and texts.

Second Floor
Mounting the main staircase the visitor reaches the general reading room. There is a seating capacity for ninety-two people and each desk is numbered. There is a reference desk strictly for genealogical inquiries and some local and family history books, mainly reference material such as census indexes and passenger lists, are on open shelves here. A microtext room adjoins the main reading room and rest rooms are conveniently located down the corridor to the east. The general reading room is a busy area, often filled to capacity, so come early. Incidentally, only pencils may be used for writing here.

Third Floor: The Card Catalogue
The third floor houses the Card Catalogue, an enormous entity. Newberry, as mentioned before, is a closed stack library, so the visitor must be able to consult the card catalogue and request materials by filling out call-slips, one for each book requested. All materials, including monographs, periodicals, and microforms have at least three cards in the Catalogue: author, title, and subject. The call number is located on the left of the card. The author, title, and call number must be carefully copied onto the call slip, not forgetting your desk number. In order to avoid laboriously writing your name and address on each slip, bring along a supply of address labels and use them. Incidentally, Newberry has its own cataloguing system and uses neither Dewey nor the Library of Congress systems.
Call-slips must then be taken down to the second floor and handed in at the genealogy desk. There is a limit on the number of books that can be requested at one time and it takes about thirty minutes to an hour for a request to be filled, so have extra requests on hand to give in as soon as your first requests are filled. That way you can work without too much of a break in your work pattern.
Readers must return books to the desk attendant when they are finished. Before leaving the room permanently, wait for clearance from the staff.

The Newberry Index
At many larger public libraries and university libraries throughout the country you will find a massive four-volume work entitled *The Newberry Index*. Published in Boston in 1960 by G.K. Hall and Company, this constitutes a very useful research tool but it is NOT a catalogue of the Library's holdings: as noted above, that fills an entire room! *The Newberry Index* is a listing of references to particular families in books, such as county histories, and periodicals held by Newberry and acquired between 1896 and 1918. The references given are not full modern bibliographic references, but usually refer to the call number of the book in which the name was found. It is unlikely that the whole book is about that family, but the reference can be found and the relevant pages photocopied.

English Genealogy at Newberry Library
The English researcher will find much to occupy him at Newberry. Types of records that have been collected include:

1) Printed parish registers e.g. *Worcestershire Parish Registers* by W. Phillimore; *Yorkshire Marriage Registers* ed. by Thomas Blagg.

2) Printed family histories: many families, particularly of the colonial period, have printed histories which stretch back to England.

3) Regimental histories: Newberry has a very strong collection of military histories.

4) County histories: notably, the Victoria County History series published in Britain earlier in the century, one set per county, and still the authoritative guide to each county.

5) Journals of county historical, record, and archaeological societies. These contain reprints of muster rolls, subsidy rolls, hearth taxes, early censuses, parish registers, vestry books, and poor law accounts, and much more of local interest.

6) Topographical dictionaries.

7) General works such as surname histories; books about population movements, and rural living conditions.

8) Handbooks to English genealogy, such as *Wills and their Whereabouts* by J. Gibson and *Key to Boyd's Marriage Index* by A.J. Camp (though the Library does not hold Boyd's Marriage Index itself).

Photocopies
Many books in suitable condition may be photocopied, but this has to be done by staff. Fill in a request for photocopying and hand it in at the desk, together with the book. Copies will either be brought to your desk or you can pick them up at the bookstore later. Alternatively, you may have them mailed.

Allen County Public Library

900 Webster Street, Box 2270
Fort Wayne, Indiana 46801-2270
TEL: (219) 424-7241
HOURS: Monday-Thursday: 9 a.m.-9 p.m.; Friday & Saturday: 9 a.m.-6 p.m.; Sunday: 1-6 p.m. (Labor Day-Memorial Day only)

The Allen County Public Library houses the Historical Genealogy Collection, one of the major collections of printed genealogical materials in the United States. The Genealogy Department began in 1961 and now has thousands of volumes, as well as fiche, microfilm, maps, and photographs. A good proportion of these relate to the United Kingdom and to England in particular.

Location
        The Public Library is a large, modern building in downtown Fort Wayne. It is situated in the north-west corner of Washington and Webster. Washington is the main thoroughfare running east-west. There is a small parking lot on the east side of Webster, facing the main entrance of the library, for which a maximum fee of $4 per day is charged.
        The Genealogy Department is located on the second floor, in the 1981 addition to the Library. The restrooms are adjacent to the department. (See sketch map.)

The Genealogy Collection has two main areas:

1) the card catalogue and index area with study area
2) the microfilm room

        Books are not on open access to the public except for some relating to the Mid-West, so request slips must be filled out using the card catalogue. A maximum of six requests at a time are permitted, and as it can take up to thirty minutes for a request to be filled, it is wise to have extra requests on hand to file as soon as your first books come.

Printed materials

1) Reference Books
        The Library has a good selection of instruction books for the researcher interested in England. These include:

-David Gardner and Frank Smith, *Genealogical Research in England and Wales.* Salt Lake City, Utah: Bookcraft, 1964 (3 volumes).

-W.E. Tate, *The Parish Chest*, third edition. Cambridge: Cambridge University Press, 1969.

-John West, *Village Records.* London: Macmillan, 1962.

-Anthony J. Camp, *Wills and their Whereabouts.* London; the author, 1974.

-*Burke's Peerage.*

-*Domesday Book* ed. John Morris, Chichester, England: Phillimore, 1975 (34 volumes).

        The library also has a selection of audio-tapes on various aspects of research.

2) Source materials
        These are books which give specific genealogical data, such as a birth record or date of the probate of a will. The coverage of each county in England varies enormously: some counties, such as Bedfordshire, are well-represented with a printed parish register

series, *Bedfordshire Wills* 1480-1519, *P.C.C. Wills* 1383-1548, and *Publications of the Bedfordshire Historical Records Society* (79 volumes). Other counties, such as Cheshire, may have only the Victoria County History. Briefly, the types of records may be summarized thus:

-Printed parish registers: look in the card catalogue under Register of Births etc., Register of Dead, Marriage Licenses.

-Printed non-conformist registers.

-Publications of the county historical, record, and archaeological societies: here you will often find name-lists such as tax rolls and muster rolls, reprinted and/or indexed.

-Wills, either in local church courts or the Prerogative Court of Canterbury. The Library has a 100-volume set of will indexes produced by the British Record Society, which covers wills from the fourteenth century to 1700.

-Victoria County Histories. Each county's history, natural history, and geography are covered in great depth, providing an important reference tool for the local historian and genealogist. Important 'county' families are given especially good coverage and their heraldic devices are usually given too.

Locating a book in the card catalogue
     Each book will have several cards representing it in the catalogue. To find a book relating to a specific place look first under the geographic location, then the subject sub-heading. For instance, if you are searching for a will index for Cornwall, look for CORNWALL, ENGLAND - WILLS. If you require muster rolls for Buxton in Derbyshire, look up DERBYSHIRE, ENGLAND - MILITARY RECORDS. For books relating to certain families, consult that surname. Be careful not to confuse place-names in the U.S. with those in England, as many places here were named after places back home. Other subject headings you may use are:

Apprentices	Inventories
Biography	Manors
Cemeteries	Maps
Census	Obituaries
Church Records and Registers	Orphans
Court Records	Probate Records
Directories	Voting Registers
Epitaphs	Wills
Gazetteers	

Microform materials

     The Library has a separate microform room which contains microfilm and fiche readers, along with copying machines in a suitably dim lighting situation. The main holdings relating to England are:

London Directory, 1677–1823
Census, 1841 and 1851 (partial)
The International Genealogical Index (IGI, 1988 edition)
Family History Registry (Church of Jesus Christ of Latter Day Saints)
Canadian Censuses 1825–1891
Passenger Lists – all the major U.S. ports.

To request a record of microform, locate the roll number by using the microform catalogue and fill out a microfilm call–slip, which should then be given to a staff member. Staff will load and unload microfilm.

Postal Inquiries
    All correspondence will be answered. Brief requests will be billed at the current rate (write for list of charges). Longer searches cannot be handled but a list of record agents will be furnished.

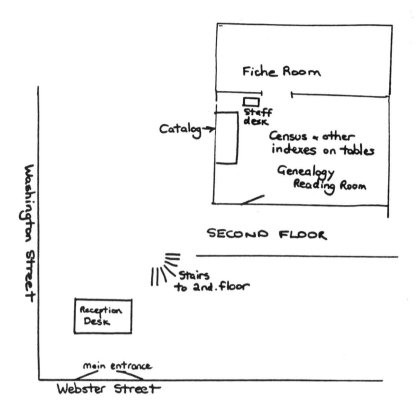

Fiche Room

Catalog →

Staff desk

Census & other indexes on tables

Genealogy Reading Room

SECOND FLOOR

Stairs to 2nd. floor

Reception Desk

Washington Street

main entrance

Webster Street

Allen Co. Library

CHAPTER 3

COPING IN ENGLAND

Flights to England from the U.S. are at least five hours duration and can be as many as twelve from the West Coast. They are usually overnight, so it is advisable to sleep enroute to avoid the worst excesses of jet-lag. Eat a good meal beforehand and settle down as soon as you are air bound, asking the stewardess not to disturb you. Avoid alcoholic beverages. After a good sleep, drink juice or milk, eat breakfast, and exercise your limbs.

Most flights to London land at Heathrow, west of the capital, or at Gatwick, to the south; but you may choose to fly to the northern city of Manchester if your research needs are in the northern counties. As soon as the descent begins, notice the rich green and yellow tapestry of fields interlaced, perhaps, with the silver ribbon of a narrow river; houses will seem squashed together. Britain is a tiny island compared to North America and space is highly prized, yet this also means that no-where is far away. A train trip from London to York takes less than four hours. Birmingham to London is only one hour by commuter plane, 1 1/2 hours by train.

At the airport, go first through immigration control (which means very long lines for foreigners); then, after collecting your luggage, negotiate customs control. Britain has instituted a two-channel system. If you have nothing to declare, go through the green channel. Only spot-checks are made here. If you do have duty to pay, go to the red channel. Officers will be waiting to tell you how much you owe. Having charted the appropriate course through customs, you will now push your trolley of luggage into Britain.

Private Transport

Through your travel-agent in the U.S. you may arrange to hire a car for the period, or part of the period you are in England. This option gives the traveler freedom from timetables, freedom to roan at will in rural areas, freedom from such annoyances as strikes.

Both Hertz and Budget Rent-a-Car offer a weekly winter rental of about $130 for a two-door standard shift, economy-size car such as the Ford Fiesta. Such a car should be adequate for two or three adults and their luggage, and would be economical in terms of petrol (gasoline), which costs about three times the American price. There are also numerous local firms which may be able to offer a competitive price, and airlines offer fly-drive holidays, which give you a break on the cost of car-hire. The leading British car rental firm is Godfrey

Davis.

When you book your vehicle, make sure that the *total* cost is quoted to you, including the Collision Damage Waiver, insurance, and drop-off charges. Car-hire firms have a sorry history of hidden costs. It is wise to purchase the Collision Damage Waiver (about $8 per day) to relieve yourself from worry over theft or accidents.

You will need a credit card for payment (in advance) otherwise you may have to leave a substantial cash deposit! Have your reservation number handy in case of mix-ups in the booking.

Most European cars have stick shifts, so if you must have an automatic, specify it and expect to pay extra. When you return your car, stop off at a service station and fill up the tank, or you will be charged top price for that.

Some points to remember when driving in England:

-drive on the left. (The steering wheel is on the right.)

-speed limits are higher than in the U.S. and the flow of traffic, even in towns, is more hectic.

-motorways have the designation M-; for example, the M1 runs from London northwards. These roads are equivalent to American express-ways. (Speed limit 70mph.)

-a roundabout is used at crossroads very often. Be prepared to halt at the edge and merge into a gap in the traffic. Signal left one exit before your intended exit. Roundabouts are not difficult to negotiate after you have tried a few.

-you may *never* turn right on a red light as is the case in some U.S. states.

-after a red light, you will see a red and amber combination before green appears. This tells you to prepare to go.

-all road signs are now European and mostly self-explanatory. A full list is given in *The Highway Code*, an inexpensive booklet available from Her Majesty's Stationery Office.

-front-seat passengers *must* use seat belts.

-children may not be seated in the front of a car.

-there are stiff penalties for speeding and driving under the influence of alcohol.

It does take some guts and determination for the foreigner to venture on Britain's roads!

Public Transport

Public transport is alive and well in Britain. The national railway network (British Rail) is very extensive and buses serve even remote areas at least once a week.

Britrail Rail passes for seven, fourteen, twenty-one, and twenty-eight days may be purchased in the U.S. through a travel agent. The pass is activated by being stamped at a ticket office on its first day of use, and can be used to go anywhere in Britain within the specified period. It is a bargain when compared to purchasing separate tickets for each journey.

British Rail uses the twenty-four-hour clock in its timetables, as do bus companies. Trains are fast, comfortable and generally reliable, though the food is a national joke. Porters are available at ail stations and should be tipped. All but very small stations have a buffet bar and waiting rooms.

The roadway rival to British Rail is the National Express Coach company. They run services to places often unserved by rail. A coach (the American bus), seats about fifty and is very comfortable; a few have lavatories in the rear and some have TVs and hostesses. The major advantages are cheapness and broad scope of destinations. The disadvantages are longer journeys and poor organization at coach stations, especially Victoria in London. There is a tourist pass scheme similar to British Rail's, but it is much cheaper and does not have to be used on consecutive days; i.e. you can use up a seven-day pass over a calendar month. This represents an advantage to the traveler who wants to stay several days at various points.

Bus companies provide local, short-distance service in cities, towns, and country areas. You may have to pay the driver as you enter or a conductor will come and collect fares. State your destination clearly. Busses are often not dependable, so be patient.

The London Underground deserves a section to itself. London is the only city in Britain with a subway system, but it is very extensive and for the first-time tourist, the most efficient mode of transport. There are nine lines or routes, covering much of metropolitan London. The Victoria and Jubilee lines, the most modern, are also the most clean and efficient. Some of the older lines, particularly the Northern, are dark and dirty, but travel is pleasant and safe from vandals. Beware of pickpockets, however - some things haven't changed since Dickens's time! Buy a ticket for your destination (you can choose your own route as long as you do not leave through a station). There are rows of ticket machines at most stations, but you need the correct change for these. Ticket offices are also open, if you do not have correct change.

Eating Out

In Britain eating out is not a pastime as it is in the U.S. and amongst families is usually reserved for very special occasions. You will not find the formidable array of fast-food places in every nook and cranny. Yes, McDonald's has infiltrated the conurbations but Britain has fare of its own to offer the discriminating visitor. I will survey the main types of eatery, from inexpensive upwards.

1) Fish and chips shops are open lunch times and evenings. Watch for the sign "frying times" on the door or window. Fish and chips (roughly equivalent but far superior to French fries) are no longer the

cheap meal they once were, but still a great British favorite, and quite reasonable. The shop-girl will surely mutter, "Salt or vinegar?" so be prepared to answer yes or no, according to whether you want your chips doused or not. Other types of food such as cornish pasties, meat pies, and peas may also be available.

2) Cafes are friendly, homelike places, offering tea, coffee, plain meals, and desserts at a very reasonable price. They are often family run, but can be found in department stores where they are called cafeterias and are self-service. Cafes in bus or coach stations are not recommended, often being dirty and the food inedible.

3) Pubs are open at lunch-times and evenings, and pub fare has an excellent reputation. The menu is usually limited to cold sandwiches, pasties, pies, or shrimp or 'chicken in a basket'; i.e., with chips. At lunch-time the Ploughman's Lunch is a must: home-made bread, fresh cheese, pickled onions, washed down with a half-pint of ale. Many pubs are in historic inns and a convivial atmosphere is almost guaranteed.

4) Restaurants are much the same as in the U.S., though a town may have only one or two. Traveler's checks and credit cards are accepted. Do not expect a salad with dinner. Dishes are not described on menus but you may ask the waiter about ingredients. Some food terms are included in Appendix E.

Manners and Customs

Much emphasis is placed upon common courtesies in England – liberal use of "please" and "thank you" is much appreciated. Queuing (lining up with infinite patience) is the national pastime at bus stops, railway stations, shops, theatres – in fact, anywhere two or more are gathered. Queue-jumping must never be practiced.

Tea drinking is not merely a way of slaking one's thirst, it is the social communion of England. If you are asked to join someone for a cup of tea, try, if at all possible, to accept the offer. Britons take milk (not cream) and possibly sugar and you will be asked your preferences.

The British policeman, or bobby, the national symbol of integrity and helpfulness, can still be seen on foot-patrol. He is usually very good at directions, and is addressed as constable (unless three stripes indicate he is a sargeant). Many terms used in Britain will be alien even to addicts of "Masterpiece Theater". Turn to Appendix E for an English/American vocabulary list.

Climate

England is predominantly a cool, damp country, hence the ubiquitous umbrella. Showers, even heavy ones, are frequent. 'Sunny periods' and 'periods of rain' are the British meteorologists' favorite phrases.

Winters bring some fog in low-lying areas near water, but do not expect the pea-soupers of Victorian London. Frost is more common than snow except in the North, and temperatures rarely fall below twenty-eight degrees Fahrenheit. A cold piercing rain is common, often with high winds.

Summers are pleasantly warm, around 65-70 degrees Fahrenheit, with rain showers, and there is no need for airconditioning. Sightseeing is enjoyable.

Spring and autumn are unpredictable seasons; it is very hard to know what to expect. Probably it is best to be prepared for the worst! Remember Keats wrote of autumn as "season of mists and mellow fruitfulness".

Electrical Gadgets

Britain's electricity supply runs on 220 volts, double that of the U.S., so any electrical appliances you take to England will require an adapter. It may be more worthwhile to use disposable razors and see a hairdresser once a week.

Currency

The units of currency are one hundred pennies (p) to one pound (£). Coins are 1p, 2p, 5p, 10p, 20p, 50p, and £1. Notes (bills) are £5, £10, £20. £1 coins are extremely unpopular and easily confused with the 10p coin; there is also a £2 coin. Visa is widely accepted, followed by American Express. Mastercard and Diner's Club are less well-known.

Telephones

The telephone system is a nationwide company. When dialing an in-town call, it is not necessary to dial the town code. Out-of-town calls will require the town code. International calls can be dialed direct anywhere in Britain and require use of the country code.

CHAPTER 4

INTERPRETING THE PAST

Interpretation Of Ancient Documents

Major obstacles in the reading of pre-nineteenth century records certainly exists for the genealogist unless he or she happens to
have studied Latin and paleography. It is essential to study and be
prepared before visiting archives or record offices; archivists are not
there to be your personal record interpreter, that is *your* job! I shall
try to make the task lighter by taking each obstacle, step-by-step,
and give exercises to help with each. Go over the exercises conscien-
tiously and repeat them at intervals.

Spelling

We tend to take uniformity in spelling for granted, so you may
be surprised to find out it is actually a very recent innovation. Before
the nineteenth century and the movement towards public education,
literate people were few and far between, and they tended to make up
their own spelling as they wrote. It is not uncommon to find the same
word spelled differently within the same sentence!
From my personal experience, I feel the best approach here is
to use you imagination together with contextual clues. Hear the word
as it would have been spoken, rather than trying to use the phonics
rules you were taught in school, and ignore odd capital letters. All
answers are at the end of the chapter.

Exercise 1A

Write the following phrases in modern English.

a) Itm one lynnen cloth
b) Itm one diapur Napkyn
c) Itm one Bason
d) Itm one Servyse boke
e) Itm one Surples for the Person

Exercise 1B

Write the following phrases in modern English.

a) Elizabeth Smyth wyff of Jno was burried the xijth of Marche.
b) Anne borne of a wayfaringe woman was xd the xxth of Marche.
c) Jan Wagit wyff of Tho: was burryed the xxvith daye of Novembre.
d) Wyllm Dunkhorne and Merry hunt war Maried the xxth of April.

Archaic Terms

Archaic words are words no longer in use. Generally, the meaning of such words can be conjectured from the context of the piece. For example: "leasowe" which I discovered in the inventory of a seventeenth-century ancestor, I inferred meant "meadow" as the rest of the section was concerned with agricultural assets. The *Oxford English Dictionary* later confirmed my conjecture.

Below is a list of some other common archaic words. For words not listed here, refer to the *Oxford English Dictionary* which should be available at your library.

ambery/aumbry – small cupboard
band – 'bond', agreement
bandcloth – linen collar
beares, beres – pillowcases
bease – cattle
bed hillings – bedclothes
ben – hardware
chaffingdish – cooking dish
cordwood – firewood
deyhouse – dairy
form – bench
fustian – type of cloth
gawne – gallon pail
hogshead – 54 gallons
hutch – small chest for clothes
keep – a safe
lather – ladder
leasowe – meadow
press – cupboard – wardrobe
pullen – poultry
quern – handmill
spence – larder
tramells – instrument for lowering & raising a kettle over a fire
trestells – a beam
trivett – a three legged cooking stand
trussing bed – trundle bed
twilleys – woolen material
virginals – small harpsichord
whitch – coffer

Abbreviations And Contractions

Because wills, registers, and legal documents were couched in jargon, it became the common practice to use abbreviations and contractions for syllables and whole words. These can be divided into several types.

1) Letters omitted completely – this was indicated by a mark above the word, an apostrophe, or mark below the word. Examples:

> comon – common
> Dmi – Domini
> Willm – William
> Mgaret – Margaret
> pfect – perfect
> prede – precede
> ppose – propose
> p'jury – perjury

2) Superior letters – the word is shortened by omission of a vowel and placing some of letters above the line. Examples:

> w^{th} – with
> w^{ch} – which
> we^{r} – were
> y^{t} – that
> y^{e} – the

Note: 'y' in the last two examples is a remnant of the Anglo-Saxon letter for 'th'.

3) Final letters omitted – this is usually represented by a period, semi-colon, or colon. Examples:

> fro: – from
> wid. – widow
> ite; – item

4) Abbreviated names. Christian names were frequently abbreviated to save time, generally according to the rules above. Examples:

> J^{no} – John
> Rich'd – Richard
> Robt – Robert
> Tho: – Thomas
> W^{m} – William
> Thoms – Thomas
> xpofer – Christopher
> Saml – Samuel
> Edwd – Edward

Handwriting

Handwriting has changed almost beyond recognition since the Tudor Age and can be the genealogist's greatest challenge.

It is not, however, an unsuperable one. Many English-speaking children learn to read and write fluently in Russian, Hebrew, and Greek, none of which uses the Roman alphabet. In paleography, we are using the Roman alphabet – the letter formations are simply different or more diverse than we, in the age of print, are used to.

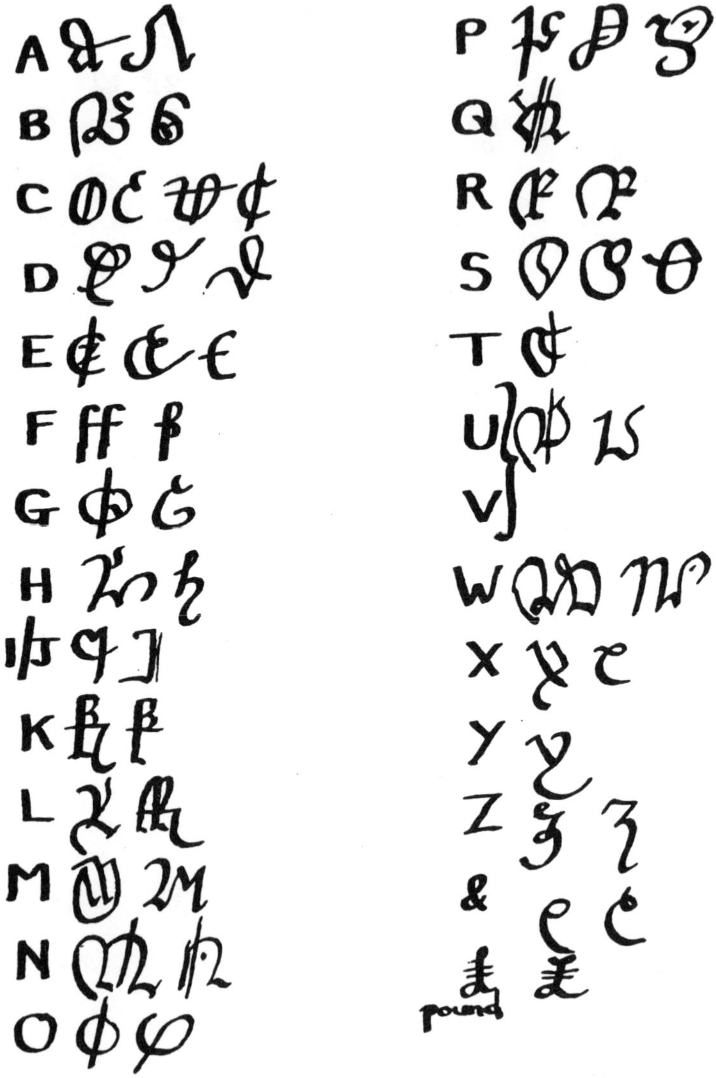

FIG. 4A

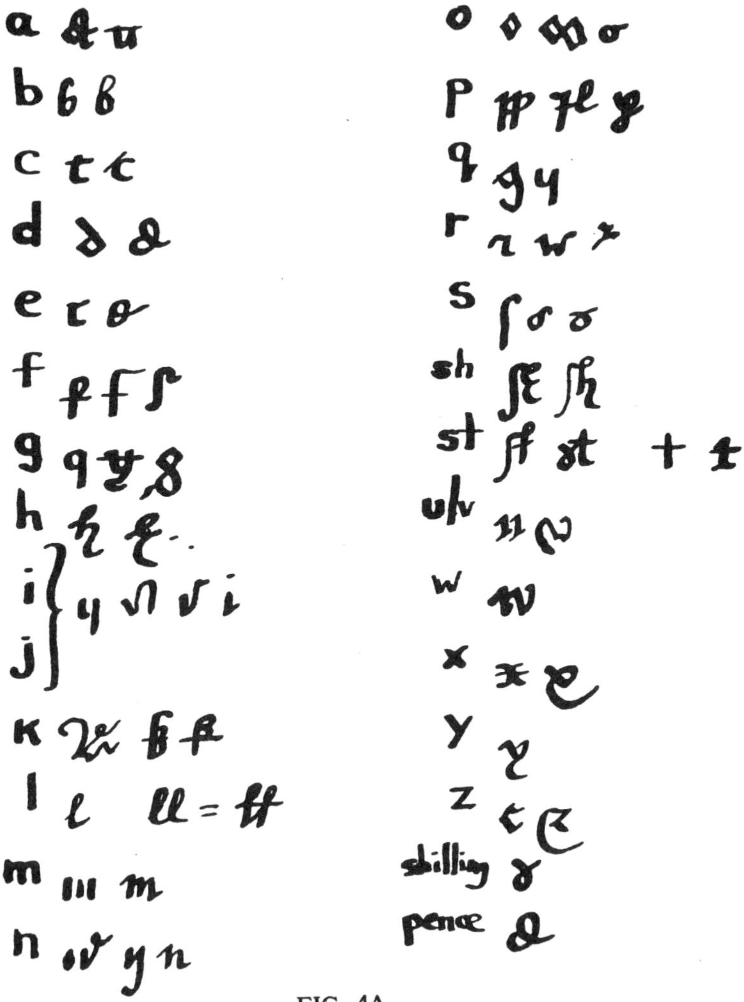

FIG. 4A

1) The Secretary Alphabet

In Fig. 4A are given various common forms of each letter. Use a narrow calligraphic nib to copy each letter at least fifty times. When you are sure you know the letter forms, try writing the alphabet without reference to the model. Go back to Exercise 1 and write them out using your new skills.

2) Recognizing Whole Words

After a good deal of alphabet practice, you should be ready to begin 'decoding' whole words. This is actually more difficult than to read whole sentences, because a sentence will usually furnish you with contextual clues. In Fig. 4B are individual words from the seventeeth century documents you will be reading later on. You may refer back to your practice alphabets the *first* time only. Later, try the section again without reference help. When you can 'read' the examples naturally, you will be ready to proceed to the next section.

3) Practice In Reading Documents

Plates 1 and 2 are examples of typical documents you will be reading: wills and inventories. Skim then first, to get the broad sense of the document, then go back and make a word-for-word transcription. Keep to the lines used in the original and do not alter spelling or expand contractions. Full transcriptions are given at the end of the chapter.

A Note On Dates

Prior to 1753, New Year's Day was held to be March 25th. Therefore, March 24th, 1642 would have been, according to our present calendar March 24th, 1643 (pushing New Year's Day back to January 1st). Exercise caution, therefore, when dating a document which precedes the nineteenth century. If necessary, write the modern date in parentheses.

Exercise 2

Change to the modern dating system, if necessary:

I) April 12, 1672
II) February 21st, 1578
III) October 9th, 1706
IV) January 3rd, 1627
V) November 11th, 1780.

Problem: how could a baby have been baptized on November 21st, 1550 and been buried March 2nd, 1550?

Reading And Interpreting Latin

Latin was the legal and ecclesiastical language of Europe

throughout the Middle Ages and remained dominant until the eighteenth century. Even if you do not intend to engage in medieval research, you may well come across parish registers and wills in Latin.

Many English words are derived from Latin and their meaning be inferred. For example, the Latin 'obiit' and English 'obituary' have a common root meaning 'death'. Many words have also changed meaning over the centuries, though, so exercise caution when translating. A comprehensive Latin word list is given in Appendix F.

Notes On Latin Grammar

1) Nouns and adjectives. Nouns can be either:

> masculine: ending in – us (e.g. dominus)
> feminine: ending in – a (e.g. puella)
> neuter: ending in – um (e.g. bellum)

The adjective then 'agrees' with the noun and has the same ending. Example:

> puella bona – a good girl
> dominus bonus – a good lord

Many words can be masculine or feminine – judge by the ending.

'Sobrinus' is a male cousin, 'sobrina' is a female cousin. In the word list this is indicated as 'sobrina/us'.

Some nouns end in other ways, such as -er, –is, or –es. All nouns 'decline', that is, change their ending according to their position in the sentence. Examples:

> Puella videt agricolam.
> The girl sees a farmer. BUT:
>
> Agricola videt puellam.
> The farmer sees the girl.

In Fig. 4C is a table of the most common endings.

2) Verbs. Latin verbs do not need pronouns such as 'I' or 'we': these pronouns are indicated by the ending of the verb. In the word list, you will find the 'I' form of the verb as it is easier to work out the other forms from this. Occasionally pronouns were used for emphasis: ego (I), te (you), nos (we).

Present tense of portare (to carry):

porto – I carry	portamus – we carry
portas – you carry	portatis – you carry (plural)
portat – he carries	portant – they carry

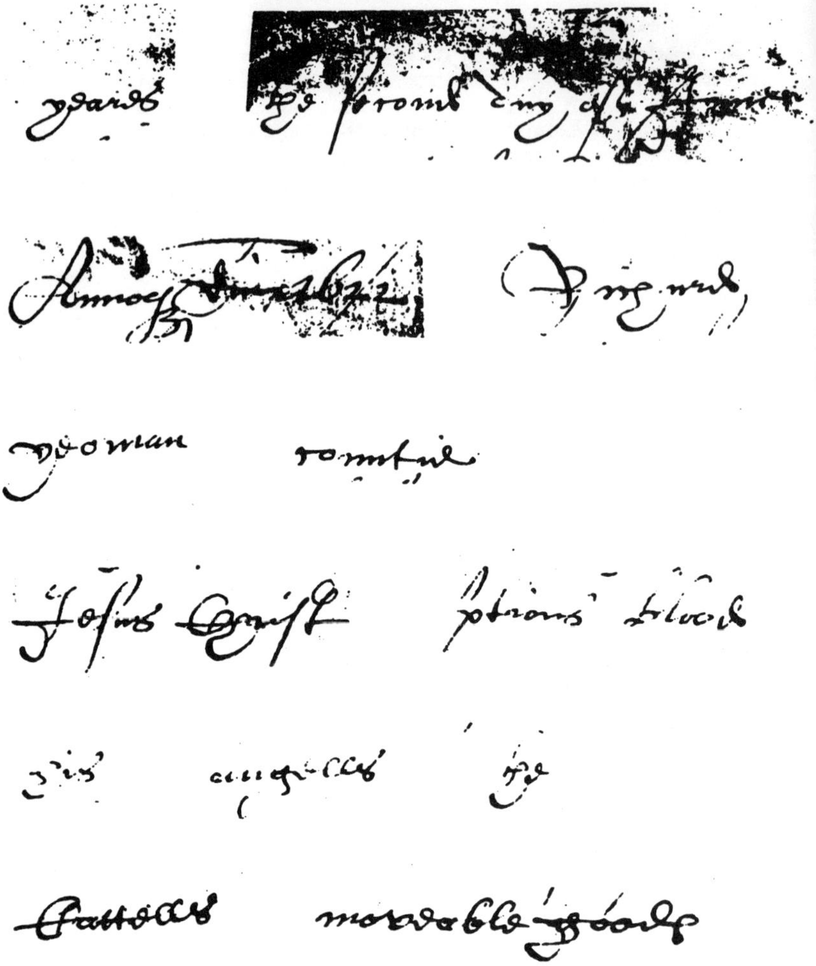

FIG. 4B

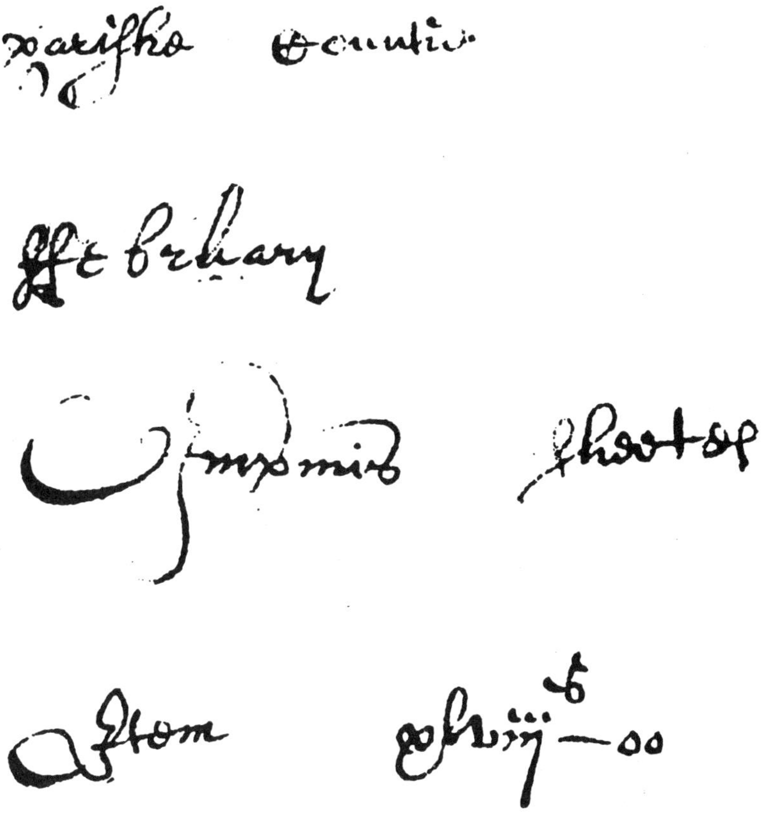

FIG. 4B

FIG. 4C TABLE OF THE MOST COMMON NOUN ENDINGS

	Masculine noun		Feminine noun		Neuter noun	
	Singular	Plural	Singular	Plural	Singular	Plural
Subject	dominus	domini	puella	puellae	castrum	castra
Object	dominum	dominos	puellam	puellas	castrum	castra
'of the'	domini	dominorum	puellae	puellarum	castri	castrorum
'to the'	domino	dominis	puellae	puellis	castro	castris

A true Inventory of the goods of Roger Woodman late of Woodrott
in the parishe of Bromsgrove in the Countie of Worcester praysed
and appraysed by the parties under named the fifth day
of this ... of ffebruary Anno Domini 1642 Annoque ...
... in manner followinge viz

Imprimis his wearinge apparell and mony in his
purse the summe of — — — — — — — — iij li — 00

Item in the ... nine sheetes one table cloth
halfe a dozen of table napkins a powder
tubbe and dable three small ... of powter
at the summe of — — — — — — — — xx s — 00

Item in the greate barne in corne, hay and
strawe att the summe of — — — — — — iij li — 00

Item in the Littell barne hay att the summe of xiij s — 00

Item Corne growinge in a feeld of land called
the Lyttell ... stubble att the summe of iij li — 00

Item thinges that may be for gotten and not apprays — 00 — vj d

Suma totalis — xj li — vij s — vj d

The apprayses
Robert Twytell
Thomas Houghting &
John Chellingworth

PLATE 2

Future: take the infinitive (portare) and drop the 're'. This is your future root.

portabo - I will carry

portabis - you will carry

portabit - he will carry

portabimus - we will corry

portabitis - you will carry

portabunt - they will carry

Past: take the root (porta) and add the endings.

portavi - I carried

portavisti - you carried

portavit - he carried

portavimus - we carried

portavistis - you carried

portaverunt - they carried

3) Medieval Spelling. Written Latin, like written English, was not uniform; words were often spelled phonetically. If you cannot translate a word, try to work out alternative spellings. Main substitutions are: j for i, i for e, v for u, s for c.

4) Medieval Dating. The Church's calendar of feasts and saints' days were used in preference to the Roman calendar. So, rather than write February 2nd, a scribe would write 'Candlemas' or one of its Latin names. Appendix F lists most major feast days. If you are flummoxed by an unknown saint, refer to the *Catholic Encyclopedia*.

5) Numerals. Words for numbers are included in Appendix F. Numbers were written thus:

j 1	vij 7	xx 20	xc 90
ij 2	viij 8	xxx 30	c 100
iij 3	ix 9	xl 40	m 1000
iv 4	x 10	l 50	
v 5	xj 11	lx 60	
vi 6	xij 12		

Answers To Exercises In This Chapter

Exercise 1A:

    a) Item one linen cloth
    b) Item one diaper napkin
    c) Item one basin
    d) Item one service book
    e) Item one surplice, for the parson

Exercise 1B:

a) Elizabeth Smith wife of John was buried the 12 of March.
b) Anne born of a wayfaring woman was christened the 20th of March.
c) Jane Waggett wife of Thomas was buried the 26 day of November.
d) William Dunthome and Mary Hunt were married the 20 of April.

Fig. 9B

I) yeare	XI) the
II) second day of June	XII) chattelles
III) Anno Domini 1622	XIII) movable goods
IV) Richard	XIV) parishe
V) yeoman	XV) countie
VI) countie	XVI) February
VII) Jesus Christ	XVII) Imprimis
VIII) precious blood	XVIII) sheetes
IX) his	XX) item
X) angelles	XXI) XXVIIIs – 00

Plate 1

A true inventory of ye goodes of Roger Wakeman late of Woodcote in the parishe of Bromsgrove in the countie of Worcestershire deceased, apraysed by the prices under named the sixth day of this ffebruary Ann^o Domi 1642: xviii in manner ffollowinge

	S	O	
Impmimis his warminge apparell and money in his purse the sume of	xx	oo	
Itm in the pler^l nine sheetes one table cloth halfe duzen of table napkines o pewter cuppe ond three small pieces of pewter at the sume of	xx	oo	
Item in the greate barne in corn and hay and strawe att the sume of	xx	oo	
Item in the littell barne haye att the sume of	xviii	oo	
Item corne growinge in a/pcell of land called the lyttell wheate leasowe at the sume of	xx	oo	
Item things that maybe for gotten and not ap^{r}aysed	oo	vj	
suma	vi^h	viij^s	vj

The ap^{r}aysers
Robert Wylde
Thomas ffaighting
John Chellingworth

1. parlour
2. aparcel

50

Plate 2

(In the name of) God Amen the second day of June in the yeare of the raigne of O^r sovreign Lord James the grace of God of England, France, and Ireland King defender of the faith ... the twentieth and of Scotland the five and fortieth Anno Dmi 1622. I Richard Hall of Chadwich yeeld (thelder?) in the prshe[1] of Bromsgrove in the countie of Worcester yeoman weake in bodie but stronge in mynde do willingly and wth a full heart, remer and give againe into the hands of my Lord God and creat^r my spirite wch he of his fatherly goodness gave unto me nothing doubting but that for his infinite mercies .... in the pcious[2] blood of his dearly beloved sonne Jesus Christ O^r only savior and redeemer he will receave my soule into his glorie and place it in the companie of heavenly angelles and blessed Sainte Ann and commending it to the earth thereof it came nothing doubling but trusting to the...of my faith and the great day of the generall Resurrection when we shall all appeare before the judgement seate of Christ and shall receave the same againe by the mightie power of God not a corruptible mortall weake and sicke bodie as it is now but an inconuptible imnortall stronge and pfect bodie in all points like unto the glorious bodie of my Lord and Saviour Jesus Christ.

1. parish
2. precious

Exercise 2
1)	April 12th 1672
11)	February 21st, 1579
111)	October 9th, 1706
IV)	January 3rd, 1628
V)	November 11th, 1780

The baby was baptized in Novenber 1550. In January, we begin dating 1551 but people then figured 1551 to begin on March 25th. Therefore March 2nd would bave been written as 1550.

NUMERALS

1	i or j	15	xv
2	ij	20	xx
3	iij	21	xxj
4	jv or iv	25	xxv
5	v	30	xxx
6	vj	50	L
7	vij	51	Lj
8	viij	90	xc
9	jx or ix	100	c
10	x/e	101	cj
11	xj	200	cc
12	xij	1000	m

GENERAL ALPHABET

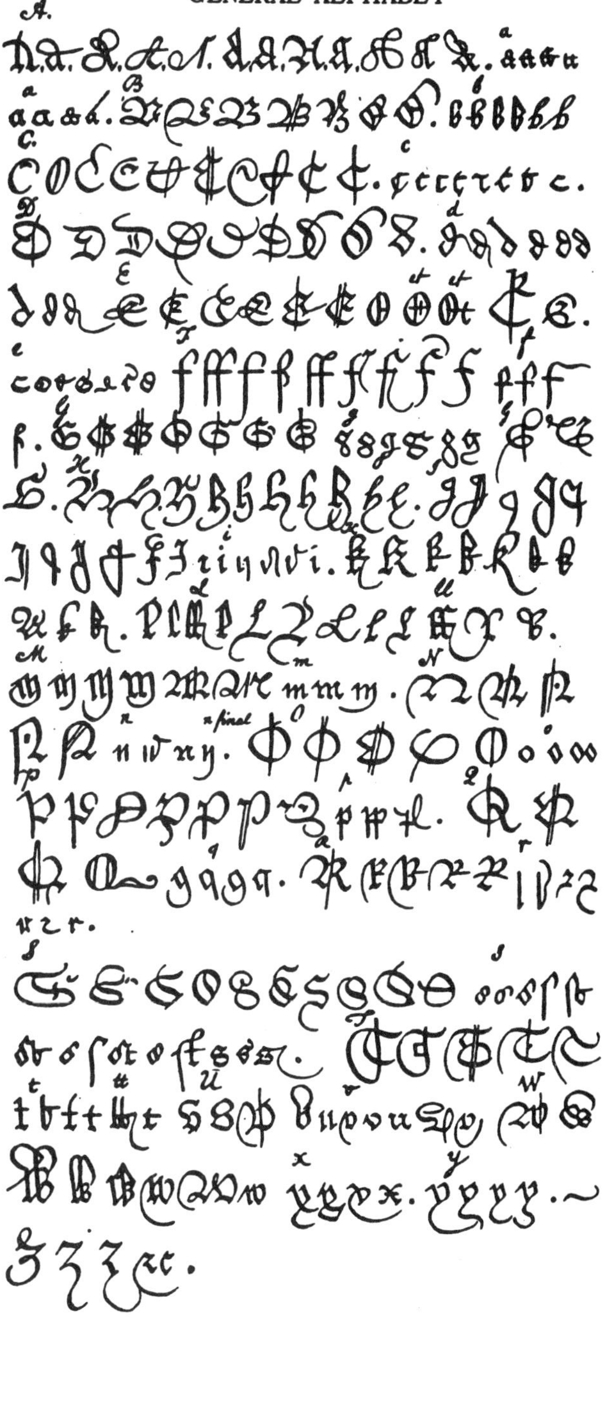

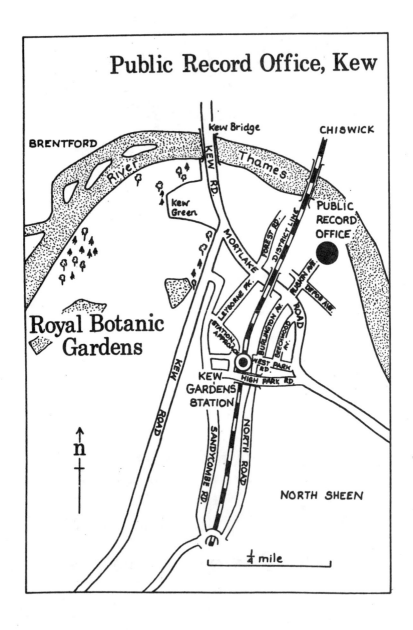

Public Record Office, Kew

BRENTFORD

Kew Bridge

CHISWICK

River

Thames

Kew Green

Kew RD.

PUBLIC RECORD OFFICE

MORTLAKE

FOREST RD.

DISTRICT LINE

RUSKIN AVE.

DEPOT AVE.

LEYBORNE PK.

PARK

BURLINGTON AV.

BEECHWOOD AV.

ROAD

Royal Botanic Gardens

STATION APPROACH

WEST PARK RD.

KEW GARDENS STATION

HIGH PARK RD.

KEW ROAD

SANDYCOMBE RD.

NORTH ROAD

NORTH SHEEN

n

¼ mile

CHAPTER 5

RECORD OFFICES AND LIBRARIES

County councils were created by an Act of Parliament in 1889 and very soon afterwards several councils began to take an active interest in the ancient documents within their jurisdiction. Bedfordshire created the first county office in the 1920's and has been followed by all other counties and major cities. Many incorporate the Diocesan Record Office.

Facilities for the researcher vary enormously. The number of staff can range from two to twenty, including professional archivists as well as technical and clerical staff. Space is often limited.

The Jurisdiction Of Record Offices

Each county or city record office varies greatly in its accessions and so it is essential to write beforehand with any specific queries you may have. Many offices have produced leaflets to help the genealogist understand the nature of their collection and what records they hold that can be of use. Below is a summary of the main types of record you may expect to find in a C.R.O.

1) Quarter Sessions Rolls. These are the documents produced by the Justices of the Peace (magistrates) in Quarter Sessions, that is, a quarterly convening of the county court. Most of the cases that came before the court involved only minor offenses, such as running an unlicensed alehouse, failure to repair a road or bridge, cases involving the poor and, in later centuries, non-Conformists and Catholics. Many counties have printed calendars (indexes) of the Quarter Sessions Rolls, which often date from the early medieval period.

2) Documents deposited with the Clerk of the Peace. The Clerk of the Peace was the clerk of the Quarter Sessions, and apart from his role as a recorder, he became guardian of various types of records. For the genealogist the most important were:

-sacrament certificates (1673-1750), which prospective officeholders had to produce to prove they were communicating members of the Chuch of England.

-a register of the estates of Catholics, describing their properties (from 1716).

-hearth tax assessments, 1662-1688. Every householder and the number of hearths he possessed was listed for tax purposes, and some copies kept by the Clerk of the Peace have survived.

-land-tax assessments: these were the basis for the electoral roll when the franchise was based on property-ownership, and so they exist from the mid-18th century to 1832. For each property the owner's name is given, plus that of the occupier and rent paid.

-freeholders (or jurors') lists: men aged 21-70 in each parish who qualified to serve on a jury were noted. Which meant those of gentry status. In general, only about four persons from each parish are mentioned, but some counties have lists from as early as 1696.

-poll-books (late seventeenth century on) list names of electors.

-registers of electors (1832 on): the Parliamentary Reform Act of 1832 widened the basis of the franchise considerably and it was extended again in 1867 and 1884. From 1832 registers of electors were printed and displayed publicly. Each entry in the register gives the voter's name, address, and the nature of their qualification, for example, amount of property owned.

3) Boards of Guardians (1834-1930). By the Poor Law Act of 1834, parishes were grouped into "unions", each of which appointed a board of Guardians of the Poor to administer the Union Workhouse, which Dickens made notorious in "Oliver Twist". The Board was required to keep registers of the poor for whom they cared, as well as minute books, of their meetings, in which they discussed specific cases. You may be lucky enough to find that an index has been prepared to these.

4) Censuses. The earliest censuses, 1801-1831, were the responsibility of the parish, and although they were supposed to have been destroyed, some survive and have found their way to the C.R.O. In these early censuses, only heads of household are mentioned by name. Most C.R.O.'s hold microfilm copies of the censuses 1841 to 1881 for their county. (Originals are in the P.R.O. in London).

5) Manorial court rolls. The manor court regulated village life in the Middle Ages. It settled minor claims and was constantly called upon to reinterpret the ancient customs of the manor and the rights and obligations of the tenants. Bromsgrove (Worcestershire) court rolls date from 1335 and its court leet still meets annually on the feast of St. John the Baptist, on a ceremonial basis, to weigh locally-produced bread and taste ale. The manor court dealt typically with vagrancy, non-payment of levies or dues, infringements of the rights of others (such as wood-gathering), or failure to perform a feudal duty. The court rolls teem with details of village life. Manorial rolls were usually written on pieces of vellum stitched together and rolled up. The writing is difficult to decipher, being in a cursive court hand, and is in Latin. However, printed editions of the rolls may be available, so check for these.

6) Parish records and Bishops' Transcripts (BT's). Parish records are more fully discussed in Chapter 8. It will, however, be noted that the trend towards depositing them in county record offices is increasing. This is not only extremely convenient for the researcher, but also comforting to know that these precious heirlooms from our ancestors are being carefully preserved for future generations.

Bishops' Transcripts, familiarly known as BT's, were begun in 1597 when an injunction was sent to all parishes requiring the priest to send an annual transcript of all the entries in his parish registers to the Bishop. Some priests were not very punctilious about this duty and some BT's have not survived the ravages of the centuries, but the remaining transcripts may be able to cover a gap in the original registers that is now missing or illegible. Occasionally, the transcripts may give facts in addition to those stated in the parish register or they may give a variant spelling of a surname.

7) Wills. Wills of most people of the rank of gentry or above before 1858 are to be found in the Public Record Office at Kew (see below) or at the Borthwick Institute in York, in the case of the northern counties. However, if the deceased did not own a substantial amount of property, the will was proved in local bishop's court, or the archdeacon's court. In this case it will now be in the diocesan record office - which often is the county record office.

The C.R.O. may have two copies of each will: the original document signed by the dying person (which are kept in annual bundles), and the full transcript entered in the court register. The will's reference number will then be identified by the surname of the first testator in the volume and the folio number - for example, Dunthorne, 162 would mean the volume beginning with the name Dunthorne, folio 162.

In many cases, a detailed inventory, or list, of the "goods, chattels and cattle" of the deceased had be added during the probate process. Usually, a small group of respectable neighbors would visit the dead person's house and write down a list of the contents, room by room, with their estimate of the value of each item or group of items appended. Many inventories give meticulous details, even to the number of sheets, chamber pots, spoons, and other items modern people would consider too trivial to mention. These inventories will not further your ancestral lines, but they will provide a fascinating look into the standard of living enjoyed then and the everyday activities of your forebears.

Wills and other probate documents are extrememly important sources of genealogical information, because their contents confirm specific relationships between the deceased and the people named by him or her, and this first-hand evidence has also been accepted by legal authorities if the will was proven. Many thousands of wills survive from the early Middle Ages, but they can also be the most difficult of sources to use. Until 1858, the courts of the Church of England had probate jurisdiction, and therefore the researcher must firstly understand the structure of these courts in order to ascertain where a will may have been probated.

The Church of England is divided into two PROVINCES: the Province of Canterbury, the senior of the two and presided over by the

Archbishop of Canterbury; and the Province of York, presided over by the Archbishop of York. Each Province is subdivided into DIOCESES, ruled by bishops.

Each diocese is usually divided into ARCHDEACONRIES, over which archdeacons preside, though in the diocese of Carlisle these were called <u>baronies</u>. The archdeaconry is further subdivided into rural deaneries, which are collections of parishes. The local probate court was usually the ARCHDEACONRY COURT, although in some dioceses there were no archdeaconry courts and the rural dean probated wills under the authority of the bishop and then sent the documentation to the bishop for registration. This happened for example in the diocese of York. Courts with higher probate authority were those of the Bishop (often called the EPISCOPAL CONSISTORY COURT) and the Archbishop (the PREROGATIVE COURT of the province). These superior courts superceded the lower court during times of INHIBITION, when the incumbency was vacant due to death, or when the superior official was making a visitation.

Basic rules for deciding where a will would be probated:

–If the deceased's estates lay <u>solely</u> within an archdeaconry, the grant could be made in the Archdeaconry court.

–If an estate was spread out between two or more archdeaconries within the <u>same</u> diocese, the episcopal court made the grant. The bishop usually had the right to grant probate in the estates of all nobility, gentry and clergy in the diocese.

–If an estate lay in more than one diocese but within a province, then the archepiscopal Prerogative Court had jurisdiciton.

–If the property lay within both provinces, Canterbury held sway.

As a general rule-of-thumb, one can assume that the smaller the estate and status of the deceased, the more likely the will was to have been proven in the local archdeaconry court. Gentry and people of middle income would have gone to the episcopal court, while the cream of society and wealthier merchants went to the Prerogative Court of the province. In practice, many wills in the southern half of the country were proven at the Prerogative Court of Canterbury when they could have been proven more locally, because that court held more weight, so to speak. All wills proven in the P.C.C. are at the Public Record Office in London. The records of the Prerogative Court of York are at the Borthwick Institute in York. (See section on Yorkshire.)

Peculiars
To every rule there is an exception, and Peculiars form a particularly complex pattern of exceptions in cases of probate. A Peculiar was formed when 'a parish or manor has jurisdiction over the grant of probate...within itself [and is] referred to as a Peculiar or Testamentary peculiar.' (Smith and Gardner, *Genealogical Research in England and Wales*, V. 2, p. 33.) In other words, the usual court was

superceded by the authority of the Peculiar Court. Royal Peculiars were generally chapels in such places as Windsor and Hampton Court that were also totally outside the usual jurisdiction. Oxford and Cambridge Universities, Eton College, and the Dean and Chapters of most cathedral churches also had peculiar jurisdictions. The records of Peculiars are often not where you might expect to find them and in the table below I shall try to indicate the whereabouts of as many as possible.

Whereabouts of wills

As a general rule, one can expect to find the following:
Archdeaconry court records - county record office
Episcopal court records - diocesan record office
Prerogative courts - P.R.O. and Borthwick Institute
Peculiars - diocesan record office

Ecclesiastical Jurisdictions Within Each County Until 1858

KEY:
A = Archdeaconry   P = Province
C = Canterbury   Y = York
D = Diocese   Pec. = Peculiar(s)
N = Notes   par. = parish(es)

Bedfordshire
P: Canterbury
D: To 1837 Lincoln & 1837-1914 Ely
A: 1) Bedford & 2) Huntingdon (par. of Everton only)
N: Pec. of Biggleswade & Leighton Buzzard at CRO. Records for Everton at Huntingdon CRO.

Berkshire
P: Canterbury
D: To 1836 Salisbury & Post-1836 Oxford
A: 1) Berkshire (records of 3 Pec. and Archdeaconry Court at Oxford CRO) & 2) Oxford (few par. near Oxford; 13 Pec. and bishop's consistory court at Wiltshire CRO

Buckinghamshire
P: Canterbury
D: To 1837 Lincoln & Post-1837 Oxford
A: 1) Buckingham & 2) St. Alban's (4 par.)
N: Records of 6 par. at Oxford CRO Eton College records 1440- 1784 at the college library. Remainder at Buckinghamshire CRO.

Cambridgeshire
P: Canterbury
D: Ely
A: Cambridge & Sudbury (diocese of Norwich)
N: Most records at Cambridgeshire CRO. Records for 12 par. of Norwich) at Norfolk CRO. Records for Archdeaconry of Sudbury &

par. of Isleham at W. Suffolk CRO.   Records for King's College, Cambridge at the college.   Remainder at Cambridge CRO.

Cheshire
    P: York
    D: Chester
    A: Chester
    N: Majority of records at CRO.   Some pre-1541 may be at Lichfield Joint Diocesan Record Office.

Cornwall
    P: Canterbury
    D: To 1876 Exeter
    A: Cornwall
    N: Most of Cornwall records destroyed in World War II.

Cumberland
    P: York
    D: 1) Carlisle & 2) Chester (1541–1856)
    A: Cumberland (most records at Carlisle CRO); Richmond (records at Lancashire CRO).

Derbyshire Co
    P: Canterbury
    D: To 1884 Lichfield
    A: Derby
    N: Derby (no archdeaconry court so most records at Lichfield Joint Diocesan Record Office.   Manor of Dale Abbey (pec.) at Nottingham CRO.)

Devon
    P: Canterbury
    D: Exeter
    A: 1) Barnstaple & 2) Exeter & 3) Totnes
    N: All records of bishop's court destroyed in World War II, but copies in Exeter City Library.   Seven par. at Cornwall CRO.   Prebendal Court of Uffculme at Wiltshire CRO.   Three par. (1836–1858) at Dorset CRO.

Dorset
    P: Canterbury
    D: To 1542 Salisbury & 1542–1836 Bristol & Post–1836 Salisbury
    A: Dorset
    N: Archdeaconry court records at Dorset CRO & indexed 61 par. at Wiltshire CRO but included in Dorset CRO's index.

Durham
    P: York
    D: Durham
    A: Durham
    N: Records of bishop's and archdeaconry court at Durham University.   Craike par. at Borthwick Institute, York.

Essex
P: Canterbury
D: London
A: 1) Essex & 2) Colchester & 3) Middlesex
N: Records of the archdeaconry courts at Essex CRO plus 12 pec. One hundred and one par. covered by Court of Bishop of London's Commissary also at CRO.

Gloucestershire
P: Canterbury
D: 1291-1541 1) Worcester & 2) Hereford; and 1541-1836 Gloucester
A: 1291-1541 Gloucester & Hereford (these records are at Worcester CRO); and 1541-1836 1) Gloucester & 2) Hereford (there were no archdeaconry courts & records of bishop's court are at Gloucester CRO. Nineteen Bristol & 16 adjacent par. in Bristol CRO.)

Hampshire
P: Canterbury
D: Winchester
A: Winchester
N: Records cover Channel Is. also & are at CRO. Has 23 pec.

Hereford
P: Canterbury
D: 1) Hereford & 2) St. David's
A: Hereford (these records are at Hereford CRO) & Brecon (8 par. near Welsh border only - were covered by Archdeacony of Brecon and episcopal court of St. David's. All records in National Library of Wales.)

Hertford
P: Canterbury
D: 1) London & 2) Lincoln
A: Middlesex, in London diocese, (34 par. in deanery of Braugham, Archdeaconry of Middlesex; records at Essex CRO) & the following two in Lincoln diocese 1) St. Alban's & Huntingdon (Hitchin division) (records at Hertford CRO for these 2 archdeaconries; records of bishop's court at Lincolnshire CRO.)

Huntingdonshire
P: Canterbury
D: To 1837 Lincoln & Post-1837 Ely
A: Huntingdon
N: All records at CRO including nine pec.

Kent
P: Canterbury
D: 1) Canterbury & 2) Rochester
A: Canterbury & Rochester
N: All records of these courts are at the Kent CRO, including those of 35 par. in the Pec. Court of the Archbishop of Canterbury in the Deanery of Shoreham.

Lancashire

     P: changes from York to Canterbury, see D:

     D: York Province for 1) To 1541 York & Post–1541 Chester

     D: Canterbury Province (before 1541) for 2) to 1541 Litchfield & Post–1541 Chester

     D: York Province (post 1541) for Manchester formed in 1847 out of Chester diocese.

     A: Richmond (for York Province, York & Chester) & Chester (for Canterbury Province)

     N: All post–1541 wills can be found at the Lancashire CRO. Prior to that, consult the Lichfield Joint Diocesan Record Office or the Borthwick Institute, York. Latter has records of the pec. of Kirk-by-Ireleth. Some grants in western deanery at Leeds Archive Sept.

Leicestershire

     P: Canterbury

     D: To 1837 Lincoln & Post–1837 Peterborough

     A: Leicester

     N: All records for the archdeaconry court are at Leicestershire CRO along with records of 3 manor courts and the Prebendal Court that covered part of Leicester. (Indexed from 1750 on.) Episcopal records at Lincoln CRO.

Lincolnshire

     P: Canterbuty

     D: Lincoln

     A: 1) Lincoln & 2) Stow

     N: Records of all wills are at the CRO. They include those of the Court of the Dean and Chapter of Lincoln (34 par.) and the pec. covering 7 parishes.

London

     P: Canterbury

     D: London

     A: 1) London (records of 50 par. at Guildhall Library) & 2) Middlesex (27 par. have their records at Greater London CRO. Court of Hustings: records at City of London CRO (Guildhall) Pec. Court of the Dean & Chapter of St. Paul's (12 par.) at St. Paul's, London. Deanery of the Arches (13 par.): records at Lambeth Palace Library. Records of the Royal Pec. of St. Katherine-by-the-Tower (1689–1775) are at Guildhall.

Middlesex

     P: Canterbury

     D: London

     A: Middlesex

     N: Commissary Court of London covered 44 par.: records at Guildhall. Pec. Court of the Archbishop of Canterbury in the Deanery of Croyden covered 4 par.: records at Kent CRO. Eight par. were under the pec. Court of the Dean and Chapter of St. Paul's (St. Paul's Library, London. Three other par. were peculiars of Westminster (Westminster Public Library). Remaining records should be at the Greater London Record Office.

Norfolk
    P: Canterbury
    D: Norwich
    A: 1) Norfolk & 2) Norwich
    N: All records at Norfolk CRO including those of the Pec.
Court of the Dean and Chapter of Norwich which covered 16 par. in and
around Norwich.

Northamptonshire
    P: Canterbury
    D: To 1541 Lincoln & Post-1541 Peterborough
    A: Northampton
    N: For records before 1541: consult Lincolnshire CRO. North-
amptonshire CRO has the records for the diocese of Peterborough and
the Archdeaconry of Northampton. Kings Sutton: records at Oxford
CRO. Records of 5 par. in pec. courts at Lincolnshire CRO.

Northumberland
    P: York
    D: Durham & (1882: Newcastle-upon-Tyne created)
    A: Northumberland
    N: Most probate records are at Durham University. Records of
6 par. under the Pec. Court of the Archbishop of York are at the
Borthwick Institute, York.

Nottinghamshire
    P: To 1839 York & Post-1839 Canterbury
    D: To 1839 York & Post-1839 Lincoln
    A: Nottingham
    N: Until 1839 the Exchequer Court of the diocese of York was
the main probate court: records at the Borthwick Institute, York.
Archdeaconry Court records at Nottingham Record Office. Thirty par.
in Pec. of Southwell and 13 other pec. at Nottinghamshire CRO.

Oxford
    P: Canterbury
    D: 1070-1546 Lincoln & Post-1546 Oxford
    A: Oxford
    N: For records before 1546, consult Lincolnshire CRO. All
post-1546 records at Oxford CRO including 3 par. in the Archdeaconry
Court of Berkshire records of the Court of the Chancellor of the University, and 30 par. in Oxford and Buckinghamshire pec.

Rutland
    P: Canterbury
    D: To 1541 Lincoln & Post-1541 Peterborough
    A: Northampton
    N: The whole county formed one rural deanery and post-1541
records are all at Northampton CRO except pec. of Liddington, Calde-
cott, and Ketton-with-Tixover, which are at Leicestershire CRO.
Records prior to 1541: consult Lincolnshire CRO.

Shropshire

P: Canterbuty

D: NORTH Lichfield & SOUTH Hereford

A: Salop

N: Wills are at the Lichfield Joint Diocesan Office and Hereford CRO respectively. Three par. in diocese of Worcester: records at Worcester CRO. Several north-west par. and pec. have records at the National Library of Wales.

Somerset

P: Canterbury

D: Bath & Wells

A: 1) Bath & 2) Wells & 3) Taunton

N: Most probate records were kept at Exeter and were destroyed during World War II. Records of 3 par. near Bristol are at Bristol City CRO.

Warwickshire

P: Canterbury

D: To 1836 1) Worcester & 2) Lichfield, and Post-1836 whole county in diocese of Worcester

A: 1) Worcester & 2) Coventry

N: Records of the Episcopal Court of Lichfield plus 19 par. in Pec. are at Lichfield Joint Diocesan Record Office. All other probate records at Worcester CRO.

Westmoreland

P: York

D: 1) Carlisle & 2) York (to 1541) then Chester

A: Barony of Appleby (for Carlisle) (the Episcopal Court of Carlisle was the probate court for this area: records at Carlisle CRO) & the following two for York/Chester: 1) Kendal & 2) Richmond (probate records of the Western Deaneries are at the Lancashire CRO. Records of the Eastern Deaneries are at Leeds Archives Dept.)

Wiltshire

P: Canterbury

D: Salisbury

A: NORTH Wiltshire & SOUTH Sarum

N: All probate records including several pec. are at Wiltshire CRO.

Worcestershire

P: Canterbury

D: Worcester

A: Worcester

N: Most records at Worcester CRO. Fifteen par. & 8 chapelries were in diocese of Hereford and records are at Hereford CRO.

Yorkshire

P: York

D: York & (in 1541 Archdeaconry of Richmond became part of diocese of Chester)

A: 1) York & 2) E. Riding & 3) Cleveland & 4) Nottingham & 5) Richmond

N: Probate records of the Exchequer Court of the Dean of York, Court of the Dean & Chapter of York and of 135 par. in pec. jurisdiction are at the Borthwick Institute, York. For the Archdeaconry of Richmond, consult Leeds Archives Dept. Fifteen par. around Northallerton have records deposited at Durham Univ. For Saddleworth and Whitewell - see Cheshire.

Staffordshire

P: Canterbury

D: Lichfield

A: Stafford

N: All probate records for the counts are at the Lichfield Joint Diocesan Record Office.

Suffolk

P: Canterbury

D: Norwich

A: WEST Sudbury (Sudbury Archdeaconry Court records are at Suffolk CRO (Bury St. Edmund's); & EAST Suffolk (records for this Archdeaconry Court are at the Suffolk CRO (Ipswich). Probate records of the Episcopal Court of Norwich are at the Norfolk CRO. Three par. in the Pec. Deanery of Bocking have records deposited at Essex CRO.)

Surrey

P: Canterbury

D: Winchester

A: Surrey

N: Records of the Episcopal Court are at the Hampshire CRO. Records of the Archdeaconry Court of Surrey are mainly at the Greater London Record Office. Twelve par. which were under the Pec. Court of the Archbishop of Canterbury in the Deanery of Croyden have their records at Kent CRO.

Sussex

P: Canterbury

D: Chichester

A: 1) Chichester (records of the Archdeaconry Court of Chichester are at the West Sussex CRO), & 2) Lewes (records of this archdeaconry court are at the East Sussex CRO. There were several pec. but records are in the geographically relevant Sussex CRO.)

Parts of a Probate Record

-WILL or TESTAMENT: The statement by the deceased showing how he wished his property to be distributed. The testator had to name at least one EXECUTOR who would arrange for the probating of the will.

-LETTERS OF ADMINISTRATION: If no executors were named, or they were all minors, or deceased, or if no will could be found, the court would arrange Letters of Adminstration to a TUTOR or CURA-TOR (i.e. a guardian) to administer the will until the executors came of age or until probate was granted.

-INVENTORY: This was an item-by-item list of the property of the deceased, often including personal property, and valued.

-PROBATE ACT: When a will had been granted probate, the court entered a summary of the will called a PROBATE ACT into the PROBATE ACT BOOK (also called a DAY BOOK) which was therefore a kind of table of contents. Sometimes the Probate Act was entered at the end of the will, or both.

-CALENDAR: This is a printed index to wills of a particular court.

Probate Terms

     Bona Notabilia - Indicates the deceased's property was worth five pounds or more.
     Commissary Court - A Court appointed by a superior authority and licenced to carry out specific functions in a district.
     Consistory Court - A court of church officials.
     Noncupative will - An oral will, legal until 1838.
     Surrogate - A deputy appointed by the ecclesiastical court to grant probate, often the parish minister.
     Peculiar - A parish or manor not under the normal jurisdiction of the local courts but basically self-governing.
     Royal Peculiar - Ususally a royal chapel totally outside the jurisdiction of the diocese it lay within.

8) Marriage allegations and bonds. When couples from different parishes wished to marry, or if they wanted to marry in a third parish, or without banns, then they had to apply for a marriage license. This meant they could furnish the diocesan office either with a BOND or an ALLEGATION. Either of these documents gave details of the couple's abode, age and occupation and the names of two sureties, one of whom was usually a parent or relative of the bridegroom. In return, they were issued with a license to marry - that is, permission.
     BONDS begin with the words "Know all men by these Present that We (the two sureties)" and involved a sum of money to be posted, although this seems rarely to have been handed over. ALLEGATIONS begin with a date and "on which day appeared personally (the groom)". Both are kept in annual bundles, but many have been indexed by ardent genealogists and local historians. Do remember that the existence of a bond or allegation is not evidence that the marriage took place, merely an indication of where and approximately when it might have happened.

9) Non-conformist and Roman Catholic records. From 1559, when the Act of Uniformity was passed, down to the early nineteenth century, it was often dangerous and costly to be a recusant - a member of a church other than the established Church of England. This group in-

cludes Baptists, Quakers, and Roman Catholics. Prosecutions for recusancy can be found in the Quarter Sessions Rolls, and as already mentioned, a register of Catholic properties was kept later on.

Quakers kept "suffering books", describing the persecution endured by its members, and also issued testimonials for members moving to another county or country (often Pennsylvania). Some of these records have been deposited in C.R.O.'s.

Most Roman Catholic registers remain in the hands of the parish priests except for Lancashire, but records of the Congregationalists, Baptists, Methodists and the Society of Friends (Quakers) are gradually finding their way into the record offices to be preserved.

10) Estate records. This category includes documents pertaining to private estates and although there may not be much of direct use in tracing a lineage, there are items which illustrate and add depth to the family history.

-Estate maps show all the field boundaries, field names (yes, every field was identified separately!), their acreages, all cottages and houses, and the names of the different owners. (See Chapter 9.)

-Enclosure maps are common from the mid-eighteenth century, when landowners consolidated their holdings and took away common land rights. They are large-scale maps, easily legible, clearly showing the pattern of land-ownership of the area. (See Chapter 9.)

-Title-deeds to land may be preserved, but these need perseverance to be interpreted.

-Farm and household accounts nay also be preserved and can serve as an extensive illustration of the history of an estate. F. G. Emmison in his book, *Archives and Local History*, gives the example of Audley End, Essex, for which almost 40,000 bills and vouchers exist for the period 1765-1832, all neatly sorted into categories and monthly bundles. In many cases, just a simple account ledger survives.

11) Family archives: letters and diaries. Many older families have turned over their collections of letters, papers, and diaries to their C.R.O. for archival storage. The Worcester C.R.O., for example, holds letters of the Pakenhams, Russells, Devereaux, Talbots, and Washingtons. There is often so much material of this type that the simple entry in the office's guide can give no indication of the richness of the find. For the researcher, this means a long process of reading and sorting, bearing in mind the problems in reading the hand of seventeenth century and earlier writers.

12) Printed and pictorial records. Besides manuscript and other documents, C.R.O.'s house a large variety of printed materials - photographs, picture postcards, town directories, and so on. There may also be a collection of the first Ordnance Survey of the county, about 1820.

13) School records. The beginning of public education in England lay with two charitable societies, which, in the early nineteenth century, founded many "British Schools" and "National Schools", the latter generally linked to an Anglican church. Later in the century, state education was built onto these foundations. For instance, the National School in Bromsgrove, Worcestershire, later became the Church of England Primary School, part of the state system. Log-books kept by the head-teacher contain references to the pupils (and their antics!) and registers of attendance were maintained on a daily basis. Registers night be useful in establishing an ancestor's age and residence.

Libraries

Local libraries may be an unexpected source of information. Many have acquired microfilm copies of the censuses for their area and may have a good collection of local newspapers. Most will have the Victoria County History and possibly other local histories, genealogies, and maps. Do be aware of their potential.

The Public Record Office

Ruskin Avenue
Richmond, Surrey TW9 4DW
TEL: 01 876 3444
HOURS: Open 9:30 a.m. - 5:00 p.m., Monday through Friday. Closed the first two weeks of October.

The Public Record Office has three repositories at present: Kew, Chancery Lane, and Portugal Street, London. Kew is by far the most valuable for genealogists in the variety of sources it offers for research, but the first-time visitor cannot expect to tap the P.R.O.'s resources to the full. It takes many visits and much experience to gain the most from each visit. That said, do not be discouraged - do your homework beforehand, come prepared with specific research objectives, but be flexible so you can follow up on new clues.
To consult public records you must obtain a reader's ticket in advance by writing to the above address. There is no charge for the ticket. When writing, take the opportunity to double-check that the records you wish to consult are at Kew; re-organizations do take place from time to time and you do not want to find yourself twenty-five miles from the correct repository! (Travel across London can be painfully slow and waste precious hours.)

Many of the records cone from governmental agencies, such as the War Office, the Admiralty, the Foreign Office, and the Treasury. The records remain classified according to their department of origin and abbreviations are used. Some of the main abbreviations you will meet are:

ADM	Admiralty
BT	Board of Trade
CO	Colonial Office
E	Exchequer

FO	Foreign Office
HO	Home Office
PC	Privy Council
T	Treasury
WO	War Office
SP	State Paper Office
PMG	Paymaster General's Office
RG	General Register Office

For example, a naval record might be designated ADM 100, an army record WO 312.

Following are the main types of records in the P.R.O.:

a) Nonconformist (or non-parochial) church registers. The P.R.O. has about 9,000 registers from churches other than the established Anglican church. They are mainly Protestant and only a few predate the eighteenth century. Early eighteenth century registers recorded baptisms, marriages and burials, but after 1754 all marriages had to be solemnnized in the Church of England, and so will not show in the nonconformist registers.

There are also a few Roman Catholic registers in the P.R.O., mainly from the northern counties of England. In general, registers remain with the priest or diocese. If you have difficulty in locating a particular Catholic parish register, write Catholic Central Library, 41 Francis Street, London SW1P IDN; or to the Catholic Record Society, c/o Miss R Rendal, Flat 5, Lennox Gardens, London SW1X 0BQ.

b) Wills prior to 1858. Before 1858 the proving or 'probate' of wills was purely an ecclesiastical matter and occurred in the Prerogative Court of the Province (York or Canterbury), or in the diocesan court. The P.R.O. has wills proved in the Prerogative Court of Canterbury (abbreviated to P.C.C.) from 1384 to 1858. Don't get too excited though – these are wills of persons of substantial means and the chances that your ancestor was such a person are very slim. If the surname you are researching is uncommon, however, it would certainly be worth searching the indexes described below. You may also hold the conviction that your ancestor was a notable and this is a way to document that idea.

Indexes To Wills:

–Camp, A.J. *P.C.C. Will Index 1750-1800*. Volume 1; Surnames A-Bh, Volume 2: Surnames Bi-Ce. Completion of this project will obviously take many decades, but it is sorely needed to update the project of the British Record Society.

–*Prerogative Court of Canterbury Wills* (British Record Society). Twelve volumes spanning 1384 to 1700. Each volume covers the wills for a specific period and indexes the deceased's names alphabetically. Many large libraries and genealogical collections hold this set.

-Card Index to P.C.C. Wills 1721-25: held by the Society of Genealogists.

When using these indexes, be careful to copy the full name of the deceased, date of death or probate, and reference number of the will.

Reading wills is not an easy task, especially those prior to the nineteenth century. See Chapter 4 for guidance in reading and interpreting these documents.

c) Tax records. Ever since Julius Caesar stood on England's shore and uttered the famous dictum "Veni, vidi, vici", the English people have been subjected to an ever-increasing tide of taxation. Fortunately for the genealogist, this means that lists have been generated for residents who might otherwise have gone unrecorded.

-The Hearth Tax, imposed between 1662 and 1674, is probably the most complete and useful of the earlier taxes. It required householders to pay a tax of two shillings on each hearth in the house. Not only do we have householders names but we can also infer their status according to the number of hearths. The most complete sets of records is for the tax collected on March 25, 1664. Many have been indexed and printed by local groups.

-The Land Tax Redemption Office Quotas and Assessments for 1798-1799 are also valuable documents. All landowners in England and Wales are listed, town by town and village by village. Sadly it remains unindexed, making a location absolutely necessary beforehand.

d) Military records. The British Army has been a regularly organized body for several hundred years. Until the mid-nineteenth century, its organization was rather looser than we now associate with that institution, but it left a mass of records for the genealogist. The Army is divided into regiments, which were often associated with a county. There are four types of regiment:

infantry	foot soldiers
cavalry	horseback soldiers
artillery	cannon-firers
engineers	constructors of bridges, roads, etc.

Each regiment consists of commissioned officers, noncommissioned officers (who have risen from the ranks) and private soldiers. Commissions were bought and sold, a practice which effectively kept them within the domain of the upper classes.

The officer classes were, perhaps inevitably, better documented than the rank and file. Look first in the *Army Lists* published annually since 1754; a complete set is available at the Society of Genealogists. This will verify your ancestor's regiment(s) and career record. The P.R.O. has a regimental list of officers for the years 1702-1823 (WO 64). If there is any indication of involvement in campaigns, consult the Medal Rolls (WO 100) for details. Genealogical information can be gleaned from applications for commissions (WO 31) and widows' pensions (WO 42).

The career of the ordinary soldier is, alas, more difficult to reconstruct, and genealogical data is very limited. After 1883 discharge papers are arranged alphabetically regardless of regiment, thus easy to locate. Before that date, however, it is totally essential to know the man's regiment before consulting the War Office records, which run into the hundreds of thousands. If you think your ancestor served in a particular campaign, consult a military history to ascertain the regiments involved. One of my Irish ancestors supposedly served in the Crimea with great distinction, but so far I have been unable to locate any reference to him. It is my only clue, though, and I continue to be guided by it. Again, if medals were awarded to the ancestor, consult the Medal Rolls (WO 100). When you have found which regiment your ancestor belonged to, you can try searching the Regular Soldiers Documents (WO 97) which detail soldiers' complete service record. The series runs from 1756 to 1913.

In the Naval records, officers are, again, much better documented than ratings are, and it is essential to know on which ship he served if he was in the Navy before 1853. Officer's careers have been published in the *Navy Lists* annually since 1814, and there are also many naval biographies such as *Commissioned Sea Officers of the Royal Navy, 1660-1815* (London, 1954). Primary sources such as the Captains Logs (ADM 51) may then be searched.

Unless his ship is known, a rating is very difficult to locate. Medal Rolls (ADM 171) can be of help. The Ship's Musters (ADM 36-39) give a great detail about the ratings, naval careers and even date and place of birth in some instances. These records survive from 1667 onwards. In the absence of a muster, Ship's Pay Books can confirm the man's presence aboard ship.

The Merchant seaman record holdings of the P.R.O. relate mainly to the years 1837-1857. They include Ship's Registers (1835-1857) and some muster rolls (1747-1834). Crew lists are accessible by reference to the Registers, but be warned that the system is complex after 1845 and you may want to leave this research to a professional.

The P.R.O. does not hold Royal Air Force records. Personnel records may be released to relatives only by applying to the R.A.F. Personnel Management Centre, Easter Ave., Barnwood, Gloucester GL4 7AN.

e) Records relating to British citizens abroad. Some registers of births, marriages, and deaths abroad were kept at various embassies and are not in the records of the Foreign Office at the P.R.O. Wills of Britons dying abroad were usually proven in the Prerogative Court of Canterbury and are therefore in the P.R.O. (See above.) These are records of many British nationals, not merely civil servants of Crown employees.

Births, marriages, and deaths at sea from 1854 to 1890 are among the records of the Board of Trade (BT 158). Deaths at sea of British nationals 1825-1880 are classified under BT 159, and births at sea 1875-1891 are in BT 160.

f) Emigrations records. Formal emigration lists have never been kept, but the following classes of documents night be useful to the American genealogist:

-BT 27 - Passenger Lists. 1890-1960: arranged by year and port of departure, they give the name, age, occupation, and last address of the passenger.

-T 47/9-12 - Register of emigrants to America, 1773-1776, for which there is a card index. The index gives name, age, occupation, reason for leaving Britain, last address, and destination.

-AO 12 - American Loyalists' Claims 1776-1831

-AO 13 - American Loyalists' Claims 1780-1835

g) Deeds. There are thousands of deeds in the Public Record Office but unfortunately there is no index to the majority of them. They are arranged in chronological order by the date of filing and there is a notation of the county in the margin. You may wish to hire a professional researcher if you are fairly confident that a deed exists and do not have the time to search on your own.

Two considerations need to be kept in mind. Firstly, that land and property ownership has until this century been the exclusive preserve of a very small class of English society. The chances that your ancestor held property are quite limited. Secondly, until the nineteenth century, there was no legal requirement to keep deeds or to record transfer of ownership. Most people held land by copyhold, a form of tenure now abolished, and transfers were recorded on the court roll of the manor. Most court rolls are held by the county record offices and many have been printed by archaeological societies.

h) Census returns.

i) Apprenticeship records.

What Not To Expect At The P.R.O. (Kew)

Formal genealogies
Anglican parish registers
Birth, marriage, or death records
Wills after 1858
Records of soldiers serving in the Boer War, World Wars I or II.

CHAPTER 6

COUNTY, CITY, AND DIOCESAN RECORD OFFICES

In this chapter I intend to list all the County and Diocesan Record Offices, some of which have branches, as well as City Record Offices and the Borthwick Institute of Historical Research in York. Details will be found of open hours, admissions policy, telephone number, and other pertinent information to the visitor, as well as details of major sources of interest to the genealogist. Many record offices have issued guides for genealogists researching their county and these have been noted.

General Guidelines

1. Many of the documents you will use are irreplaceable and can be damaged quite easily. They should be handled with great care.
2. Always use pencil, never ballpoint or fountain pen.
3. Learn to use the indexes and call number system. Most record offices operate on a paging system, by which you request an item or items. An assistant then retrieves the item(s) from the archives, a process which may take up to half an hour.
4. Generally documents cannot be ordered thirty minutes before lunch or the close of the office.
5. Smoking, eating, and drinking are never allowed in search rooms.
6. Children under school age should not be taken to record offices, and older children should only be taken if they are sufficiently mature not to disturb others.
7. Do not attempt to trace maps or other documents without permission.
8. Return documents to the staff when work is complete.
9. If the documents are bundled, keep them in the same order in which they were received.

The County Archive Research Network

Due to serious thefts from certain record offices in England over the past few years, a number of offices have banded together to form the County Archive Research Network. Sad to say, amateur genealogists and family historians have probably played a part in this state of affairs, and in order to preserve genealogical documents for our future generations, the Network has instituted a central registry of record office users. The reader must fill in a form giving name, address in the U.S.A. and England, telephone number, likely date of departure from the U.K., and signature. Identification containing name, address, and signature must be produced: a U.S. driving license or passport would fill the requirements. You will then be issued a reader's ticket valid for four years at all participating record offices, at no cost.

On arriving at a participating record office, the visitor will need to sign the visitors' book and enter his ticket number. A member of staff then checks the signature against that on the ticket. Generally, the visitor will have to surrender his ticket during the visit, retrieving it only when all documents borrowed have been surrendered. Allow time for this end-process.

If the visitor forgets or loses his ticket, he may be allowed access to limited classes of materials after filling in a temporary registration form, but these materials will probably be only printed sources, reference works, and so on.

Lost or stolen tickets should be reported immediately to the Network so that valuable archives are in no way jeopardized. Of course, tickets should never be loaned to others. You may obtain your ticket from the first participating record office you visit. So far, counties involved are:

Berkshire	Hampshire
Buckinghamshire	Kent
Cambridgeshire	Lancashire
Cleveland	Norfolk
Cornwall	Northumberland
Cumbria	Nottinghamshire
East Sussex	Suffolk
Essex	Wiltshire
Greater Manchester	Worcestershire

Other record offices may also require identification, signing of a visitor's book, and so on. Some restrict what may be carried into the search room, banning briefcases and other large bags.

You will always find staff on hand to help with minor problems, but do not expect them to read or interpret your documents! Have specific research aims mapped out ahead and, if necessary, make an appointment with the archivist who may be able to advise you before you begin.

Below follows a complete list of all the present-day English counties with their respective county, diocesan, and city record offices grouped together. Where a record office has not yet been established, I have indicated in which other record offices relevant information may be found.

AVON

This county was created in 1974 from Bristol, Bath, and parts of Gloucestershire and Somerset. At present it has no county record office and materials relating to the areas formerly in Gloucestershire and Somerset are in those record offices. (See below for addresses).

Bath Record Office
    The Guildhall
    Bath BA1 5AW
    TEL: 0225-46111 ext. 2421
    Hours: Monday-Friday: 9 a.m.-1 p.m.; 2-5 p.m. (closes at
4.30 p.m. on Fridays)
    POSTAL INQUIRIES: queries are accepted on a limited basis
without fee.
    SEAT RESERVATIONS: not necessary
    PHOTOCOPIES: 10p (letter size); 20p (legal size)
    PARISH REGISTERS: The record office holds no original or
microfilmed registers but has bound typescript volumes (indexed) for
80% of Bath parishes. They also hold duplicate registers for Unitarian
and Methodist churches, both Primitive Methodist and Wesleyan.
    WILLS: The office holds some copies of eighteenth to twenti-
eth century wills.
    CENSUSES: Bath Reference Library, Queen Square, holds
microfilm copies of Bath censuses, 1841-1881.

    Bristol Record Office
    The Council House
    College Green
    Bristol BS1 5TR
    TEL: 0272-266031 Ext. 442
    HOURS: Monday-Thursday: 9.30 a.m.-4.45 p.m.   Friday: 9.30
a.m.-4.15 p.m. (by appointment only)
    POSTAL INQUIRIES: Accepted for a fee of L-6.90 per hour.
    SEAT RESERVATIONS: Necessary.
    PHOTOCOPIES: 17p (letter-size); 23p (legal-size) plus L-1
handling charge plus postage.
    PARISH REGISTERS: 85% of city registers are held.   These
may not be photocopied.
    NON-PAROCHIAL   REGISTERS: Baptist,   Congregational,
Methodist, Roman Catholic, Society of Friends, Unitarian, United
Reformed.
    WILLS: The office has wills dating from 1546.
    OTHER SOURCES: Hearth taxes (seventeenth century)

BEDFORDSHIRE

    Bedfordshire County Record Office
    County Hall
    Bedford MK42 9AP
    TEL: 0234-63222 ext. 2833
    HOURS: Monday-Friday: 9 a.m.-1 p.m.; 2-5 p.m.
    POSTAL INQUIRIES: These are accepted but a two-hour time
limit is set so be brief and to the point.
    SEAT RESERVATIONS: Not necessary.
    PHOTOCOPIES: 20p per sheet, all sizes
    PARISH REGISTERS: Almost 100% of registers up to the
1940's are held.
    NON-PAROCHIAL REGISTERS: Some   Baptist,   Methodist,
Moravian, Roman Catholic and Congregational.

IGI: The fiche for Bedfordshire, Buckinghamshire, Cambridge-shire, Huntingdonshire, Hertfordshire, Northamtonshire, and London are held.

CENSUSES: available on microfilm for 1841-1871.

WILLS: These date from about 1480 and have been partially indexed.

OTHER SOURCES: Hearth taxes (seventeenth century), Bish-op's Transcripts.

BERKSHIRE RECORD OFFICE
Shire Hall
Shinfield Park
Reading RG2 9XD
TEL: 0734-875444 ext. 3182

HOURS: Tuesday & Wednesday: 9 a.m.-5p.m. Thursday: 9 a.m.-9 p.m. Friday: 9 a.m.-4.30 p.m.

SPECIAL NOTE: Documents are produced at intervals of 45 minutes. No documents are produced between 12.30 and 2 p.m. Member of the County Archive Research Network.

POSTAL INQUIRIES: are accepted for a fee, details of which are sent on request.

SEAT RESERVATIONS: Very necessary as there are only sixteen seats in the search room.

PHOTOCOPIES: 35p per sheet plus a handling charge of one pound sterling.

PARISH REGISTERS: 80% of the registers for the county prior to 1900 are held. Berkshire is in the Archdeaconry of Berkshire, which also covers parts of Oxfordshire.

NON-PAROCHIAL REGISTERS: The Berkshire Record Office has relatively few; mainly Quaker and Methodist.

IGI: the entire IGI for England (1978 edition) is held plus the 1984 edition for Berkshire.

WILLS: The office has wills dating from the sixteenth century to 1857 but wills from Berkshire will more likely be found in the Oxford or the Wiltshire Record Office.

CENSUS: The 1851 census of Reading, indexed, is held.

BUCKINGHAMSHIRE RECORD OFFICE
County Hall
Aylesbury, Buckinghamshire HP20 1UA
TEL: 0296-382587

HOURS: Tuesday-Thursday: 9 a.m.-5.15 p.m. Friday: 9 a.m.-4.45 p.m. Late opening: First Thursday of the month (by appointment only).

NOTE: A member of the County Archive Research Network.

POSTAL INQUIRIES: Initial, brief postal inquiries accepted.

SEAT RESERVATIONS: This is recommended as space is limited.

PHOTOCOPIES: "Volumes, large maps, and parish registers are not photocopied. Other documents at the discretion of the archiv-ist." Cost: 18p (letter size) and 23p (legal size).

PARISH REGISTERS: Approximately 95% of Buckinghamshire registers prior to 1880 are held and are usually available to microform. The Archdeaconry of Buckingham covers the some area as the pre-1974 county.

NON-PAROCHIAL REGISTERS: thirty-three registers are held from denominations including Baptist, Independant, Congregational and Methodist churches (1765-1837) and Quaker registers 1656-1837 on microfilm.

CENSUSES: The censuses for Buckinghamshire 1841-1881 are available in the County Reference Library, housed in the same building as the Record Office.

DIOCESAN RECORDS: Until 1845 the archdeaconry of Buckingham was part of the diocese of Lincoln, so relevant records such as probate and marriage bonds may be in the Lincolnshire Archives Office. However, this office does hold Bishop's Transcripts for 1600-1840, including those of the peculiars. A catalogue is available for reference in the search room.

OTHER RECORDS: The record office has the IGI for Buckinghamshire and adjacent counties, the Protestation returns of 1642 for part of the county, wills for the Archdeaconry of Buckingham including Slough, 1483-1858.

PRINTED SOURCES:
    The Certificate of Musters for Buckinghamshire in 1522, Buckinghamshire Record Society, v. 17, 1973. (11,500 or more names, indexed.)
    Subsidy Rolls for Buckinghamshire, 1524. Buckinghamshire Record Society, v. 8, 1944. (About 8,000 names.) Typed index in search room.
    The Buckinghamshire 'Posse Comitatus' of 1798, Buckinghamshire Record Society, v. 22, 1985. Over 23,000 males aged 15-60 listed and indexed.

CAMBRIDGESHIRE RECORD OFFICE
(see also HUNTINGDONSHIRE)
    Shire Hall
    Cambridge CB3 OAP
    TEL: 0223-317281
    HOURS: Monday-Thursday: 9 a.m.-12.45 p.m.; 1.45-5.15 p.m. Friday: 9a.m.-12.45 p.m.; 1.45-4.15 p.m. (5.15-9 p.m. by appointment only)
    POSTAL INQUIRIES: These are accepted but time is strictly limited.
    SEAT RESERVATIONS: Not necessary to book a seat, but advisable for microfilm readers. A member of the Archive Network.
    PHOTOCOPIES: 15p (letter size); 20p (legal size)
    PARISH REGISTERS: The record office holds about 98% of registers for the old county of Cambridgeshire.
    NON-PAROCHIAL REGISTERS: Originals are held for Methodist, Baptist, Congregational, Roman Catholic, and Quaker congregations. Microfilm copies of Baptist, Catholic Apostolic, Congregational, Countess of Huntingdon, Methodist, Presbyterian, and Quaker registers are also held.
    CENSUSES: The complete returns for the county on microfilm are held for the years 1841-1871.
    OTHER SOURCES: The office has the IGI for Cambridgeshire

and all adjoining counties. With regard to probate records, the archivist, Mr. Michael Farrar, writes: "It is probable that the local probate records (Ely Consistory, Ely Archdeaconry, Peculiar of Thorney) beginning 1449, ending 1858, will be transferred to this office within the next year from their present home in Cambridge University Library." This would be 1989-1990. Hearth tax records (seventeenth century) are held on microfilm, and land tax records are also held.

CHESHIRE RECORD OFFICE & CHESTER DIOCESAN RECORD OFFICE
Duke Street
Chester CH1 1RL
TEL: 0244-602574
HOURS: Monday-Friday: 9.15 a.m.-4.45. p.m.
POSTAL INQUIRIES: These are accepted if they are fairly specific in nature i.e. as to name, date, and place.
SEAT RESERVATIONS: Necessary.
PHOTOCOPIES: All sizes: 20p. Copies from microfilm of parish registers and newspapers are 60p per sheet (minimum charge L-1).
PARISH REGISTERS: Approximately 85% of the county is held.
NON-PAROCHIAL REGISTERS: Those of Methodist, Unitarian, Quaker, Congregational, Presbyterian, and Baptist congregations are held.
OTHER SOURCES: These include the IGI for Cheshire, hearth taxes (seventeenth century), the censuses for Cheshire 1841-1871, and wills dating from 1545.
PUBLICATIONS: Summary guide to the office costs L-2 plus postage.

CLEVELAND
County Archives Department
81 Borough Road
Middlesborough
Cleveland TS1 3AA
HOURS: Monday-Thursday: 9 a.m.-1 p.m.; 2-4.30 p.m. Friday: 9 a.m.-1 a.m.; 2-4 p.m.
POSTAL INQUIRIES: The Cleveland Record Office does not engage in research for postal inquiries.
SEAT RESERVATIONS: These are necessary.
PHOTOCOPIES: Copies are available at 10p per sheet or 15p per sheet of microform printout.
PARISH REGISTERS: About 90% of the county's parish registers are held in the original or on microfilm.
NON-PAROCHIAL REGISTERS: The Office also has Methodist congregational records.
OTHER SOURCES: The censuses, 1841-1881, for the area covered by the new county.
GEOGRAPHICAL NOTE: Cleveland was created in 1974 from the south-east tip of Co. Durham and the north-east tip of Yorkshire. It is small in area but covers the metropolitan area of Middlesborough and Stockton-on-Tees.

CORNWALL RECORD OFFICE
County Hall
Truro
Cornwall TR1 3AY
NOTE: A member of the County Archive Research Network.
TEL: 0872-73698
HOURS: Tuesday-Thursday: 9.30 a.m.-1 p.m.; 2-5 p.m.
Friday: 9.30 a.m.-1 p.m.; 2-4.30 p.m. Saturday: 9-noon.

POSTAL INQUIRIES: These are accepted and a rate of L-9 per hour will be invoiced to the researcher.

SEAT RESERVATIONS: An appointment is absolutely necessary. In general, only two items are issued at a time, excepting microfilm reels which are issued one at a time.

PHOTOCOPIES: L-2.40 for I-ID sheets (surface mail) or L-3.79 (airmail). Payment must be made in sterling by International Money Order or banker's draft.

PARISH REGISTERS: 95% of the parishes in Cornwall have deposited their registers: 241 out of 257 parishes.

NON-PAROCHIAL REGISTERS: Most of nineteenth century Cornwall was Methodist and the Cornwall Record Office holds more than two hundred Methodist registers. In addition, the Society of Friends (Cornwall Monthly Meeting) has voted to deposit its records. There are also Baptist and Congregational registers.

CENSUSES: The returns for Cornwall 1841-1871 are held on microfilm. There is a charge of L-1 per reel consulted.

WILLS: The record office holds wills from 1600-1857 for the Archdeaconry of Cornwall. Records of twenty-eight parishes that were peculiars of the Diocese of Exeter were destroyed in World War II. There are no wills for the period 1649-1660. There are seven volumes containing indexes to wills and administrations, arranged alphabetically by parish 1570-1649, 1660-1857, in the office.

OTHER SOURCES: Bishop's Transcripts. (Some parishes were in the diocese of Truro and are at the Devon Record Office). Tithe maps for most of the 212 ancient parishes.

PUBLICATIONS: *Sources for Cornish Family History* (1988; 35pp.) L-3.50 by surface or L-4.50 airmail. *Brief Guide to Sources* (rev. 1985; 67 pp.) L-3.50 by surface or L-5.50 airmail. *Index to Cornish Probate Records, 1600-1649*, in 4 parts, each costing L-2.75 by surface or by airmail. Pt. 1 covers surnames A-D. Part 2 E-K, Part 3 L-R, Part 4 S-Z.

CUMBRIA
Cumbria is a new county created in 1974 from Cumberland, Westmoreland, the Furness area of Lancashire and part of the old West Riding of Yorkshire. The record office has three locations. The area they cover will be indicated with each one. All participate in the County Archive Research Network.

Cumbria Record Office
The Castle
Carlisle
Cumbria CA3 8UR
GEOGRAPHICAL AREA: Covers former county of Cumberland.

TEL: 0228-23456 ext. 2416

Cumbria Record Office
140 Duke Street
Barrow-in-Furness
Cumbria LA14 1XW
GEOGRAPHICAL AREA: Covers Furness area of Lancashire.
TEL: 0229-31269

Cumbria Record Office
County Offices
Kendal
Cumbria LA9 4RQ
GEOGRAPHICAL AREA: Covers former county of Westmoreland and the Sedbergh part of the West Riding of Yorkshire.
TEL: 0539-21000 Ext. 329
HOURS: (At all branches) Monday-Friday: 9 a.m.-5 p.m.
POSTAL INQUIRIES: These are accepted but they must be very limited and specific.
SEAT RESERVATIONS: This is not necessary but bear in mind to bring your readers' ticket if you already have one or identification to apply for one.
PHOTOCOPIES: 15p (letter size); 20p (legal size). The assistant archivist, Mr. D.M. Bowcock, writes: 'Most documents can be photocopied unless they are too large, too fragile, or [under] copyright.'
PARISH REGISTERS: Most Cumbrian registers over one hundred years old are now in the Cumbria Record Office at the appropriate branch. Very few are available in microform.
NON-PAROCHIAL REGISTERS: The office has registers from various denominations including Baptist, Roman Catholic, Church of Scotland, Congregational, Inghamite, Methodist, Presbyterian, Quaker and Unitarian.
WILLS: The following probate records are available:
Diocese of Carlisle 1564-1858 (originals)
Diocese of Carlisle, 1727-1941 (registered copy wills)
Docker peculiar, 1686-1770
Ravenstonedale peculiar, 1691-1851
Temple Sowerby peculiar, 1580-1816.
OTHER SOURCES: The Cumberland census for 1841 and 1851 available at the Carlisle branch. The IGI for the entire Cumbria historic area will soon be available. Hearth taxes for Cumberland (circa 1664) and Carlisle (circa 1673) are held. In addition, the Carlisle branch has the Cumberland Protestation returns (1642).
PUBLICATION: *Cumbrian Ancestors* cost L-2.50 plus L-.15 airmail postage.

DERBYSHIRE RECORD OFFICE
County Education Department
County Offices
Matlock, Derbyshire DE4 3AG
TEL: 0629-580000 Ext. 7347
HOURS: Monday-Friday: 9.30 a.m.-1 p.m.; 2-4.45 p.m.

POSTAL INQUIRIES: These are limited to one search per inquirer and a fee of L-3.50 is charged.

SEAT RESERVATIONS: It is recommended that you reserve a seat in advance.

PHOTOCOPIES: 10p (letter size); 15p (legal size)

PARISH REGISTERS: Over 80% of the county's parish registers are held by the Record Office.

NON-PAROCHIAL REGISTERS: The office also holds registers from the Methodist, Baptist, Congregational, and Roman Catholic Churches in original. Quaker records are held on microfilm only.

WILLS: Before 1858 Derbyshire wills were proved in the court of the diocese of Coventry and Lichfield so relevant records will be at the Lichfield Joint Record Office (see West Midlands). The wills proven at the Derby Probate Registry, 1858-1928, are in the Derbyshire Record Office.

BISHOP'S TRANSCRIPTS: None are in the record office. They are also at the Lichfield Joint Record Office.

DEVON

This county has four record offices: three county branches and a diocesan office. The branches each cover a geographical area of the county.

Devon Record Office
Castle Street
Exeter EX4 3PU
AREA COVERED: East Devon.
TEL: 0392-273509
HOURS: Monday-Thursday: 9.30 a.m.-5 p.m. Friday: 9.30 a.m.-4.30 p.m. Saturday: 9.30 a.m. - noon (first & third Saturday of each month).

POSTAL INQUIRIES: These are accepted for a fee of L-5 for thirty minutes or L-9 per hour's work. Research is conducted by the county genealogist, a specially appointed professional.

SEARCH ROOM FEE: There is a charge of one pound per day or ten pounds per year for use of the search room.

SEAT RESERVATION: This is not necessary, but as some classes of material are stored elsewhere, it is advisable to write ahead giving details of what you wish to see.

PHOTOCOPIES: 15p (letter size); 25p (legal size). The minimum order by post is 50p.

PARISH REGISTERS: The record office has 98% of the registers of the county EXCEPT those for Plymouth, some West Devon parishes and the North Devon area parishes, which are at the respective branch offices.

NON-PAROCHIAL REGISTERS: The office has registers from Methodist, Baptist, Congregational, and Unitarian churches, and from the Society of Friends (Quakers).

CENSUSES: The record office does not have census returns but they are available for the years 1841-1881 on microfilm at the nearby Westcountry Studies Library, Castle Street, Exeter. (Tel: 0392 273422 for an appointment for a microfilm reader.)

IGI: The fiche for Devon and Cornwall are also at the Westcountry Studies Library.

WILLS: Very few Devon wills survived the Second World War. There are seventy-five wills dating 1555-1765 from the records of the Orphans' Court of the City of Exeter and some earlier city wills. Copies of the P.C.C. wills for the area, 1812-1857, are available at the record office.

BISHOP'S TRANSCRIPTS: These are available for almost all Devon and Cornwall parishes but coverage is not complete for all years. The transcripts after 1812 were badly damaged and the series only goes to 1850 anyway. The BT's begin in the late sixteenth century but there are large gaps in the seventeenth century.

OTHER SOURCES: Lists of Freemen of the City of Exeter, 1226-present; Voters' lists, 1832-present.

West Devon Record Office
Unit 3, Clare Place,
Coxside
Plymouth PL4 OJW
AREA COVERED: Approximately the area west of Dartmoor.
TEL: 0752-264685
HOURS: Monday-Thursday: 9.30 a.m.-4.50. p.m.   Friday: 9.30 a.m.-4.20 p.m. Also the first Wednesday of each month: 5-7 p.m.

POSTAL INQUIRIES: These are accepted and brief searches will be made for a fee.   Please ask for a quote when you write with details of your research.

SEAT RESERVATIONS: It is advisable to book a seat, particularly for the period April to October. *A charge of one pound sterling per day is levied for use of the search room.*

PHOTOCOPIES: As main branch.   Copies from fiche: 15-20p per sheet.

PARISH REGISTERS: Microfiche copies cover Devon 100% for the pre-1837 era. Approximately 12% of the originals are held here.

NON-PAROCHIAL REGISTERS: A limited number are held: mainly Methodist, and some Baptist, Congregational, and Society of Friends (Quakers).

WILLS: The West Devon branch has copies of the P.C.C. wills for its area, before 1858.

North Devon Record Office
North Devon Athenaeum and Local Studies Centre
North Devon Library and Record Office
Barnstaple, Devon EX32 7EJ
TEL: 0271 47119
HOURS: Monday, Tuesday, Friday: 9.30 a.m.-5 p.m.   Wednesday, Saturday: 9.30 am-4 p.m. Thursday: 9.30 a.m.-7 p.m.

PARISH REGISTERS: Originals of the North Devon parishes are held here, the remainder of the county on fiche.

OTHER INFORMATION: as the other branches *including the one pound charge per day.*

Exeter Dean and Chapter Archives
The Cloister Library
Exeter Cathedral Library

Diocesan House
Palace Gate, Exeter EX1 1HX
TEL: 0392 72894 or 273063
HOURS: Monday-Friday: 2-5 p.m. by appointment only.

DORSET RECORD OFFICE
County Hall
Dorchester
Dorset DT1 1JX
TEL: 0305-204411
HOURS: Monday-Friday: 9 a.m.-1 p.m.; 2-5 p.m.
POSTAL INQUIRIES: Research can be conducted at a cost of L 6 per hour, preferably paid in advance. Searches are limited to two hours per request.
SEAT RESERVATIONS: It is strongly urged that you reserve a seat in advance.
PHOTOCOPIES: 15p (letter size) and 30p (legal size). A fee of 50p extra is charged for documents staff have to search for. Parish registers and other fragile documents may not be copied but may be photocopied from a microfilm if such exists.
PARISH REGISTERS: 97% of Dorset parish registers are held at the county record office but please note that Bournemouth and Christchurch are in the Winchester diocese and will therefore be found at the Hampshire Record Office (see below). The Dorset Record Office is the Diocesan Record Office for the diocese of Salisbury.
NON-PAROCHIAL REGISTERS: These include Methodist, Congregational, Quaker, and Roman Catholic.
IGI: The archivist has ordered the Dorset segment, and it should soon be available.
WILLS: The Record Office holds wills dating from 1557.
OTHER SOURCES: The tithe apportionment maps (circa 1836) are held for most Dorset parishes.

DURHAM COUNTY RECORD OFFICE
County Hall
Durham DH1 5UL
TEL: 091-386-4411 ext. 2474 or ext. 2253
HOURS: Monday, Tuesday, Thursday: 8.45 a.m.-4.45 p.m. Wednesday: 8.45 a.m.-8.30 p.m. Friday: 8.45 a.m.-4.15 p.m.
POSTAL INQUIRIES: Staff cannot answer research inquiries, apart from indicating records which are deposited, but a list of record agents can be supplied.
SEAT RESERVATIONS: It is necessary to make an appointment.
PHOTOCOPIES: Available at 20p per sheet.
PARISH REGISTERS: Most of the parishes in the ancient county have now deposited their registers at the Durham County Record Office. This includes areas now in the counties of Tyne and Wear and Cleveland.
NON-PAROCHIAL REGISTERS: The County Record Office holds records from Methodist, Congregational, and United Reformed congregations.
OTHER SOURCES: The Record Office holds the IGI for the

entire country and microfilm of the censuses 1841-1881 for the pre-1974 county. It also has seventeenth century hearth taxes.

UNIVERSITY OF DURHAM
DEPARTMENT OF PALEOGRAPHY AND DIPLOMATIC
5 The College
Durham DH1 3EQ
TEL: 091-374-3610

HOURS: Monday-Friday: 10 a.m.-1 p.m.; 2-5 p.m. (during university vacations). During university terms the office is also open 5-8 p.m. on Tuesday evenings by appointment only.

POSTAL INQUIRIES: Research cannot be undertaken by staff, but a list of record agents can be supplied.

SEAT RESERVATIONS: Although not strictly necessary, it is advisable to make an appointment.

PHOTOCOPIES: Copies, photostats, or microfilms can be made of most documents. Write for details of price.

DIOCESAN RECORDS:
Bishop's Transcripts: c.1760-1840 (with some gaps)
Marriage License Bonds and Allegations: 1664-twentieth century.

Probate records: Wills: 1540-1857 Inventories: from the sixteenth to the eighteenth centuries. [The index to the wills has been microfilmed by the L.D.S. church and is available through local Family History Centers.]

Tithe apportionment plans: 1830's and 1840's
Inclosure plans: eigthteenth & nineteenth centuries
Inclosure awards: sixteenth to nineteenth centuries
Apprenticeship, Freemen, and Guild records from the Middle Ages.

ESSEX RECORD OFFICE
County Hall
Chelmsford, Essex CM1 1LX
TEL: 0245-492211 Ext. 20067

HOURS: Monday: 10 a.m.-8.45 p.m.; Tuesday-Thursday: 9.15 a.m.-5.15 p.m.; Friday: 9.15-4.15p.m.

GEOGRAPHIC NOTE: This is the principal record office for the county and covers the whole of the historic county except the north-east and south-east which are covered by branches at Colchester and Southend-on-Sea respectively. (This includes the modern London boroughs of Barking, Havering, Hewham, Redbridge, and Waltham Forest.)

POSTAL INQUIRIES: These are accepted for a fee of L-7 per hour. Payment should be by international money order in sterling.

SEAT RESERVATIONS: This is advisable, particularly for a microfilm reader. Essex Record Office is a member of the County Archive Research Network.

PHOTOCOPIES: 22p (letter size); 32p (legal size). Parish registers for which there are microform copies may not be copied, nor may tithe awards, enclosure awards, or archival maps larger than letter-size.

PARISH REGISTERS: 80% of the county's parish registers are

held, either in the principal office or the two branches. Parish records of the Deanery of Waltham Forest are at Vestry House Museum and Archives, Walthamstow.

NON-PAROCHIAL REGISTERS: The record office has registers from Methodist, United Reformed Church, Roman Catholic, Baptist, and Quaker congregations.

OTHER SOURCES: IGI for all England; censuses 1841-1881; hearth taxes (seventeenth century); Protestation returns; wills from the fifteenth century on.

PUBLICATIONS: F.G. Emmison, *Guide to the Essex Record Office*, (Essex Record Office, 1969); *Handlist of Parish and Nonconformist Registers in the Essex Record Office*. (Both available from the E.R.O.)

GLOUCESTERSHIRE RECORD OFFICE
Clarence Row
Alvin Street
Gloucester GL1 3DW
TEL: 0452 425295

HOURS: Monday-Friday: 9 a.m.-1 p.m.; 2-5 p.m. (Thursday open to 8 p.m.)

SEAT RESERVATION: None is necessary. A charge of one pound per day is levied for the use of the search room.

POSTAL INQUIRIES: These are accepted but a fee may be charged for a lengthier search.

PHOTOCOPIES: 30p per sheet.

PARISH REGISTERS: 75% of the county's parish registers are held. There are also registers from most non-conformist sects.

DIOCESAN RECORDS: The diocesan archives of Gloucester date from 1541. They include bishop's transcripts from about 1600 and wills 1541-1941; also marriage records from the Gloucester Consistory Court.

OTHER SOURCES: The 1851 census for Gloucestershire; the IGI segment for the county; hearth taxes, 1671-1672.

PUBLICATIONS: *Handlist of the contents of the Gloucestershire Record Office* L-6.50; *Gloucestershire Family History* L-1.50; Gloucestershire parishes (map) 40p. Please add postage to above prices.

HAMPSHIRE RECORD OFFICE
20 Southgate Street
Winchester SO23 9EF
TEL: 0962-846154

HOURS: Monday-Thursday: 9-4.45 p.m. Friday: 9-4.15 p.m. Saturday: 9-noon (October-March) *By Appointment Only* [April-September: 2nd & 4th Saturday of the month only.]

POSTAL INQUIRIES: These are accepted on a limited basis. No census searches are carried out.

SEAT RESERVATIONS: There is no need to reserve a seat in the search room but it is advisable to reserve a microfilm reader. All documents for Saturday visits must be ordered in advance. Hampshire is a member of the County Archive Research Network.

PARISH REGISTERS: The archivist writes: "It is difficult to

judge the proportion of registers still held by parishes, although on the whole most have retained only current or recently completed registers." Most are on microfiche to save wear and tear on the originals. Some originals are at the Portsmouth City Record Office, Southampton Record Office and Guildford Muniment Room (see below) but fiche copies are in most cases available at the main record office in Winchester.

NON-PAROCHIAL REGISTERS: These include Baptist, Congregational/United Reformed, Quaker, and Roman Catholic. Some of these are on fiche only.

OTHER SOURCES: The census returns for Hampshire on microfilm, 1841–1881; the IGI segment for the county; hearth taxes for 1665 on microfilm.

DIOCESAN RECORDS: The records of the Diocese of Winchester are at the Hampshire Record Office. They include wills from about 1500 and Bishop's Transcripts. Marriage records date from the early seventeenth century but there are several gaps in the series.

Portsmouth City Records Office
3 Museum Road
Portsmouth PO1 2LE
TEL: 0705   829765
HOURS: Monday–Friday: 9.30 a.m.–1 p.m.; 1.30 p.m.–5 p.m. (4 p.m. Friday) Thursday: open until 7 p.m.
POSTAL INQUIRIES: Limited
SEAT RESERVATIONS: Not necessary
PHOTOCOPIES: 10p (letter size); 20p (legal size)
PARISH REGISTERS: This office has parish records of the rural deaneries of Portsmouth, Alverstoke, and Havant, though the archivist could not give a figure as to what percentage have been deposited.
DIOCESAN RECORDS: The City Records Office is the principal diocesan records office for the diocese of Portsmouth.
OTHER SOURCES: Records of Portsmouth area nonconformist and Roman Catholic churches have been deposited.

Southampton City Record Office
Civic Centre
Southampton SOG 4XR
TEL: 0703 223855 (ext. 2251) or 832251
HOURS: Monday–Friday: 9 a.m.–1 p.m.; 1.30–5 p.m.
POSTAL INQUIRIES: Limited research can be done.
SEAT RESERVATIONS: No appointment or booking necessary.
PHOTOCOPIES: 15p (letter size); 25p (legal size). Permission to copy depends on the condition of the document.
PARISH REGISTERS: 90% of Southampton City's parishes have deposited their registers here.
NON–PAROCHIAL REGISTERS: The office has Methodist and Congregational registers.
WILLS: Two local solicitors' firms have deposited wills dating from 1659–1918. They are indexed.
OTHER SOURCES: Hearth taxes (1662); Window taxes (circa 1760–1770); Rate and tax assessments 1552 onwards; Examinations

as to settlement (1711-1901: indexed to 1858); Examinations for bastardy (1811-1839: indexed). [These last three types of document are from the Corporations records.]

PUBLICATIONS: *Guide to Southampton Records* 45p. *Main Record Sources for Genealogical Information* 20p (leaflet).

HEREFORDSHIRE

Since 1974 Herefordshire has been part of the new county of Hereford and Worcester, but it has retained its own county record office with jurisdiction for the same geographical area as before 1974.

HEREFORD RECORD OFFICE

The Old Barracks
Harold Street
Hereford HR1 ZQX
TEL: 0432-265441

HOURS: Monday: 10 a.m.-1 p.m.; 2-4.45 p.m. Tuesday, Wednesday, Thursday: 9.15 a.m.-1 p.m.; 2-4.45 p.m. Friday: 9.15 a.m.-1 p.m.; 2-4 p.m.

POSTAL INQUIRIES: A genealogical panel handles inquiries at a rate of L-6 per hour.

SEAT RESERVATIONS: This is necessary.

PHOTOCOPIES: 15p per sheet

PARISH REGISTERS: 80% of the county's parishes have deposited their registers.

NON-PAROCHIAL REGISTERS: The record office also has Methodist, Quaker, and Congregational registers.

WILLS: Wills proved in the diocese of Hereford from 1540-1858 are in the Hereford Record Office. (Note: The Diocese of Hereford also includes parts of Shropshire and Powys).

OTHER SOURCES: Bishop's Transcripts (diocese of Hereford); hearth taxes (seventeenth century); censuses (1841-1871); IGI for the entire country.

HERTFORD COUNTY RECORD OFFICE

County Hall
Hertford SG13 8DE
TEL: 0992-555105

HOURS: Monday-Thursday: 9.15-5.15 Friday: 9.15-4.30 p.m.

POSTAL INQUIRIES: Up to two hours of research can be undertaken for a fee. Please write to the archivist for details.

SEAT RESERVATIONS: It is necessary to make an appointment in advance.

PHOTOCOPIES: Copying is permitted when the document is in a suitable condition. Prices not given.

PARISH REGISTERS: The record office holds 95% of the pretwnetieth century registers of the county.

NON-PAROCHIAL REGISTERS: There are also Quaker, Methodist, Baptist, and Independant church records at the Hertford Record Office.

WILLS: Wills from the Archdeaconry of Huntingdonshire (Hitchin division) from 1557-1857 and from the Archdeaconry of St. Alban's 1415-1858 are at this office.

OTHER SOURCES: IGI for the entire country; hearth taxes for the county (on microfilm).

HUMBERSIDE
Humberside is a new county forged out of the area of Yorkshire around Hull and the northern part of Lincolnshire around Grimsby. The County Record Office has two branches, the northern half being centered in Beverley, the southern half in Grimsby.

HUMBERSIDE COUNTY RECORD OFFICE
County Hall
Beverley,
North Humberside HU17 9BA
TEL: 0482-867131 Ext. 3394
HOURS: Monday, Wednesday, Thursday: 9.15 a.m.–4.45 p.m. Tuesday: 9.15 a.m.–8 p.m. Friday: 9.15 a.m.–4 p.m.
POSTAL INQUIRIES: These are accepted.
SEAT RESERVATIONS: It is necessary to make an appointment.
PHOTOCOPIES: 15p (letter size); 10p (legal size). Plus Value Added Tax (VAT) at 15% (European equivalent of sales tax.)
PARISH REGISTERS: 98% of the parishes in the Archdeaconry of the East Riding of Yorkshire have deposited their registers.
NON-PAROCHIAL REGISTERS: Other denominations which have deposited registers are: Baptist, Congregational, Methodist, Presbyterian/United Reformed, Roman Catholic, Quakers, Swedenborgian, Unitarian, Unitarian Baptist Society.
OTHER SOURCES: The office has the IGI for Yorkshire (1984 edition) and microfilm copies of hearth taxes from the Public Record Office pertaining to the area.
PUBLICATIONS: *Handlist of Parish Registers on Deposit* (25p plus postage). *Handlist of Non-Anglican Church Records on Deposit* (25p plus postage).

SOUTH HUMBERSIDE AREA RECORD OFFICE
Town Hall Square
Grimsby, South Humberside DN31 1HX
TEL: 0472-35381
HOURS: Monday–Thursday: 9.30 a.m.–noon; 1–5 p.m. Friday: 9.30 a.m.–noon; 1–4.15 p.m.
POSTAL INQUIRIES: These are accepted.
SEAT RESERVATIONS: It is not necessary to book a seat but if you wish to speak with the archivist for advice, please write for an appointment.
PHOTOCOPIES: 10p per sheet.
PARISH REGISTERS: None are held in the South Humberside Area Record Office. All parishes in this area have deposited their records with the Lincolnshire Record Office.
NON-PAROCHIAL RECORDS: Again, the office has no registers of non-conformist congregations but does have the membership books of the Grimsby and Horncastle Methodist Circuit from 1769 to 1823.
CENSUSES: Microfilms of returns of the 1851–1881 censuses

for the Grimsby area are held at the Central Library, adjacent to the Record Office.

BURIAL RECORDS: The office has the following cemetery records: Ainslie Street Cemetery 1855-1943 (indexed), Scartho Road Cemetery 1889-1941 (indexing in progress).

SHIPPING RECORDS: Grimsby is a major shipping and fishing port so these records should be noted: Grimsby registers of British ships 1824-1925 (indexed), Register of Grimsby merchant marine apprentices 1879-1919, Register of Grimsby fishing apprentices 1880-1937 (indexed), Grimsby merchant vessel crew lists 1863-1913 (indexed), Grimsby fishing vessel crew lists 1884-1914.

DIOCESAN RECORDS: This area is part of the diocese of Lincoln so all wills proved before 1858 and Bishop's Transcripts relating to the area will be found at the Lincolnshire Archives Office (see below).

OTHER SOURCES: Register of electors (Grimsby and Cleethorpes) 1863-present. Grimsby Borough sacrament certificates 1679-1791. Rate books 1883-1974. Poor Law Records for Grimsby Union 1895-1948 (births and deaths). There is restricted access to this set of records due to their nature and recent date.

HUNTINGDON COUNTY RECORD OFFICE
Grammar School Walk
Huntingdon PE18 6LF
TEL: 0480 56165
HOURS: Monday-Thursday: 9 a.m.-3.45 p.m.; 1.45 p.m.-5.15 p.m. Friday: as above but closes at 4.15 p.m. Saturday: open the second Saturday of the month, 9 a.m. to noon, by appointment only.

POSTAL INQUIRIES: These are limited to very specific topics.

SEAT RESERVATIONS: It is not necessary to reserve a general seat, but it is essential to reserve a microfilm reader. The Huntingdon County Record Office is a member of the County Archive Research Network.

PARISH REGISTERS: Most of the county's parishes have deposited their registers up to 1800. Microfilm copies are held of other parishes as well as many Cambridgeshire parishes.

NON-PAROCHIAL REGISTERS: Those deposited in this office include Baptist, Congregational, Methodist (both Wesleyan and Primitive Methodist), and, on microfilm, Moravian.

IGI: All sections of the IGI for modern Cambridgeshire (including Huntingdonshire) and the surrounding counties are available. The nearby Huntingdon Library has the complete IGI.

CENSUSES: The Record Office has the returns for 1841-1881 for all of Huntingdonshire and the Soke of Peterborough and some parishes in adjacent counties. It also has the 1861 census of Cambridgeshire and the Isle of Ely. Indexing of the 1851 census is in progress and should be completed soon.

WILLS: These date from 1479 to 1857 for the Archdeaconry of Huntingdon. The Record Office also has administrations, 1559-1857, and inventories, 1607-1857, as well as records of the peculiars of Brampton, Buckden, Leighton Bromswold, and Stow Longa, with indexes. Indexes to the probate records of the Prerogative Court of

Canterbury (1383-1700) are available on fiche.

MARRIAGE RECORDS: Allegations and bonds for marriage licenses in the Archdeaconry of Huntingdon, 1662-1883, with index.

Index of all marriages in Huntingdonshire and the Cambridgshire parish of Thorney, 1754-1837.

Boyd's Index of Marriages for Camridgeshire and the Isle of Ely, 1538-1625, 1676-1837 (microfilm) with a supplement 1801-37.

DIOCESAN RECORDS: Bishop's Transcripts for Huntingdonshire, 1604-1874, with many gaps.

ISLE OF WIGHT COUNTY RECORD OFFICE
26 Hillside
Newport
Isle of Wight P030 2EB
TEL: 0903-823820
HOURS: Monday-Friday: 9.30 a.m.-5 p.m.

POSTAL INQUIRIES: Only very brief inquiries are answered. Any research taking longer is referred to a record agent, who charges a fee.

SEAT RESERVATIONS: Although it is not essential to reserve a seat ahead, you must do so for a microfilm reader.

PHOTOCOPIES: 10p per sheet

PARISH REGISTERS: The Record Office has all the island's parish registers on deposit.

NON-PAROCHIAL REGISTERS: Registers representing most major denominations are held.

OTHER SOURCES: IGI (all England); censuses for the county; hearth taxes; a Consolidated Index of names from various manuscript sources, around 360,000 names in all.

KENT ARCHIVE OFFICE
County Hall
Maidstone, Kent ME14 1XJ
TEL: 0622-671411
HOURS: Tuesday-Friday: 9 a.m.-4.30 p.m.

POSTAL INQUIRIES: The Kent Archives Office does not deal with postal inquiries. A record agent will have to be engaged to conduct research there on your behalf.

SEAT RESERVATIONS: It is necessary to book a seat ahead of time.

PHOTOCOPIES: 18p-36p per page, depending on size.

PARISH REGISTERS: The Kent Archives Office holds approximately 70% of the registers for the county, either in the original or on microfilm. If the records of the particular parish in which you are interested is deposited elsewhere, the archivist should be able to indicate the location.

NON-PAROCHIAL REGISTERS: The office has a few nonconformist registers, mainly Methodist.

OTHER SOURCES: Hearth taxes (seventeenth century); wills dating from the fourteenth century. Microfilm copies of census returns for the county are at the nearby Reference Library.

NOTE: In June 1989 the Cathedral Archives in Canterbury was be linked with the County Archive Office. The Cathedral has 75% of the parish registers for the Archdeaconry of Canterbury and wills 1570-1639.

LANCASHIRE RECORD OFFICE
Bow Lane
Preston, Lancashire PR1 2RE
TEL: 0772-54868
HOURS: Tuesday: 10 a.m.-8.30 p.m.   Wednesday-Friday: 10 a.m.-5 p.m.

GEOGRAPHICAL NOTE: The Manchester area of the ancient county is now covered by the Greater Manchester Record Office and the Liverpool area is now in Merseyside but has a city record office. Both these offices will be found described after the Lancashire Record Office. The Furness area of the ancient county is now part of Cumbria (see Cumbria Record Office.)

POSTAL INQUIRIES: Although the Lancashire Record Office will answer inquiries of a genealogical nature, the time is very restricted: two years per parish; therefore your information must be as accurate as possible. A list of record agents can be furnished by the office.

SEAT RESERVATIONS: It is not necessary to book ahead. The Lancashire Record Office is a member of the County Archive Research Network.

PHOTOCOPIES: 20p per sheet plus VAT.

PARISH REGISTERS: The Lancashire Record Office has 90% of the parishes in the dicoese of Blackburn and parts of Liverpool and Bradford. The diocese of Manchester is not included.

NON-PAROCHIAL REGISTERS: The office has registers from the following denominations: Roman Catholic, Baptist, Congregational, Inghamite, Methodist, Presbyterian, United Reformed and Society of Friends (Quakers).

WILLS: There are probate records dating from the sixteenth century. Lancashire wills were proven either in the Diocese of Chester for those living in the county south of the river Ribble, or in Richmond for those to the north of the river. Indexes are available.

HEARTH TAXES: The Record Office has some originals for 1664 as well as microfilm copies of the Lancashire hearth tax records at the Public Record Office.

OTHER SOURCES: The IGI (1981 edition) for the whole country is available. Census records are held by the district libraries.

PUBLICATIONS: *Handlist of Genealogical Sources* (revised March 1986) 114 pp., lists all parish registers, Bishop's Transcripts, and non-conformist registers held and gives details of probate jurisdiction. Cost: L-3 plus postage.

LIVERPOOL RECORD OFFICE
Brown Picton and Homly Libraries
William Brown Street
Liverpool L3 8EW
TEL: 051-207-2147 Ext. 34
HOURS: Monday-Friday: 9 a.m.-9 p.m.   Saturday: 9 a.m.-5 p.m.

POSTAL INQUIRIES: These can only be accepted if they are

very specific.

SEAT RESERVATIONS: Not necessary.

PHOTOCOPIES: 15p per sheet.

PARISH REGISTERS: 90% of the city's parishes have deposited originals or microiorm copies.

NON-PAROCHIAL REGISTERS: Registers have been deposited from Methodist, Congregational, and Baptist churches in the city. There are also Jewish records, mostly dating from after 1837. Thirty Roman Catholic parishes have deposited registers and eventually all Catholic parishes will place their registers here.

DIOCESAN RECORDS: The Liverpool Record Office has the archives of the diocese of Liverpool, which covers Merseyside, parts of Lancashire, Cheshire and Greater Manchester. As this diocese is of fairly modern foundation, it will not have bishop's transcripts or probate records.

CENSUSES: The census returns for the city of Liverpool 1841–1881 are held on microfilm. Street indexes are available. There is also an Ecclesiastical Census for Liverpool for 1851 on microfilm.

OTHER SOURCES:

IGI for the whole country

Liverpool Workhouse: birth records 1841–1914; admissions and discharges, 1841–1914

Newspapers from 1756

Obituaries from 1879 on

City trade directories 1766–1970

Monumental inscriptions transcribed from Liverpool cemeteries

Poll books and electoral registers from 1734 on

Printed parish registers of Lancashire and probate indexes of the Prerogative Court of Canterbury.

GREATER MANCHESTER RECORD OFFICE

56 Marshall Street

New Cross

Manchester M4 5FU

TEL: 061–832 5284

HOURS: Monday–Friday: 9 a.m.–5 p.m. Second and fourth Saturdays of the month: 9 a.m.–noon.

POSTAL INQUIRIES: Inquiries of a limited nature and length can be dealt with.

SEAT RESERVATIONS: This is not necessary except for the index material from St. Catherine's House, London. A member of the County Archive Research Network.

PHOTOCOPIES: Documents may be copied subject to condition. The cost is 10p (letter–size) and 15p (legal size).

PARISH REGISTERS: None.

NON-PAROCHIAL REGISTERS: The Record Office holds some Methodist marriage registers.

WILLS: Indexes to Manchester wills 1857–1938 are held.

LEICESTERSHIRE RECORD OFFICE

57 New Walk

Leicester LE1 7JB

TEL: 0533-544566

HOURS: Monday-Thursday: 9.15 a.m.-5 p.m.   Friday: 9.15 a.m.-4.45 p.m. Saturday: 9.15-12.15 p.m.

GEOGRAPHICAL NOTE: The Leicestershire Record Office covers the ancient counties of Leicester and Rutland. Rutland ceased to exist as a separate county in 1974.

POSTAL INQUIRIES: These are limited to twenty minutes each and therefore must be very specific. No charge is levied for the service.

SEAT RESERVATIONS: There is no system of seat reservation at the Leicestershire Record Office, searchers being accepted on a first-come, first-served basis. It is a member of the County Archives Research Network.

PHOTOCOPIES: 15p (letter size); 20p (legal size)

PARISH REGISTERS: 90% of the parishes in Leicestershire and the former Rutlan have deposited their registers.

NON-PAROCHIAL REGISTERS: The Record Office has registers representing all the non-conformist denominations.

CENSUSES: Returns for Leicestershire and Rutland are held on microfilm for the years 1841-1881. There is an index for the Borough of Leicester for 1851.

WILLS: There are wills dating from 1496 to 1940 at the Record Office. Those from 1750 have been indexed.

MARRIAGE INDEX: The Record Office has an index for the Borough of Leicester, 1801-1837, in four volumes. The rest of the county for the years 1801 to 1837 is currently being indexed by Mr. R.E.A. Makins of Leicester.

OTHER SOURCES: Hearth taxes (seventeenth century) available on microfilm; Protestation returns (1642) for only three towns; the IGI for Leicestershire and Rutland.

PUBLICATIONS: *Family Forbears: A Guide to Tracing your Family Tree in the Leicesterhsire Record Office*, Jerome Farrell, 48 pp., 1987 (L-3.45 plus postage). The Leicesterhsire Family History Society has also published: *Leicestershire Military Index Vol. 1: Leicestershire & Rutland Marines enlisted 1755-1820* (price: L-1.95 by surface mail or L-3.25 airmail), *Vol. 2 Leicestershire & Rutland Chelsea Out Pension Applications 1815-1831* (price: L-2.45 by surface mail or L-3.00 airmail). *1851 Census Index* in eleven volumes, covering these registration districts and sub-districts: 1. Ibstock, 2. Market Bosworth, 3. Market Harborough, 4. Enderby, 5. Hinckley, 6. Burbage and Earl Shilton, 7. Denton and Measham, 8. Atherstone, Hartshorne, and Leake, 9. Whitwick, 10. Blaby, 11. Billesdon. (Write for price details.) These are obtainable from Mrs. H. Schutlka, 121 Station Road, Countesthorpe, Leicester. Remittances should be in sterling and payable to the Leicestershire Family History Society.

LINCOLNSHIRE ARCHIVES OFFICE

The Castle
Lincoln LN1 3AB
TEL: 0522-25158

GEOGRAPHICAL NOTE: The northern tip of the county around Grimsby is now part of Humberside (see above).

HOURS: Monday-Friday: 9.15 a.m.-4.45 p.m.

POSTAL INQUIRIES: These are handled at a charge of L-7.50 per hour. A list of record agents can also be furnished if you prefer.

SEAT RESERVATIONS: It is absolutely essential to write or telephone for an appointment.

PHOTOCOPIES: By post: 25p (letter size) and 50p (legal size) per sheet. At the office, the costs are 15p and 30p respectively.

PARISH REGISTERS: 90% of those over one hundred years old have been deposited and these are currently being microfilmed.

NON-PAROCHIAL REGISTERS: Methodist registers from the 1830's on; Congregational, Society of Friends from the late seventeenth century to 1837; and two Roman Catholic parishes.

CENSUSES: The 1841 and 1881 returns for Lincolnshire are held on microfilm.

WILLS: Indexes and abstracts are available for wills 1271-1935 for the diocese of Lincoln. The actual wills date to 1941.

OTHER ECCLESIASTICAL RECORDS: Bishop's Transcipts, 1561-1812 and 1813-1840's: marriage licence bonds 1574-1846; records of the Dean and Chapter of Lincoln Cathedral.

OTHER SOURCES: IGI for the whole country; an index of Quaker personal names compiled by the late H.W. Bruce; voters' lists.

PUBLICATIONS: *List of deposited Parish Registers*, (L-1 plus postage). *List of deposited Non-Parochial Registers*, (L-1.30 plus postage). *Diocesan Handlist*, (L-2.20 plus postage).

LONDON

This section deals with repositories in London which cover local records, as opposed to the national repositories described in Chapter 5 and Chapter 7.

GREATER LONDON RECORD OFFICE
40 Northampton Road
London EC1R 0HB
TEL: 071-633-6851
UNDERGROUND: Faringdon
HOURS: Tuesday-Friday: 9.30 a.m.-4.45 p.m.

POSTAL INQUIRIES: The Greater London Record Office does not carry out searches for patrons. It will however answer questions relating to documents in the archives.

SEAT RESERVATIONS: It is not necessary to make an appointment.

PHOTOCOPIES: Some documents may be copied, depending on format, but this does not include bound volumes. Cost is 25p per sheet.

PARISH REGISTERS: The Record Office does hold parish registers from London and the ancient county of Middlesex but is unable to quantify them at present. I suggest you write to the Archivist requesting information on the particular registers in which you are interested. [The modern county of Greater London also includes parts of Surrey and Kent.]

NON-PAROCHIAL REGISTERS: The Record Office does hold Methodist registers.

WILLS: The Greater London Record Office holds wills from

several courts which held jurisdiction in London and the surrounding areas. The main courts used were the Episcopal Consistory Court of London, the Commissary Court of the Bishop of Winchester in the Archdeaconry of Surrey, the Archdeaconry Court of Surrey and the Archdeaconry Court of Middlesex (Middlesex Division). For records of other lesser-used courts, see A.J. Camp's *Wills and their Whereabouts* London, 1974.

OTHER SOURCES: Hearth taxes. Affiliated to the Record Office is a photograph library (Tel: 633-6859) and a map and print collection (Tel: 633-7193).

Corporation of London Records Office
P.O. Box 270
Guildhall, London EC2P 2EJ
TEL: 071-260-1251

UNDERGROUND: St. Paul's. Go north up Aldermanbury, turning right into Love Lane. Skirt the north side of the Guildhall and go in by the second entrance, almost at Basinghall Avenue.

HOURS: Monday-Friday: 9.30 a.m.-4.45 p.m.

POSTAL INQUIRIES: Searches in regard to specific inquiries can only be made on a very limited basis.

SEAT RESERVATIONS: It is not usually necessary to reserve a seat but it may be helpful in some cases. I particularly recommend those with little time to do so.

PARISH REGISTERS AND NON-PAROCHIAL REGISTERS: The Guildhall Library has no parish or non-conformist registers.

WILLS: The Corporation of London Records Office holds wills from the Court of Hustings dating from 1258 to 1688. They are calendared in two volumes, both of which are on reference at the record office. The two-volume set is also available for purchase for L-40.

TAX ASSESSMENTS: These include orphans, land, poll tax and marriage tax assessments, and are mostly for the timespan 1673-1698. The only set indexed is the marriage tax assessment of 1695, which is indexed in two parts: the first part as *London Inhabitants Within the Walls 1695* edited by D.V. Glass (London Record Society, Vol. 2, 1966); the second part, which covers inhabitants outside the walls, as a typescript index at the Corporation of London Records Office.

FREEDOM RECORDS: Admittance to the Freedom of a city is a practice dating from medieval times. It was an essential step for any person wishing to engage in trade or a craft in that particular city but was only allowed through three methods: Patrimony, that is, being the child of a freeman of the city born after the date of his father's admission; Servitude, that is, having served a term of apprenticeship to a freeman of the city; or Redemption, that is, paying a higher fee.

Many cities retain Freedom records, but none in such great number as the City of London. No-one under twenty-one years old was admitted and until 1835, admittance was through membership in one of the City Companies; i.e., guilds.

Records at the Corporation of London Record Office date from 1681 to 1916, and personal name indexes are available there for consultation. Note that Freedom records prior to 1681 were destroyed by fire and that post-1916 records are at the Chamberlain's Court.

Reference: "Some Genealogical Sources in the Corporation of London Records Office", Betty Masters, *Genealogist's Magazine* Vol. 20, Nos. 10 & 11 (June and September 1982).

Guildhall Library
London EC2P 2EJ
TEL.: 01-606-3030 ext. 1863 or 01-260-1863 [After April 1990 01 becomes 071]
HOURS: Monday-Saturday: 9.30 a.m.-4.45 p.m.
SPECIAL NOTE: Although housed in the same building as the Corporation of London Records Office, this is a totally separate record office. Address mail to The Keeper of Manuscripts.
POSTAL INQUIRIES: These are not accepted. You will have to engage a record agent to search records here.
SEAT RESERVATION: Not necessary.
PHOTOCOPIES: No bound volumes or large papers may be copied. Other items may be copied at a cost of 16p per sheet. Copies from a microfilm reader/printer cost 20p per sheet.
PARISH REGISTERS: This office has 98% of the parishes of the City of London either in the original or microfilm copies.
NON-PAROCHIAL REGISTERS: Records from Independent, Methodist, Presbyterian, and Baptist congregations are held, as well as miscellaneous printed transcripts and some foreign churches.
OTHER SOURCES: The IGI for the City of London, wills from 1374, and land taxes. In the printed books section: the IGI for the entire country and censuses ior London.

MERSEYSIDE – see Lancashire.

NORFOLK RECORD OFFICE
Central Library
Norwich NR2 4NJ
TEL: 0603-761349
HOURS: Monday-Friday: 9 a.m.-5 p.m. Saturday: 9 a.m.-noon.
POSTAL INQUIRIES: These are accepted on a limited basis and a charge of L-8.17 plus VAT per hour is made. A list of record agents may also be furnished if desired.
SEAT RESERVATIONS: It is advisable to reserve a seat in advance. The Norfolk Record Office is a member of the County Archive Research Network.
PHOTOCOPIES: 27p per sheet plus packing and postage.
PARISH REGISTERS: The Norfolk Record Office has about 80% of the registers from parishes within the county. Most are originals but some are on microfilm.
NON-PAROCHIAL REGISTERS: The office has registers from Baptist, Congregational, Methodist, Quaker, and Unitarian churches.
DIOCESAN RECORDS: The Norfolk Record Office is also the record office of the Diocese of Norfolk. It holds wills proved in the diocesan court from 1370 to 1858 and other wills to 1941. It also has a series of Bishop's Transcripts for the diocese, which, though incomplete, provide a good back-up to the parish registers.
OTHER SOURCES: The office has a few hearth tax records

(seventeenth century).

CENSUSES: The adjacent Local Studies Library within the same building has microfilm copies of the census returns for Norfolk, 1841-1881, and the IGI for the entire country.

PUBLICATIONS: *List of Parish Registers Deposited*, L-1.20 plus postage). *List of Microfilm and Manuscript Copies of Parish Registers not held by the Record Office*, (70p plus postage). *Guide to Genealogical Sources (Norfolk)*, (L-2 plus postage).

NORTHAMPTONSHIRE RECORD OFFICE

Delapre Abbey
Northampton NN4 9AW
TEL: 0604-762129

HOURS: Monday, Tuesday, Wednesday: 9 a.m.-4.45 p.m. Thursday: 9 a.m.-7.45 p.m Friday: 9 a.m.-4.15 p.m. Saturday: 9 a.m.-12.15 p.m. (two Saturdays a month).

POSTAL INQUIRIES: Inquiries which are very specific are accepted.

SEAT RESERVATIONS: It is appreciated by the staff if you reserve a place in advance.

PHOTOCOPIES: 10p per sheet plus postage.

PARISH REGISTERS: The Record Office has 80% of the registers of the Diocese of Peterborough but please note that Rutland registers are at the Leicestershire Record Office.

NON-PAROCHIAL REGISTERS: Registers from United Reformed, Methodist and Quaker congregations are held.

DIOCESAN RECORDS: The Northamptonshire Record Office is also the Diocesan Record Office for the diocese of Peterborough. Wills date from 1640 and also include those from the archdeaconry of Northampton. There is a series of Bishop's Transcipts running from about 1706 to 1860.

OTHER SOURCES:

Census returns for the county from 1841, 1851, 1871, and 1881 are held and there is an index of parishes

Hearth tax records (17th century)

Register of electors from 1832 on

Trade directories, 1784-1940; professional directories.

The IGI for the county (1981 edition) is also held.

INDEXES: There is a Personal Names Index for consultation, which is not, however, a comprehensive index of all the records deposited. A Marriage Licence Index and Settlement Index are currently being compiled.

PUBLICATION: *List of Parish and Nonconformist Registers* (50p).

NORTHUMBERLAND COUNTY RECORD OFFICE

Melton Park
North Gosforth
Newcastle-upton-Tyne NE3 5QX
TEL: 091-236 2680

HOURS: Monday: 9 a.m.-9 p.m.; Tuesday-Thursday: 9 a.m.-5 p.m.; Friday: 9 a.m.-4.30 p.m.

POSTAL INQIRIES: The Northumberland Record Office offers a

comprehensive record-searching service at a cost of L-4.50 per half-hour (plus VAT). Inquiriers should send a deposit of L-4.50 and an indication of the maximum time they want spent on the search. The balance will then be billed to them. Please send for the 'Application for a Genealogical Search' form.

SEAT RESERVATIONS: It is necessary to reserve a seat. A member of the County Archive Research Network.

PHOTOCOPIES: These are available for a charge.

PARISH REGISTERS: The Record Office holds all parish registers of the county to 1900 on microfilm.

NON-PAROCHIAL REGISTERS: The Office has registers from United Reformed, Methodist, Baptist, Roman Catholic, and Quaker congregations.

OTHER SOURCES: The IGI for the whole country; censuses 1841-1881 for the county; Protestation Returns (1642) and wills from 1858. See also TYNE AND WEAR and UNIVERSITY OF DURHAM (for diocesan records)

NOTTINGHAMSHIRE ARCHIVES OFFICE and
SOUTHWELL DIOCESAN RECORD OFFICE
County House
High Pavement
Nottingham NG1 1HR
TEL: 0602-504524
HOURS: Monday, Wednesday-Friday: 9 a.m.-4.45 p.m. Tuesday: 9 a.m.-7.15 p.m. Saturday: 9 a.m.-12.15 p.m.

POSTAL INQUIRIES: The Office handles occasional *limited and specific* inquiries but all others are referred to record agents.

SEAT RESERVATIONS: It is not necessary to book ahead of time but note that this office is part of the County Archives Research Network.

PHOTOCOPIES: Available at 10p and 20p for letter and legal size respectively.

PARISH REGISTERS: The Nottinghamshire Archives Office holds 100% of the parish registers of the county before 1900 on microfiche.

NON-PAROCHIAL REGISTERS: Most denominations are represented in the Archives' collection, particularly Methodist, Quaker, Baptist, and Congregational.

OTHER SOURCES: Wills from about 1500; hearth taxes (seventeenth century) and Protestation Returns (1642) on microfilm; IGI for Nottinghamshire and adjacent counties; 1851 census on microfilm.

Department of Mamuscripts and Special Collections
University Library
University Park
Nottingham NG7 2RD
TEL: 0602-484848 ext. 3440
MARRIAGE RECORDS: The University of Nottingham holds part of the records of the Archdeaconry of Nottingham, namely bonds and allegations for marriage licenses issued by the court of the Archdeaconry from 1594-1884. Mrs. L. Shaw, the Assistant Keeper

of Manuscripts, writes that several publications have provided abstracts of the marriage bonds, and that the Department is currently working on a further volume covering 1771-1780.

PRINTED SOURCES:

T.M. Blagg and F.A.A. Wadsworth, eds. *Abstracts of Nottinghamshire Marriage Licences Archdeaconry Court 1577-1700; Peculiar of Southwell, 1588-1754*, (British Record Society LVIII, 1930).

T.M. Blagg and F.A.A. Wadsworth, eds. *Abstracts of Nottinghamshire Marriage Licences Archdeaconry Court 1701-1753; Peculiar of Southwell, 1755-1853*, (Britsh Record Society LX, 1935).

T.M. Blagg, ed. *Abstracts of the Bonds and Allegations for Marriage Licences in Archdeaconry Court of Nottingham 1754-1770*, (Thoroton Society Record Series, Vol. X, Parts I and 11, 1946-47).

T.M. Blagg, ed. *Nottinghamshire Marriage Bonds 1791-1800: Abstracts of the Bonds for Marriage Licences of the Archdeaconry Court of Nottingham*, (University of Nottingham Library, 1987).

OXFORD COUNTY RECORD OFFICE

County Hall
New Road
Oxford OX1 1ND
TEL: 0865-815203
HOURS: Monday-Thursday: 9 a.m.-5 p.m.   Friday: 9 a.m.-4 p.m.

POSTAL INQUIRIES: These are accepted at a cost of L-6 per hour, with a maximum of three hours' research.

PHOTOCOPIES: Available on a sliding scale of cost.

PARISH REGISTERS: The Oxford County Record Office holds about 85% of the parish registers for the county, either in the original or microform. Many pre-1837 registers are typed and indexed.

NON-PAROCHIAL REGISTERS: There are a few at the Oxford County Record Office, mainly Quaker, Methodist, and Independent.

MARRIAGE INDEX: An Index to Oxfordshire Marriages, 1538-1837, will become available on microfiche during 1989.

DIOCESAN RECORDS: The Oxford County Record Office is now the Diocesan Record Office, formerly the function of the Bodleian Library, Oxford.   It therefore holds Bishop's Transcipts, marriage bonds and allegations, and probate records for the diocese of Oxford, formed in 1546.   Other probate records held include those of thirty peculiars.

OTHER SOURCES: The IGI for the entire country.

NOTE: Microfilm copies of the censuses are available at the Central Library, Westgate, Oxford.

RUTLAND see Leicestershire

SHROPSHIRE COUNTY RECORD OFFICE

The Shirehall
Abbey Foregate
Shrewsbury SY2 6ND
TEL: 0743-252851 or 252853

HOURS: Monday-Thursday: 9.30 a.m.-5 p.m. (closed for lunch 12.40-1.20 p.m.) Friday: 8.45 a.m.-4 p.m.

POSTAL INQUIRIES: The County Record Office does accept short inquiries (about twenty minutes) without charge. Longer searches cost I9 per hour.

SEAT RESERVATIONS: It is necessary to book both a seat in the search room and a microfilm reader.

PHOTOCOPIES: Suitable documents may be copied at a cost of 20p per sheet (minimum postal order charge of L-1).

PARISH REGISTERS: The Shropshire Record Office holds about 80% of the registers for the county up to 1812, but a smaller percentage thereafter.

NON-PAROCHIAL REGISTERS: The Office also has Methodist, Congregational, and Baptist records.

OTHER SOURCES: The IGI for Shropshire and adjacent counties; copies of wills dating 1858-1940; hearth taxes (seventeenth century) and a few land taxes.

SOMERSET RECORD OFFICE
Obridgge Road
Taunton, Somerset TA2 7PU
TEL: 0823-337600

HOURS: Monday: 10.30 a.m.-4.50 p.m.; Tuesday-Thursday: 9 a.m.-4.50 p.m.; Friday: 9 a.m.-4.20 p.m.; Saturday: 9.15 a.m.-12.15 p.m. (by appointment only).

POSTAL INQUIRIES: The Somerset Record Office charges L-2 per hour for postal inquiries.

SEAT RESERVATIONS: The archivist writes: "To ensure a seat or a reader it is advisable to give between three and seven days notice of an intended visit."

PHOTOCOPIES: Large maps and bound volumes may not be photocopied. Other documents may be copied at a cost of 20p per sheet.

PARISH REGISTERS: The Record Office holds about 98% of the parish registers of the county before the boundary changes of 1974 and so includes those from the southern part of the new county of Avon.

NON-PAROCHIAL REGISTERS: The Office holds registers representing the following denominations, though by no means fully covering the county: Methodist, Baptist, Unitarian, Bible Christian, United Reformed, Quaker, Roman Catholic.

OTHER SOURCES: Microfilms of the census returns for Somerset, 1841-1881; the IGI for Somerset and the west of England; wills dating 1812-1857; printed and indexed hearth tax records (seventeenth century); printed and indexed Protestation returns (1642).

STAFFORDSHIRE COUNTY RECORD OFFICE
County Buildings
Eastgate Street
Stafford ST16 2LZ
TEL: 0785-223121 ext.8380

HOURS: Monday-Thursday: 9 a.m.-1 p.m.; 1.30 p.m.-5 p.m.; Friday: 9 a.m.-1 p.m.; 1.30-4.30 p.m.; Saturday: 9.30 a.m.-1 p.m. (by appointment only).

POSTAL INQUIRIES: The Staffordshire County Record Office has a limited paid service for searches in parish registers only. Please write to the Archivist for details.

SEAT RESERVATIONS: It is advisable to book a seat in the search room and obligatory for a microfilm reader.

PHOTOCOPIES: Maps and large volumes may not be copied. Present cost of copying other material is 18p per sheet, cost reviewed annually.

PARISH REGISTERS: The Record Office holds 95% of the pre-1885 parish registers for the county.

NON-PAROCHIAL REGISTERS: The office has some Methodist records, and a few Quaker and United Reformed.

OTHER SOURCES: Microfilms of the censuses, 1841-1881; printed editions of the hearth taxes (seventeenth century); and microfilm of the Protestation returns of 1642.

SUFFOLK

The county has two Record Offices, dividing the county roughly into east and west, centered on Ipswich and Bury St. Edmunds respectively.

Suffolk Record Office
Raingate Street
Bury St. Edmunds
Suffolk 1P33 1RX
TEL: 0284-763141 ext. 2522 (On Saturday: 0284-756020)
HOURS: Monday-Thursday: 9 a.m.-5 p.m.; Friday: 9 a.m.-4 p.m.; Saturday: 9 a.m.-1 p.m.; 2-5 p.m.

POSTAL INQUIRIES: These are dealt with at a charge of L-7 for the first hour of research and L-3.50 for each half-hour thereafter.

SEAT RESERVATIONS: It is not necessary to book ahead. Please note, however, that this office is a member of the County Archive Research Network.

PHOTOCOPIES: Obtainable at a cost of 20p per sheet (letter-size) and 25p (legal size). Printouts from microform cost 60p for the first sheet and 25p for subsequent sheets.

PARISH REGISTERS: This office holds 98% of the registers for the western half of Suffolk.

NON-PAROCHIAL REGISTERS: Baptist, Methodist, Congregational, Unitarian, Presbyterian, and Quaker records are held, some on microfilm.

OTHER SOURCES: The IGI for Suffolk, Cambridgeshire, Essex and Norfolk; microfilms of the censuses for 1841-1881; wills dating from 1354.

PRINTED SOURCES: Sylvia Coleman, "Hearth Tax Returns for the Hundred of Blackbourne, 1662", *S.I.A. Proceedings* Vol. 32, pp. 168-192, (1973). S.H.A. Henrey, ed. "Suffolk in 1674, Hearth Tax Returns", *Suffolk Green Books* No. 11 (1905).

Suffolk Record Office
St. Andrew House
County Hall
Ipswich IP4 2JS

TEL: 0473-230000 Ext. 4235 (Saturday: 0473-230732)

HOURS: Monday-Thursday: 9 a.m.-5 p.m.; Friday: 9 a.m.-4 p.m.; Saturday: 9 a.m.-1 p.m.; 2-5 p.m.

POSTAL INQUIRIES: As at the Bury branch.

SEAT RESERVATIONS: It is helpful to book ahead but not essential. A member of the County Archive Research Network.

PHOTOCOPIES: As at Bury.

PARISH REGISTERS: The Ipswich branch of the Suffolk Record Office has about 95% of the parish registers for the eastern half of the county.

NON-PAROCHIAL REGISTERS: The Office has original and microfilm records from Methodist, Baptist, Congregational, Roman Catholic, Quaker, and Presbyterian congregations.

DIOCESAN RECORDS: The Ipswich branch has the wills proven in the court of the Archdeaconry of Suffolk from 1444-1858 and also wills to 1940. These are all indexed. It also has Bishop's Transcripts from 1560 on.

OTHER SOURCES: Marriage index for the county 1538-1837 on microfilm; The IGI for Suffolk and microfilm of the censuses 1851-1871; Hearth taxes (seventeenth century); and Protestation returns (1642).

PUBLICATIONS: *Guide to Genealogical Sources*, L-3.75 plus postage.

SURREY

GEOGRAPHICAL NOTE: The ancient county of Surrey included the modern boroughs of Croydon, Lambeth, Southwark, and Wandsworth, which were formed in 1889. The Surrey Record Office therefore holds ancient records of what are now parts of London.

SURREY RECORD OFFICE
County Hall
Penrhyn Road
Kingston-upon-Thames,
Surrey KT1 2DN

TEL: 081-541-9065

HOURS: Monday-Wednesday: 9.30 a.m.-4.45 p.m.; Friday, Second and fourth Saturday of the month: 9.30 a.m.-12.30 p.m. (by appointment only).

POSTAL INQUIRIES: These are dealt with only if brief and specific. A list of private record agents can be furnished for lengthier inquiries.

SEAT RESERVATIONS: It is necessary to make an appointment.

PHOTOCOPIES: 20p per sheet.

PARISH REGISTERS: The Surrey Record Office holds 95% of the parish registers of parts of the dioceses of Southwark and Guildford. It holds vestry records for the whole county, however. (For Guildford, see below)

OTHER SOURCES: IGI for Surrey and the census returns on microfilm for the area covered by the modern county, 1841-1881 (i.e. not including the boroughs of Croydon, Lambeth, Southwark, Wandsworth, Kingston-upon-Thames, Richmond-upon-Thames, Sutton, and

Merton, which are parts of London.)

GUILDFORD MUNIMENT ROOM
Castle Arch
Guildford
Surrey GU1 3SX
TEL: 0483-573942
HOURS: Tuesday-Thursday: 9.30 a.m.-12.30 p.m.; 1.45-4.45 p.m.; First and third Saturday of the month: 9.30-12.30 p.m. (by appointment only).
POSTAL INQUIRIES: The archivist can only answer the briefest of specific searches.
SEAT RESERVATIONS: It is necessary to book ahead.
PHOTOCOPIES: Photocopying is permitted only when it will not damage the document. Parish registers may never be copied. The cost is 20p per sheet.
PARISH REGISTERS: This office holds about 75% of the parish registers of the Diocese of Guidford as originals. Those registers which have been microfilmed are available for consultation at the Surrey Local Studies Library, 77 North Street, Guildford GU1 4AL
NON-PAROCHIAL REGISTERS: The Guildford Muniment Room has very few non-conformist records, representing Methodist, Congregational, Baptist, and Unitarian.
OTHER SOURCES: Land taxes for 1735 for the hundred of Godalming.

SUSSEX
The ancient county of Sussex was divided in 1974 into two new counties: East Sussex, which covers the area of Brighton and eastward; and West Sussex, the area to the west of Brighton almost to Southampton. Each new county has its own record office.

EAST SUSSEX RECORD OFFICE
The Maltings
Castle Precincts
Lewes
East Sussex BN7 1YT
TEL: 0273-482349
HOURS: Monday-Thursday 8.45 a.m.-4.45 p.m.; Friday 8.45 a.m.-4.15 p.m.
POSTAL INQUIRIES: Searches are limited to thirty minutes' duration for which there is a charge of L2. For more extensive research, a list of professional record agents can be supplied. In addition, office staff do not search microfilm (including censuses).
SEAT RESERVATIONS: It is not essential to make an appointment. Member of County Archive Research Network.
PHOTOCOPIES: Material in good condition may be copied at a cost of 15p per sheet plus 35p postage. The cost of printout from microform is 20p-25p per sheet plus 50p postage.
PARISH REGISTERS: All but two of the ancient ecclesiastical parishes of the county have deposited their registers at the East Sussex Record Office.
NON-PAROCHIAL REGISTERS: The Office holds records

from the following sects: Baptists, Congregationalists, Methodists, Independents, and Countess of Huntingdon Connexion (an off-shoot of Methodism).

OTHER SOURCES: Wills dating from the sixteenth century; microfilm copies of the census returns 1841-1881; hearth taxes (seventeenth century).

WEST SUSSEX RECORD OFFICE
County Hall
Chichester
West Sussex P019 1RN
TEL: 0243-777983
HOURS: Monday-Friday: 9.15 a.m.-12.30 p.m.; 1.30-5 p.m.

POSTAL INQUIRIES: These are accepted but write to the archivist for details.

SEAT RESERVATIONS: An appointment is not strictly necessary but would be appreciated by the archivist.

PHOTOCOPIES: Copying facilities are available. Cost on request.

PARISH REGISTERS: The West Sussex Record Office holds 100% of the parish registers for the county up to the mid-nineteenth century.

NON-PAROCHIAL REGISTERS: Most of those held are from 1837 onwards. They include records from Baptist, Congregationalist, Countess of Huntingdon Connexion, Independent Calvinist, Methodist, Presbyterian, Roman Catholic, and Quaker congregations.

OTHER SOURCES: Wills dating from 1482; Protestation returns (1642); land taxes; the IGI for the county and microfilm of the census returns.

PUBLICATION: *Genealogist's Guide to the West Sussex Record Office.*

TYNE AND WEAR
This new county was formed in 1974 from the south-east tip of Northumberland around Newcastle-upon-Tyne and the north-east tip of County Durham around Sunderland. It is a heavily industrialised area.

TYNE AND WEAR ARCHIVES SERVICE
Blandford House
Blandford Square
Newcastle-upon-Tyne, NE1 6JA
TEL: 091-232-6789
HOURS: 8.45 a.m.-5.15 p.m. daily. Closed Saturday and Sunday.

POSTAL INQUIRIES: These are accepted if they are short and specific.

SEAT RESERVATIONS: Microfilm readers need to be booked but otherwise an appointment is not strictly necessary.

PHOTOCOPIES: Documents in suitable condition may be copied at a cost of 20p per sheet.

PARISH REGISTERS: The Tyne and Wear Archives Service has microfilm copies of the ancient parish registers now within its jurisdiction.

NON-PAROCHIAL REGISTERS: The Archive Service has records from the following sects: Methodist, Presbyterian, Congregational, Quaker, Unitarian, and Jewish.

OTHER SOURCES: Microfilm copies of the censuses and the IGI for the county. The archivist writes: 'Many other groups of records, e.g. guild, business/industrial, court, local authority, hospital, contain information of use to genealogists, and these form the majority of our holding.'

WARWICKSHIRE

NOTE: Warwickshire lost some of its western territory to the new county of the West Midlands (see below) in 1974, including Birmingham and Coventry.

WARWICK COUNTY RECORD OFFICE
Priory Park
Cape Road
Warwick CV34 4JS
TEL: 0926-410410 Ext. 2508

HOURS: Monday-Thursday: 9 a.m.-1 p.m.; 2-5.30 p.m.; Friday: 9 a.m.-1 p.m.; 2-5 p.m.; Saturday: 9 a.m.-12.30 p.m.

POSTAL INQUIRIES: These are not handled at the Warwick County Record Office, but the archivist is able to supply a list of private record agents who reside locally.

SEAT RESERVATIONS: It is unnecessary to make an appointment but bring along identification in order to be issued with the Record Office's reader ticket.

PHOTOCOPIES: Parish registers may never be copied. Small documents in suitable condition may be copied at a cost of 15p per sheet (letter-size) and 20p for legal-size. A photostat service for books, newspaper files, and larger maps is available and takes about one month.

PARISH REGISTERS: The Warwick Record Office holds about 95% of the non-current parish registers for the county. It also has registers from most of the main non-conformist sects.

OTHER SOURCES: The IGI for the county; a few wills; hearth tax records and Protestation returns (1642) on microfilm.

DIOCESAN RECORDS: As there is no diocese of Warwick, most wills and Bishop's Transcripts will either be at Worcester or the Joint Diocesan Record Office in Lichfield (see West Midlands).

PUBLICATIONS: *Church of England and Nonconformist registers and census returns* (50p including postage) lists the Office's holdings in these areas. It includes a map showing parishes and diocesan boundaries. The map is available separately for 35p.

WEST MIDLANDS

NOTE: A new county formed in 1974, the County of the West Midlands covers Birmingham, Coventry, West Bromwich, Dudley, and Walsall, all of which were formerly in other counties. There is no record office as yet for the county but several smaller archives and libraries are of note to the genealogist.

BIRMINGHAM REFERENCE LIBRARY
Chamberlain Square
Birmingham 83 3HQ
TEL: 021-235-4511
HOURS: Monday-Friday 9 a.m.-6 a.m.; Sat. 9 a.m.-5 p.m.
The Birmingham Reference Library has a large collection of printed parish registers and local history materials relating to the Birmingham area and surrounding counties. It also has the IGI and censuses for Birmingham.

Coventry City Record Office
Room 220
Broadgate House
Coventry
TEL: 0203 832418
HOURS: Monday-Thursday: 8.45-4.45 p.m.; Friday: 8.45-4.15 p.m.; Saturday: 8.45-noon.
POSTAL INQUIRIES: These are accepted.
SEAT RESERVATIONS: It is advisable to make an appointment for weekdays and essential at weekends.
PARISH REGISTERS: There are no parish registers at the Coventry City Record Office.
NON-PAROCHIAL REGISTERS: The Office has the records of the Coventry Primitive Methodist Circuit for the nineteenth and twentieth centuries, and also registers of thirteen Methodist churches, one Baptist and one Unitarian.
CENSUS RECORDS: 1841-1871 census returns are held on microfilm.
OTHER SOURCES: Apprenticeship records, 1781-1963; trade directories, 1874-1960; electoral registers, 1877-1980.

JOINT DIOCESAN RECORD OFFICE
Bird Street
Lichfield
Staffordshire WS13 6PN
TEL: 0543-256787
HOURS: Monday, Tuesday, Thursday, Friday: 10 a.m.-5.15 p.m.; Wednesday: 10 a.m.-4.30 p.m.
POSTAL INQUIRIES: Short inquiries can be handled, for instance, of one or two particular dates and places. Searches in the manuscript calendar of wills (see below for details) can be carried out at a cost of L-6 per hour or part thereof.
SEAT RESERVATIONS: It is essential to make an appointment ahead.
PHOTOCOPIES: Available at 18p per sheet.
PARISH REGISTERS: The Joint Diocesan Reocrd Office has microfilm copies of the parish registers of the four ancient parishes of Lichfield only.
NON-PAROCIAL REGISTERS: None.
WILLS: The Joint Diocesan Record Office has calendars of wills dating from about 1520 to 1857 which were proved in the Consistory Court of the Diocese of Lichfield. This diocese covered Staffordshire and Derbyshire, the northeastern half of Warwickshire, and the

northern half of Shropshire. They are arrranged by initial letter of the deceased's surname and within each letter by year.

OTHER SOURCES: Bishop's Transcripts; the IGI for the counties of the diocese; copies of the census returns for Lichfield and district are available at the Lichfield Library.

WESTMORELAND - see CUMBRIA

WILTSHIRE COUNTY RECORD OFFICE
County Hall
Trowbridge
Wiltshire BA14 8JG
TEL: 0225-753641 Ext. 3502
HOURS: Monday, Tuesday, Thursday, Friday: 9 a.m.-12.30 p.m. & 1.30-5 p.m.; Wednesday: 9 a.m.-12.30 p.m. & 1.30-8.30 p.m.

POSTAL INQUIRIES: These are accepted but only on a very limited basis.

SEAT RESERVATIONS: An appointment is not needed for the search room but for use of microfilm readers. A member of the County Archive Research Network.

PHOTOCOPIES: Only suitable documents may be copied at a cost of 15p per sheet plus VAT.

PARISH RECORDS: About 98% of the parish registers for Wiltshire are held in the original, the remainder are on microfilm.

NON-PAROCHIAL REGISTERS: The Wiltshire County Record Office has records from the following sects: Quaker, Baptist, Methodist, United Reformed, and Unitarian.

OTHER SOURCES: Wills from 1540; the IGI for England; census returns for 1841-1881 on microfilm.

WORCESTER RECORD OFFICE
County Hall
Spetchley Road
Worcester WR5 ZNP
TEL: 0905-763763 Ext. 3612
HOURS: Monday: 10 a.m.-4.45 p.m.; Tuesday-Thursday: 9.15 a.m.-4.45 p.m.; Friday: 9.15 a.m.-4 p.m.

POSTAL INQUIRIES: These cannot be handled except for specific inquiries relating to the Office's holdings. A list of record agents is obtainable from the office, however.

SEAT RESERVATIONS: It is necessary to book a microfilm reader though not a seat in the searchroom. A member of the County Archive Research Network.

PHOTOCOPIES: Available at 15p per sheet.

PARISH REGISTERS: The Worcester Record Office holds. about 90% of the parish registers for the diocese of Worcester which includes not only Worcestershire but also parts of Warwickshire.

NON-PAROCHIAL REGISTERS: The Record Office holds records of Baptist, Methodist, Presbyterian, Quaker, Congregational and Roman Catholic congregations.

DIOCESAN RECORDS: Wills dating from 1451 to 1858; Bishop's Transcripts.

OTHER SOURCES: The IGI for all England (1988 edition);

census returns for the county on microfilm for 1841–1881; local electoral registers 1843–1939; trade directories 1790–1972 (original and microfilm).

NOTE: Hearth tax records are kept at another branch of the Worcester Record Office at Fish Street, Worcester, but as a rule material of genealogical interest has been concentrated at County Hall.

YORKSHIRE

Yorkshire used to be the largest county in England and was divided into three administrative areas called Ridings: East, West, and South. In 1974 three new counties were created: North Yorkshire (the largest in area), West Yorkshire (centered around Bradford, Halifax, and Huddersfield) and South Yorkshire (which includes Sheffield, Rotheram, Doncaster, and Barnsley). West Yorkshire and South Yorkshire are heavily industrialised areas. The Sedburgh area is now in Cumbria and the Beverley-Hull area is now in Humberside. Hull however has its own Record Office (see below for details County Hall.)

NORTH YORKSHIRE COUNTY RECORD OFFICE
Northallerton
N. Yorkshire DL7 8AD
TEL: 0609–780780 Ext. 2455
HOURS: Monday, Tuesday, Thursday: 9 a.m.–4.50 p.m.; Wednesday: 9 a.m.–8.50 p.m.; Friday: 9 a.m.–4.20 p.m.; (closed 1–2 p.m. each day unless an arrangement is made with the staff).

POSTAL INQUIRIES: Searches are made at a charge of L-8.20 per hour with a minimum charge of L-4.10. Inquiries should be specific as to date and place.

SEAT RESERVATIONS: It is necessary to make an appointment at least six to eight weeks in advance, stating the documents needed or the precise nature of the subject being studied. A telephone appointment is preferable.

PHOTOCOPIES: Up to four sheets cost 76p with 19p for each additional sheet plus L-1.23 packing and postage. Copies from microfilm cost 52p for the first sheet and 26p for subsequent sheets plus L-1.83 handling and postage.

PARISH REGISTERS: Most of the county's registers are on deposit at the North Yorkshire Record Office but a few are at the Borthwick Institute in York, the Leeds Archives Dept, West Yorkshire Record Office (see below for these) or the Humberside Record Office (see relevant entry)

OTHER SOURCES: The 1851 census returns for the county are held on microfilm; poll books 1807–35; electoral registers, 1832–75; apprenticeship records; muster rolls.

NOTE: Copies of the searches carried out by the staff are filed with other genealogical information in the record office and may be consulted by other readers on payment of a fee. By this means, a person can be put in touch with others working on his genealogy.

PUBLICATIONS: *Guide No. 2 Parish Registers, Census Returns, Land Tax assessments, Tithe Apportionments, Enclosure Awards in the Record Office*, L-1.25. *Guide No. 5 North Yorkshire Parish Registers*, L-

1.00. *Guide No. 6 North Yorkshire Gazeteer of Townships and Parishes*, L1.00. A map showing the ancient parishes and chapelries of Yorkshire can be purchased for L3.00 plus postage.

SOUTH YORKSHIRE COUNTY RECORD OFFICE
This office was abolished on April 1, 1986 by the Metropolitan County Council and its holdings have been passed to:

SHEFFIELD RECORD OFFICE
Central Library
Surrey Street
Sheffield S1 1XZ
TEL: 0742-734756
HOURS: Monday-Friday: 9.30 a.m.-5.30 p.m.; Saturday: 9 a.m.-1 p.m.; 2-4.30 p.m. (All documents must be ordered in advance by noon on Friday.)
POSTAL INQUIRIES: Only short searches can be handled.
SEAT RESERVATIONS: It is preferable that an appointment be made.
PHOTOCOPIES: Available, the cost varying with the size.
PARISH REGISTERS: About 80% of the parishes currently in the South Yorkshire boundaries have deposited their registers.
NON-PAROCHIAL REGISTERS: Mainly Methodist records have been deposited but the Sheffield Record Office also has some Quaker, Congregational, and Presbyterian records.
OTHER SOURCES: The IGI for the county; the census returns 1851-1871 with the following indexes on microfiche: 1851 Sheffield, Wortley, Bradfield, Ecclesfield; 1871 - same towns. (NOTE: An 1851 index to Rotherham is now at the Rotherham Central Library, Howard St., Rotherham, South Yorkshire.) Hearth tax records are held in printed form.

WEST YORKSHIRE ARCHIVES SERVICE HEADQUARTERS
Registry of Deeds Building
Newstead Road
Wakefield
West Yorkshire WF1 ZDE
TEL: 0924-367111 Ext. 2352
HOURS: Monday: 9 a.m.-8 p.m.; Tuesday-Thursday: 9 a.m.-5 p.m.; Friday: 9 a.m.-1 p.m.
POSTAL INQUIRIES: The Archives Service can carry out brief searches but longer inquiries are referred to record agents. The office can supply a list of agents.
SEAT RESERVATIONS: No need to make an appointment.
PHOTOCOPIES: These are available at a cost of 20p per sheet plus packing and postage.
PARISH REGISTERS: The West Yorkshire Archives Service has about 90% of the county's registers on deposit. All those within the diocese of Wakefield are held on microfilm.
NON-PAROCHIAL REGISTERS: The office also has many non-conformist registers, mainly Methodist.
DIOCESAN RECORDS: Because West Yorkshire is in the diocese of Wakefield, which was formed out of the diocese of Ripon

in 1888, and Ripon itself was of fairly recent creation, all Bishop's Transcripts and wills before 1858 are on deposit at the Borthwick Institute in York (see below).

OTHER SOURCES: The West Yorkshire Archive Service has one important source that is not often available elsewhere: The Registry of Deeds for the West Riding. Between 1704 and 1970 it was the custom to register title deeds, such as conveyances, leases, mortgages, wills, and abstracts of title. These records cover the whole of the former West Riding including the cities of Leeds, Bradford, Sheffield and Halifax. There is a vast name index and a place index for the periods 1704-1787 and 1885-1923. There is also a separate index of wills for 1704 to 1879. Searching the indexes in person is free, but a L-6 charge per search is made if the staff do the search. A further L-6 fee is payable for a copy of the document found. These fees are payable in advance to Wakefield Metropolitan District Council in sterling. If, however, no reference is found, the L-6 copy fee will be refunded.

The West Yorkshire Archives Service also has the IGI for Yorkshire, and copies of the Protestation Returns for the West Riding. Microfilm copies of the censuses are at the Wakefield District Library Headquarters, Balne Lane, about five minutes' walk away.

Copies of wills proved in Wakefield 1858-1941 are on deposit here and the national probate calendars 1858-1936 are also available.

PUBLICATION: *Guide to the West Yorkshire Archive Service for Family Historians.* Price: L-1.75 plus postage.

OTHER BRANCHES:

West Yorkshire Archive Service, Bradford
15 Canal Road
Bradford BD1 4AT
TEL: 0274-731931
HOURS: Monday-Wednesday: 9.30 a.m.-1 p.m.; 2-5 p.m.; Thursday: 9.30 a.m.-1 p.m.; 2-8 p.m.; Friday: 9.30 a.m.-1 p.m. By appointment only.

West Yorkshire Archive Service, Calderdale
Central Library
Northgate House
Northgate
Haliiax HX1 1UN
TEL: 0422-57257 Ext. 2636
HOURS: Monday, Tuesday, Thursday, Friday: 10 a.m.-5.30 p.m.; Wednesday: 10 a.m.-noon. By appointment only.

West Yorkshire Archive Service, Kirklees
Central Library
Princess Alexandra Walk
Huddersfield HD1 2SU
TEL: 0484-513808 Ext. 207
HOURS: Monday-Thursday: 9 a.m.-8 p.m.; Friday, 9 a.m.-4 p.m. By appointment only.

West Yorkshire Archive Service
    Yorkshire Archaeological Society
    Claremont
    23, Clarendon Road
    Leeds LSZ 9NZ
    TEL: 0532-456362
    HOURS: Monday (unless open the previous Saturday), Thursday, Friday: 9.30 a.m.-5 p.m.; Tuesday, Wedneseday: 2-8.30 p.m. First and third Saturday of the month: 9.30 a.m.-5 p.m. By appointment only.
    Many parish registers have been printed by the Yorkshire Parish Register Society, which is now a section of the Yorkshire Archaeological Society. The Society also holds a number of manorial collections, including Wakefield from the thirteenth century to 1925. There is a name index to 1559 for the Wakefield collection.

West Yorkshire Archive Service, Leeds
    Chapeltown Road
    Sheepscar
    Leeds LS7 3AP
    TEL: 0532-628339
    HOURS: Monday to Friday: 9.30 a.m.-5 p.m. by appointment only. Note: Restricted service between noon and 2 p.m.
    SEAT RESERVATIONS: An appointment is necessary.
    PARISH REGISTERS: Almost all the registers from the Archdeaconry of Leeds have been deposited.
    NON-PAROCHIAL REGISTERS: Sheepscar office has records of the Yorkshire Congregational Union (1813-1968), several United Reformed churches, and many Methodist circuits for the Leeds area.
    DIOCESAN RECORDS: The Sheepscar office has the records of the diocese of Ripon, formed in 1836. It also has the records of the Archdeaconry of Richmond, as follows:
        Bishop's Transcripts from the late seventeenth century
        Tithe awards
        Original wills, adminstrations & inventories, 1521-1837
        Register of wills, 1474-90, 1503 [the original wills no longer exist], 1529-85, 1720-37, 1783-88.
        Index of wills c.1427-1857.
        Probate records of the following peculiars are also held: Altofts (1622-77), Arkengarthdale with New Forest and Hope (1698-1812), Hunsingore (1607-1839), Knaresborough (1640-1858), Masham (1576-1699), Middleham (1722-1854).
    OTHER SOURCES: Records of the Leeds Board of Guardians and Public Assistance Committee (1844-1948); Records of the Leeds School Board (1870-1903).
        PUBLICATION: *Leeds Archives, 1938-1988: an illustrated guide*, (L-6.50).

BORTHWICK INSTITUTE OF HISTORICAL RESEARCH
    St. Anthony's Hall
    Peasholme Green
    York YO1 2PW
    TEL: 0904-642315

HOURS: Monday-Friday: 9.30 a.m.-12.50 p.m.; 2-4.50 p.m.

POSTAL INQUIRIES: These are accepted at a charge of L-5 per half-hour. The parishes and dates must be fairly concise for the search-request to be accepted, however.

SEAT RESERVATIONS: This is absolutely necessary. One needs to give up to two months' notice of an intended visit.

PHOTOCOPIES: Copies are available at a cost of 25p per sheet (letter-size) and 50p per sheet (legal-size). The contents of a probate file (will, inventory, probate or administration bond) can be copied for an overall fee of L-1.75 plus postage and packing.

PARISH REGISTERS: About 33% of the registers of the diocese of York are held, including those of the former West Riding, which form the Archdeaconry of York.

NON-PAROCHIAL REGISTERS: The Borthwick Institute has registers of the following denominations: Methodist, Catholic Apostolic, Quaker, and two Roman Catholic parishes.

WILLS: The Borthwick Institute holds the original probate records of the Prerogative Court of York from 1389 to 1858. This court was the superior court in the Province of York, which covered the dioceses of York, Durham, Carlisle, Chester, plus the Isle of Man. The will of a deceased person who owned property in more than one of these dioceses would have been proved by the P.C.Y.

OTHER DIOCESAN RECORDS: Bishop's Transcripts and other records dating from 1215.

OTHER SOURCES: IGI (Yorkshire); copies of Protestation Returns (1642) for three York parishes.

PUBLICATIONS: *A list of the parochial and non-conformist registers on deposit at the Borthwick Institute*, 80p. *A Guide to Genealogical Sources in the Borthwick Institute of Historical Research*, C.C. Webb, 1981, L-2 plus postage. *An Index of Marriage Bonds and Allegations in the Peculiar Jurisdiction of the Dean and Chapter of York, 1613-1839*, compiled by E.B. and W.R. Newsome, 1985, L-7.00 plus L-2 surface mail. *An Index to the Archbishop of York's Marriage Bonds & Allegations, 1830-1839*, compiled by E.B. and W.R. Newsome, 1986, L-10.00 plus L2.50 surface mail. (Further volumes covering the periods 1820-1829 and 1810-1819 are available for the same cost.)

KINGSTON-UPON-HULL RECORD OFFICE
Guildhall
Kingston-upon-Hull
North Humberside HU1 2AA
TEL: 0482-222015 or 222016
HOURS: Monday-Friday: 8.30 a.m-5 p.m.

POSTAL INQUIRIES: Searches cannot be performed for overseas inquirers. The office will answer inquiries as to their holdings, however.

SEAT RESERVATIONS: Advisable to make an appointment.

PHOTOCOPIES: 10p per sheet.

The Kingston-upon-Hull Record Office houses primarily the records of the city which is of modern origin. It does not have Anglican parish registers - these would be at the North Humberside County Record Office in Beverly - but it does have some non-conformist registers, mainly Methodist and United Reformed from the city of Hull itself. There are neither wills nor census records deposited at the Hull City Record Office.

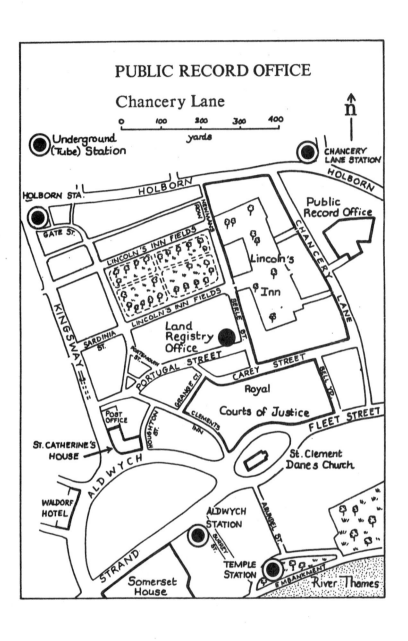

PUBLIC RECORD OFFICE

Chancery Lane

0   100   200   300   400
yards

n

Underground (Tube) Station

CHANCERY LANE STATION

HOLBORN STA.

HOLBORN

HOLBORN

Public Record Office

GATE ST.

NEWMAN'S ROW

LINCOLN'S INN FIELDS

Lincoln's Inn

CHANCERY LANE

KINGSWAY

SARDINIA ST.

LINCOLN'S INN FIELDS

SERLE ST.

Land Registry Office

PORTSMOUTH ST.

PORTUGAL STREET

CAREY STREET

BELL YD.

Royal Courts of Justice

GRANGE CT.

POST OFFICE

(HOUGHTON) ST.

CLEMENTS INN

FLEET STREET

ST. CATHERINE'S HOUSE

ALDWYCH

St. Clement Danes Church

WALDORF HOTEL

ALDWYCH STATION

ARUNDEL ST.

SURREY ST.

TEMPLE STATION

EMBANKMENT

STRAND

Somerset House

River Thames

CHAPTER 7

OTHER LONDON RECORD REPOSITORIES

The Public Record Office

Chancery Lane
London
Hours: 9:30 a.m.–5:30 p.m. weekdays

The original copies of census records, taken every ten years from 1841 to 1881, are housed with the Domesday Book and other fragile materials at the P.R.O. in Chancery Lane. They are not available for use. Microfilm copies may be consulted, free of charge, at the Public Record Office, Chancery Lane. If you do not have a P.R.O. reader's ticket, a day-pass can be obtained without a fuss at the entrance.

Be warned: this is a busy place! If you cannot arrive at the opening time, try the lunch hour. You may feel intimidated by the hoards of people who really look as if they know what they are doing, but you will soon feel like an old hand. Come prepared with as much information as possible about the families for whom you are searching. If they lived in a large town, have a street address. (Was the ancestor or a sibling born in a census year? Obtain the birth certificate for their residence.)

The Office has its own system for obtaining the microfilm needed and large posters hung on the walls explain what you need to do: a slip must be filled in with the correct reference numbers for the enumeration district, street, etc., which are to be found in indexes. Despite lack of time, try not to rush. Write legibly: preprinted forms prove very useful and time saving.

Censuses are probably the single most vital public record to genealogists. They should be used with care and intelligence. When searching an area for a surname, particularly a rare one, note all the individuals with that name. They may tie in later. Often it is important to have all the siblings' names in a family, in order to identify it definitely. Perhaps you see what you believe to be an enumerator's error; do not be tempted to correct it automatically. Later you may not remember whose error it was, or even that it was an error.

Some notes on British censuses:

Dates Taken:

7 June 1841
30 March 1851
8 April 1861
3 April 1871
4 April 1881

The 1841 census was the first, not destroyed, to record names. Ages in it are rounded to the nearest five years. Some abbreviations used:

/	end of one family
//	end of house
Y/N	Yes or No
N.K.	Not Known
Ind.	Independent means
J.	Journeyman
F.W.K.	Framework knitter
F.S./M.S.	Female or male servant
Agr. or Ag. Lab.	Agricultural Laborer

The 1851 and later censuses give:
        actual age
        place of birth
        relationship to head of household
        marital status

St. Catherine's House (birth & marriage certificates)

10 Kingsway
London WC2B 6JP
Telephone: 01-242-0262
Hours: 8:30 a.m.-4:30 p.m. weekdays

The General Registry Office houses all the birth, marriage, and death records since they were legislated by Parliament - July 1st, 1837. Only the indexes are available directly to the public for consultation, and these occupy many hundreds of volumes in the Office's reading rooms. Actual certificates must be purchased when the appropriate entry has been located in the index.

The indexes are located on the ground floor of the building, which in American terms is the first floor. A new reading room has been built at the rear of the building and the marriage indexes are now housed there. These obviously take up much more space than the births and deaths, because for each marriage, two names are indexed. The indexes for the first quarter century or so after 1837 are handwritten and all the volumes are very large and heavy. Bring your own muscles. There is no place to sit but slanted reading tables at waist level run between the stacks.

Indexes for births, marriages, and deaths are all arranged in basically the same format. Each calendar year is divided into four quarters, and each quarter may occupy several volumes. Within the quarter, names of all persons mentioned are in alphabetical order by surname and then by Christian name. The actual dates of the events are not given, only the registration district, volume, and page number of the entry in the actual register. Remember that parents had forty-two days to report a birth, so if it occurred near the end of a quarter, it might not appear until the next quarter.

DETAILS YOU CAN EXPECT TO FIND ON CERTIFICATES

Birth (Full Certificate)

Child's full name
Name of mother
Name of father
Occupation of father or status
Address
Date and time of birth

Birth (Short Certificate)

Child's full name
Date of birth

Marriage

Names of bride and groom
Their marital statuses
Their addresses at time of marriage
Names of the witnesses to the marriage (usually two)
Occupation or status of the couple
Place and date of ceremony
Whether marriage was after banns or with license

Death

Name and address of deceased
Place and time of death
Cause of death
Age of deceased
Name of attending doctor

The fee for a certificate is I5.00 and they take about forty-eight hours to prepare, so you can either return to St. Catherine's House and pick them up yourself or have then posted to your hotel.

Other indexes:

Births and deaths at sea: 1 July, 1837 to 31 December, 1874
British births abroad since 1 July, 1849
Army returns of births, marriages and deaths from 1761
Royal Air Force returns of births, marriages, and deaths since 1920

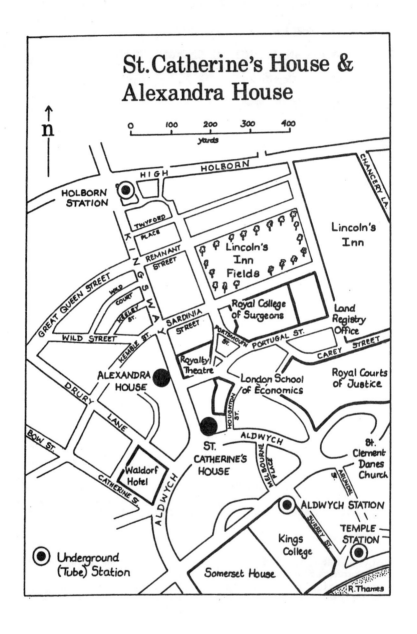

St. Catherine's House & Alexandra House

n

0   100   200   300   400
yards

CHANCERY LA.

HIGH   HOLBORN

HOLBORN
STATION

TWYFORD
PLACE

Lincoln's
Inn

REMNANT
STREET

Lincoln's
Inn
Fields

GREAT QUEEN STREET

WILD
COURT

KEELEY
ST.

K
I
N
G
S
W
A
Y

SARDINIA
STREET

Royal College
of Surgeons

Land
Registry
Office

WILD STREET

KEMBLE ST.

PORTSMOUTH
ST.

PORTUGAL ST.

CAREY   STREET

ALEXANDRA
HOUSE

Royalty
Theatre

London School
of Economics

Royal Courts
of Justice

DRURY

LANE

HOUGHTON   ST.

St.
Clement
Danes
Church

BOW ST.

ALDWYCH

ST.
CATHERINE'S
HOUSE

ALDWYCH

MELBOURNE PLACE

ARUNDEL ST.

Waldorf
Hotel

CATHERINE ST.

ALDWYCH STATION

TEMPLE
STATION

Kings
College

SURREY ST.

⊙ Underground
(Tube) Station

Somerset House

R. Thames

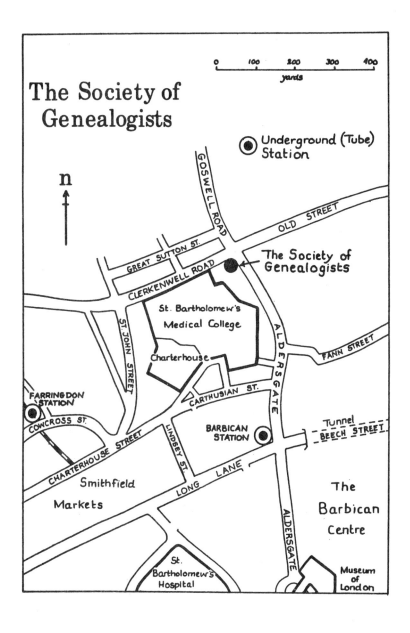

The Society of
Genealogists

◉ Underground (Tube)
Station

n

↑

GOSWELL ROAD

OLD STREET

GREAT SUTTON ST.

CLERKENWELL ROAD

The Society of
Genealogists

St. Bartholomew's
Medical College

ST. JOHN STREET

Charterhouse

ALDERSGATE

FANN STREET

CARTHUSIAN ST.

FARRINGDON
STATION

COWCROSS ST.

LINDSEY ST.

BARBICAN
STATION

Tunnel

BEECH STREET

CHARTERHOUSE STREET

Smithfield

Markets

LONG   LANE

The

Barbican

Centre

ALDERSGATE

St.
Bartholomew's
Hospital

Museum
of
London

Scale: 0   100   200   300   400
yards

The Society of Genealogists

14, Charterhouse Buildings
Goswell Road,
London EC1M 7BA
Tel: 01-251-8799
Hours: Closed Mondays.   Open Tuesday, Friday, and Saturday 10
a.m.-6 p.m.   Wednesday and Thursday 10 a.m.-8 p.m.

The Society of Genealogists has undoubtedly the most important collection of genealogical materials in the British Isles.   It was
founded in 1911 "to promote and encourage the study of genealogy"
and although it once had the exclusive atmosphere of a London gentleman's club, it has now shaken off that image and has become a
modern organization, ready and willing to help all family historians.
The Society boasts the distinguished patronage of H.R.H. Prince
Michael of Kent as its president, with the eminent genealogist A.J.
Camp serving as director.   In July 1984, the Society moved from the
extremely cramped house it had always occupied in South Kensington
to a new and modern facility in the East End.   One does not have to
be a member of the Society to use its extensive library.   Fees are,
however, charged to non-members on the following basis:

L-2 for an hour
L-5 for half a day
L-7.50 for a day or a day and an evening.

These charges are very reasonable, especially when compared
with the rates charged by professional genealogical researchers.   The
Society will also undertake research for nonmembers at a cost of
$13.50 for an hour or $72 per day.   A minimum of one or two days'
work in advance is required, and you must be very specific about
dates, names, and places when setting research goals.   The obvious
advantage to this method is that the members who will do the research for you know the collection very well, to a degree that you, the
outsider, cannot hope to match.
You may wish to consider membership in the Society, which
costs $43 for the first year and $28 annually thereafter.   Prospective
members must find a proposer and seconder, preferably people who
arc already members, and each person's application is scrutinized
before acceptance.   In other words, membership is not automatic on
paying of dues.   You will receive the Society's quarterly, *Genealogist's
Magazine*, obtain Society publications at a discount, and also be
entitled to a lower research fee.   You may also wish to subscribe to a
quarterly newsletter, *Computers in Genealogy*, l5 a year.   Meetings are
held regularly.

1) Parish register transcripts.   This category covers baptismal,
marriage, and burial records of the Church of England.   The Society
has no original registers, but it does house about 8,000 transcripts.
Some are complete copies, others are only extracts.   They usually
cover the period 1538 to 1812 or 1837, but some cover the later nineteenth century.   A complete listing of the parishes for which copies

are held is found in *Parish Register Copies: Society of Genealogists Collection*, obtainable from the Society for L2.80. Occasionally you will find a Bishop's Transcript, or BT, instead of the original register. These were exact copies of registers which the local priest was supposed to send to his bishop periodically, and often they have served to cover gaps in the originals. But remember, a BT transcript is a copy of a copy, and there has been more room for error to creep in. Invaluable as register transcripts are, they should be used with great care, and the original register should always be consulted as confirmation of your findings, even if only by mail. The transcripts at the Society are arranged by county, and interspersed with them are local histories, publications of local record, and archaeological societies of the county. There are also about 600 nonconformist register transcripts in the collection.

2) Directories and poll books. City and county directories have been published in Britain for several centuries and the Society has a large collection. Most directories will list only people of some substance – tradesmen, landowners, factory owners, clergy, and professional men. Well-to-do widows are also listed in general. Occupation and street address are usually given. The Society also has clergy and medical directories. Poll books are lists of people eligible to vote and can be helpful, but bear in mind that prior to the Reform Acts of 1832 and 1864, the franchise was given to relatively few property-owners.

3) Army and Navy lists. The Army Lists are a type of military directory, published annually since 1754. Each edition lists all the officers currently serving in the armed forces and gives an account of his career to date, including regiment, ranks held, battles, and any medals awarded. The Society possesses a complete run of these and the Navy Lists, which is the seafaring equivalent. There is also an annual R.A.F. List but as it is of post-World War I origin, it may not be of much interest to the genealogist.

4) Calendars of Wills before 1858. Calendars are lists or indexes of documents – in this case, wills. Prior to 1858, probate was an ecclesiastical matter and wills were proved in either the Prerogative Court of Canterbury (southern counties) – abbreviated to P.C.C.; or the Prerogative Court of York (northern counties) – abbreviated to P.C.Y. All the original P.C.C. wills are in the Public Record Office at Kew: the P.C.Y. wills are in the Borthwick Institute in York. In a minority of cases, when the deceased lived in a special type of parish called a peculiar, the will was proved in the archdeacon's court and will be found in the County Record Office.

The P.C.C. wills are kept in large bound volumes and until 1841 the volumes were marked not by their year but by the first name in it. The individual will was then identified by a number, which is the folio number. A folio is a group of pages, possibly up to sixteen, so it is necessary to search all the pages in the folio until the correct will is located. Ex: Trenley, 178 indicates the register for 1742, folio 178.

Names of the P.C.C. registers of wills:

Abbott, 1729
Abercrombie, 1801
Adderley, 1800
Adeane, 1506
Alchin, 1654
Alen, 1546
Alenger, 1540
Alexander, 1775
Anstis, 1744
Arden, 1840
Arran, 1759
Arundell, 1580
Ash, 1704
Aston, 1714
Auber, 1730
Audley, 1632
Aylett, 1655
Ayloffe, 1517
Babington, 1568
Hakon, 1579
Bargrave, 1774
Barnes, 1712
Barrett, 1708
Barrington, 1628
Bath, 1680
Beard, 1830
Bedford, 1732
Bellas, 1776
Bence, 1676
Bennett, 1508
Berkley, 1656
Bettesworth, 1752
Bevor, 1791
Bishop, 1790
Blamyr, 1501
Bodfelde, 1523
Bogg, 1769
Bolein, 1603
Bolton, 1724
Bond, 1696
Bowyer, 1652
Box, 1694
Boycott, 1743
Brent, 1653
Bridport, 1814
Brodrepp, 1738
Brook, 1728
Browne, 1740
Browning, 1719
Bruce, 1664
Brudenell, 1585
Bucke, 1551
Buckinghan, 1721

Bunce, 1674
Busby, 1751
Butts, 1583
Byrde, 1624
Caesar, 1763
Calvert, 1788
Cambell, 1642
Cann, 1685
Capell, 1613
Carew, 1576
Can, 1667
Chaynay, 1559
Chayre, 1563
Cheslyn, 1761
Clarke, 1625
Cobhan, 1597
Coke, 1669
Coker, 1693
Collier, 1777
Collingwood, 1810
Collins, 1780
Coode, 1550
Cope, 1616
Cornwallis, 1783
Cottle, 1682
Coventry, 1640
Crane, 1643
Cresswell, 1818
Crickitt, 1811
Crumwell, 1536
Crymes, 1565
Dale, 1621
Daper, 1572
Darcy, 1581
Daughtry, 1577
Degg, 1703
Derby, 1736
Dixy, 1594
Dodweil, 1793
Dogett, 1491
Dorset, 1609
Drake, 1596
Drax, 1683
Drury, 1590
Ducarel, 1785
Ducie, 1735
Duke, 1671
Dycer, 1675
Dyer, 1701
Dyke, 1690
Dyngeley, 1537
Edmunds, 1746
Eedes, 1706

Effingham, 1817
Ellenboro', 1819
Ely, 1808
Ent, 1689
Erskine, 1824
Essex, 1648
Eure, 1672
Evelyn, 1641
Exeter, 1797
Exton, 1688
Fagg, 1715
Fairfax, 1649
Fane, 1692
Farquhar, 1833
Farrant, 1727
Fenner, 1612
Fetiplace, 1511
Fines, 1647
Foot, 1687
Fountain, 1792
Fox, 1716
Gee, 1705
Glazier, 1756
Gloucester, 1835
Goare, 1637
Godyn, 1463
Gostling, 1782
Greenly, 1750
Grey, 1651
Hale, 1677
Hare, 1684
Harrington, 1592
Harris, 1796
Harte, 1604
Harvey, 1639
Hay, 1778
Hayes, 1605
Heatfield, 1813
Heber, 1827
Hele, 1626
Henchman, 1739
Hene, 1668
Herne, 1702
Herring, 1757
Herschell, 1822
Heseltine, 1804
Hogen, 1533
Holder, 1514
Holgrave, 1504
Holman, 1794
Holney, 1571
Horne, 1496
Howe, 1799

Hudleston, 1607
Hutton, 1758
Hyde, 1665
Irby, 1695
Isham, 1731
Jankyn, 1529
Jenner, 1770
Juxon, 1663
Kent, 1820
Kenyon, 1802
Ketchyn, 1556
Kidd, 1599
King, 1679
Lane, 1709
Langley, 1578
Laud, 1662
Lawe, 1614
Lee, 1638
Leeds, 1713
Legard, 1767
Leicester, 1588
Lewyn, 1597
Lisle, 1749
Liverpool, 1829
Lloyd, 1686
Loftes, 1561
Logge, 1479
Lort, 1698
Loveday, 1809
Luffenam, 1423
Lusbington, 1807
Lynch, 1760
Lyon, 1570
Macham, 1789
Major, 1787
Mansfield, 1821
Marche, 1401
Marlbro, 1722
Marriott, 1803
Martyn, 1574
May, 1661
Maynwaryng, 1520
Meade, 1618
Mellershe, 1559
Mico, 1666
Milles, 1487
Montague, 1602
Moone, 1500
More, 1554
Morrison & Crynies, 1565
Nabbs, 1660
Nelson, 1805
Neveil, 1593

Newcastle, 1795
Nicholl, 1838
Noel, 1700
Noodes, 1558
Norfolk, 1786
North, 1681
Norwich, 1837
Ockham, 1734
Oxford, 1812
Pakenham, I815
Parker, 1619
Paul, 1755
Pell, 1659
Pembroke, 1650
Penn, 1670
Peter, 1573
Pett, 1699
Pile, 1636
Pinfold, 1754
Pitt, 1806
Plymouth, 1726
Poley, 1707
Populwell, 1548
Porch, 1525
Potter, 1747
Powell, 1552
Price, 1733
Pye, 1673
Pykering, 1575
Pyne, 1697
Pynning, 1544
Reeve, 1678
Richards, 1823
Richmond, 1723
Ridley, 1629
Rivers, 1644
Rockingham, 1784
Romney, 1725
Rous, 1384
Rowe, 1583
Rudd, 1615
Rushworth, 1765
Russell, 1633
Ruthen, 1657
Rutland, 1S88
Sadler, 1635
Sainberbe, 1591
St. Albans, 1825
St. Eloy, 1762
St. John, 1631
Savile, 1622
Scott, 1595
Scroope, 1630

Seager, 1634
Searle, 1753
Secker, 1768
Seymer, 1745
Shaller, 1720
Sheffelde, 1569
Simpson, 1764
Skinner, 1627
Smith, 1710
Soame, 1620
Spencer, 1587
Spert, 1541
Spurway, 1741
Stafford, 1606
Stevens, 1773
Stevenson, 1564
Stokton, 1454
Stonard, 1567
Stowell, 1836
Strahan, 1748
Streat, 1562
Sutton, 1828
Swabey, 1826
Swann, 1623
Tashe, 1553
Taverner, 1772
Tebbs, 1831
Teignmouth, 1834
Tenison, 1718
Tenterden, 1832
Thower, 1531
Tirwhite, 1582
Trenley, 1742
Trevor, 1771
Twisse, 1646
Tyndall, 1766
Vaughan, 1839
Vere, 1691
Vox, 1493
Wake, 1737
Wallop, 1600
Walpole, 1798
Warbuton, 1779
Watson, 1584
Wattys, 1471
Webster, 1781
Weldon, 1617
Welles, 1558
Whitfield, 1717
Windebanck, 1608
Windsor, 1586
Wingfield, 1610
Wood, 1611

Woodhall, 1601
Wootton, 1658
Wrastley, 1557

Wynne, 1816
Young, 1711

The Society of Genealogists holds the three indexes to P.C.C. wills.

5) Boyd's Marriage Index. Percival Boyd was an eminent member of the Society of Genealogists who, before the age of the micro-chip and word processor, decided to compile an index of all the marriages in England from 1538 to which he could have access. This was, indeed, a lifetime's work and was still nowhere near completion when Mr. Boyd died in 1955. He had read through all the printed parish registers and transcripts at the society and for each made an index slip. At certain stages, he compiled his findings into typed volumes. There are three series of volumes to the Boyd's Marriage Index:

First Series. This was compiled on a county basis. Since Boyd had access only to printed registers, many parishes were not included, or only portions of a register, if it was abstracted. If there is an M on the spine, men's names only are indexed in the volume; W means women's names indexed; - indicates a mixed index; MW means both men's and women's names are indexed, but separately. Within each volume, the time span is divided into ten periods. Counties covered in the first series are:

Cambridgeshire
Cornwall
Cumberland
Derbyshire
Devon
Durham
Essex
Gloucestershire

Lancashire
London and Middlesex
Norfolk
Northumberland
Sonerset
Staffordshire
Suffolk
Yorkshire

Second series. This is known as the Miscellaneous Marriage Index and covers 1538-1837 only. It indexes printed calendars of marriage licenses, marriages mentioned in *Gentleman's Magazine* (a 'society' periodical), and counties not in the first series. However, the series is not arranged by county.

Third series. An alphabetical index of over one million names left over after Mr. Boyd's death and not included by him in the first two series. They were arranged by the Genealogical Society of Salt Lake City into alphabetical order.

Each reference to a marriage in the three series consists of only one line. For example, if you consulted the Norfolk Marriage Index Brides section for the late eigthteenth century, letter G, you would find:

Year Female Male Where

1794 GUYTON, Easter (married to) Dunthorn, George at Thursford.

For a fuller account of the ceremony, it would be necessary to consult the printed parish register at the Society of Genealogists or, preferably, the original, which in this case is held at the Norfolk County Record Office. This would give details of age, residence, and marital status. Boyd's is an invaluable research tool but no substitute for the actual documentary source.

6) Printed and typescript family histories and genealogists. The Society has a large collection, comprising volumes presented by members and those acquired by purchase.

7) London 'Society' periodicals and newspapers. In this category are included publications such as *Gentleman's Magazine*, which began in 1731 as a chronicle of the main social events in the lives of the upper classes – betrothals, "coming out" into society, weddings, bereavements, and so forth. Each annual volume is indexed, by surname only, though there are cumulative indexes for 1731–1786 and 1786–1810. Marriages are indexed to 1768; biographical notices and obituaries are indexed to 1780. Obituaries from *The Times* are also kept.

8) Pedigrees submitted to the Society.

9) Records of the East India Company. The East India Company was begun in 1601 strictly as a trading company, but in the eighteenth century began to expand its powers in India in such a way that by the India Act of 1784 it actually became the government of India. It had two classes of employees, both British emigres: merchants, who were recompensed with their profits; and civil servants, who worked for a salary. The Company's position declined after the Indian Mutiny of 1857, which caused India to come directly under the rule of the Crown, but for almost two centuries it kept records of the British men and their families who served it. Further information can be found in G. Hamilton-Edward's *In Search of Ancestry*, London, Phillimore, 1974 (new edition).

10) The Great Slip Index: 800 boxes of indexed biographical material collected by the Society, containing about three million references.

11) The International Genealogical Index (IGI) contains references to millions of baptisms and other events throughout the world, but mainly in England and Wales. The Index is on microfiche and is continually being updated.

Principle Probate Registry

Somerset House,
Strand, London WC2R 1LP
Tel: 01-405-7641
Hours: 10 a.m.-4:30 p.m., Monday-Friday

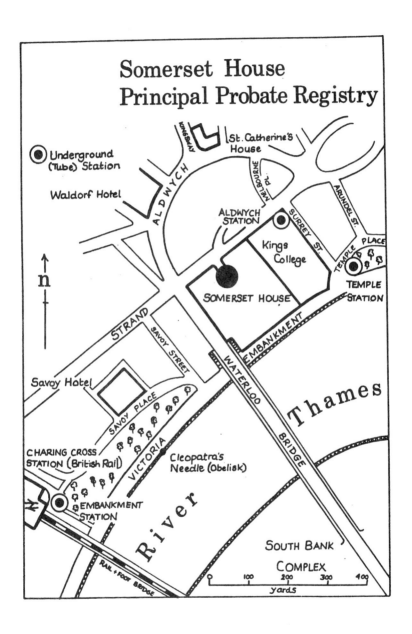

Somerset House
Principal Probate Registry

KINGSWAY

St. Catherine's
House

ALDWYCH

MELBOURNE PL.

ARUNDEL ST.

Underground
(Tube) Station

Waldorf Hotel

ALDWYCH
STATION

SURREY ST.

TEMPLE PLACE

Kings
College

SOMERSET HOUSE

TEMPLE
STATION

n

STRAND

SAVOY STREET

EMBANKMENT

WATERLOO

Savoy Hotel

SAVOY PLACE

Thames

VICTORIA

CHARING CROSS
STATION (British Rail)

Cleopatra's
Needle (Obelisk)

BRIDGE

EMBANKMENT
STATION

River

RAIL + FOOT BRIDGE

SOUTH BANK

COMPLEX

0   100   200   300   400

yards

Somerset House, as it is generally known, houses all wills from January 11, 1858. The wills are all indexed, as are letters of administration, which give details of how the estates of those who died intestate were disposed of. From 1858 to 1870, wills and administrations were indexed in separate volumes, but as the labeling on the spines is not very distinct, be sure you have checked the correct volume. Copies of wills can be obtained for 25p (about 40 cents) each. Originals of wills can be consulted without charge, but you may not copy out the contents word for word!

The Principal Probate Registry also accepts postal applications for searches. Write and ask for form PR100. You will need to know the deceased person's surname, forenames, date of death and address at time of death. The total cost is I2 (about $3). which is non-refundable even if no will is found. Payment should be made by international money order, available from banks, and in pounds sterling.

Post-1858 wills can be most useful, not only in clarifying the various relationships within a family, but also because specific addresses are given which can lead to results when searching the censuses.

The British Library

a) Reading Room at the British Museum, Great Russell St.
   Telephone: 01-363-1544
   Hours: Monday through Saturday 9.00 a.m.-5.00 p.m.

The Reading Room of the British Museum is the equivalent of the U.S. Library of Congress. It houses virtually every book ever published in Britain, including local histories and biographies, perhaps even books written by your ancestor. Many, of course, are rare and you may find a long sought-after genealogy or city directory. Make out a list beforehand of what you hope to locate.

It is necessary to apply for a reader's ticket well in advance. If you are not absolutely sure you will be visiting the Reading Room. do not hesitate to apply for a card anyway - better to be safe than sorry.

b) Newspaper Library
   Colindale Ave., London NW9
   Telephone: 01-20S-6039 or -4788

All nineteenth and twentieth century newspapers, provincial and foreign before 1800 are housed at the Newspaper Library. As you can imagine, the volume of material is staggering, so it is essential to have a specific date and location for your search. You will fill in a request slip and a page will bring you the papers from the stacks.

Newspapers are a very useful tool for the genealogist, capable of providing information which might otherwise have gone unrecorded. This is particularly true of obituaries. My grandmother's obituary revealed that my grandfather had been a city councillor and she had therefore been given a civic funeral.

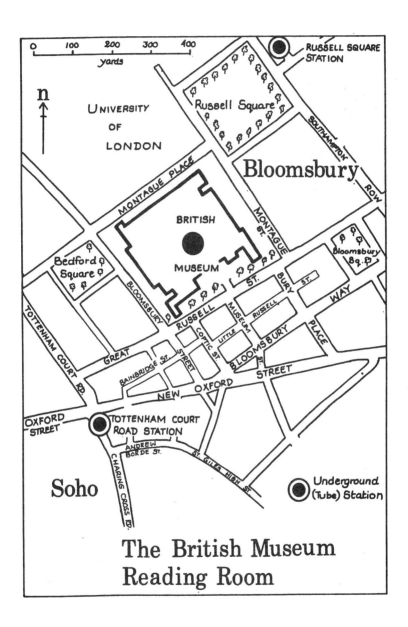

0   100   200   300   400
yards

n

UNIVERSITY
OF
LONDON

RUSSELL SQUARE
STATION

Russell Square

Bloomsbury

SOUTHAMPTON ROW

MONTAGUE PLACE

BRITISH

MONTAGUE ST.

Bedford
Square

MUSEUM

Bloomsbury
Sq.

BLOOMSBURY

ST.

BURY

ST.

WAY

TOTTENHAM COURT RD.

GREAT

RUSSELL

COPTIC ST.

STREET

LITTLE

MUSEUM

RUSSELL

BLOOMSBURY

STREET

PLACE

BAINBRIDGE ST.

NEW   OXFORD   STREET

OXFORD
STREET

TOTTENHAM COURT
ROAD STATION

ANDREW
BORDE ST.

ST. GILES HIGH ST.

CHARING CROSS RD.

Soho

Underground
(Tube) Station

The British Museum
Reading Room

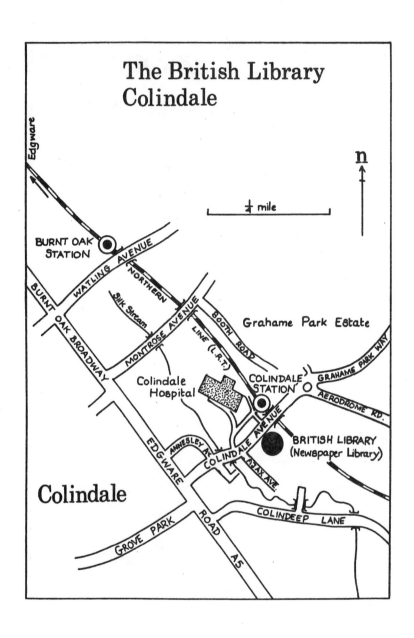

The British Library
Colindale

L.D.S. Branch Library

64-68 Exhibition Road
London SW 2
Telephone: 01-589-8561

Located conveniently near the South Kensington underground station, the L.D.S. Library has the microfiche IGI standard English genealogical reference books, and microfilm of many parish registers.

CHAPTER 8

RESEARCH IN AND AROUND THE PARISH CHURCH

The parish is probably the most ancient unit of ecclesiastical and civil administration in England. Parishes had almost certainly evolved by 1066 and many stand today in the boundaries they occupied in 1291. Thomas Cromwell, Henry VIII's Vicar-General, was the first to hint at a civil or administrative use of the parish when he instituted the registering of baptisms, marriages, and burials.

The Poor Law Act of 1601 created the 'civil' parish, which usually corresponded to the ecclesiastical one, and gave the parish council or 'vestry' new powers and obligations, which mainly concerned the care of the poor and indigent, thus creating a series of records about a class of society which would otherwise be undocumented.

Many of the parishes have deposited all their records at their county or diocesan record office, especially since the General Synod of the Church of England passed its 1978 measure requiring archival-quality depositories for such documents, but many still remain in the parishes. Fees or a donation are asked for searches.

Main Types of Parish Record of Use to Genealogists

a) Baptism, marriage, and burial registers. Until the nineteenth century, baptisms, burials, and marriages were generally entered in one book, rather mixed and not easily searched. Very early registers may be in Latin. To determine the earliest date for which registers survive in your parish, consult A. M. Burke's *Key to the Ancient Parish Registers of England and Wales*. Note that all marriages had to be performed in the Church of England, except Jews and Quakers, hence many Catholics and Non-conformists held two ceremonies.

b) Banns books: after 1753. "Banns" refers to the notice of marriage called out in the parishes of the couple for three consecutive weeks before the wedding. These may give more information than the marriage register, but remember that the marriage may not necessarily have taken place! (Before 1753, banns were usually recorded in the register.)

c) Ratepayers' lists: "Rates" are the English equivalent of property taxes and so ratepayers' lists will show the names of those who owned property within the parish.

d) Vestry minutes. The vestry was the ruling body of the parish, a group of men elected or appointed to run the affairs of the parish. After the passing of the Elizabethan Poor Law, their duties became much more civic and less ecclesiastical, having to deal with the poor parishioners, vagrants, apprenticeships, and much more. In many cases, the vestry had a very hard-headed attitude, almost un-Christian, refusing shelter and care to those for whom it did not have a legal responsibility. The vestry appointed church wardens, parish constables (fore-runners of the police), and overseers of the poor. All these officials reported regularly to the vestry. W. E. Tate, author of *The Parish Chest*, states that "vestry minutes are among the most interesting of parish records." Particularly if your ancestor was from the working, agricultural, or servant classes of society, you may be lucky enough to find many references to their upkeep.

e) Records of the Overseers of the Poor include:

-settlement certificates, which were in effect passports for paupers. A pauper - that is, a person with no visible means of support such as a trade - had to have proof of his parish of origin, usually the parish where he was born or apprenticed, in order to be accepted in another parish. If he ever became reliant on the poor law provisions, he would be returned to his settlement parish. On arrival at the new parish, the pauper handed his settlement certificate to the vestry. Settlement certificates may show if any other family members accompanied the pauper and what age they were.

-account books. Up to 1834 (when the new Poor Law Act was passed) the account books are extremely detailed. All moneys disbursed were accounted for in detail, and such items as fathers of bastards, apprenticeship arrangements for pauper children, and vagrant passes are often mentioned.

f) Apprenticeship records, mainly after 1757. Pauper children were apprenticed at cost to the parish and apprenticeship constituted legal 'settlement' in the parish. Apprenticeship indentures give name of child and age, and domicile, name, parish, and trade of master, and years of indenture.
    When a parish issued a certificate of settlement, it acknowledged its obligation to give relief to the recipient if he became a pauper. The settlement parish might not be the recipient's present address, but where he or she would be sent if impoverished.

g) Burial-in-woolen certificates (1666-1814). In 1666, parliament enacted a law requiring burial in woolen and a certificate to show it, to promote Britain's flagging wool industry. Within eight days of burial, someone present at the funeral had to furnish the affidavit - stating that the corpse's shroud had been woolen. Enforcement of the law did lapse some time before its repeal in 1814.

h) Censuses. As noted in Chapter 7 the earlier national censuses (1801-1831) were taken by the parish constables and although they were supposed to have been destroyed after all the computations were made, many constables copied their own returns into the vestry minutes or registers. An inquiry on this matter is certainly worthwhile.

Other documents that list all male citizens are:

-the poll-tax lists. Poll ("head") taxes were levied on all men over sixteen in 1641, 1660, 1666, and 1677. In parishes where the lists survive, they can be very useful as they often describe the relationships between people on the list, presumably to distinguish them.

-the 1641 Protestation Returns. At the beginning of the English Civil War, Parliament was very nervous of pro-Royalist feelings in the country and so ordered every male of eighteen years or older to take an oath "protesting" his loyalty to the Parliamentary cause and to sign his name (or make his mark) to that effect. Almost all did so, and lists were also made of those who refused. The original returns are in the Record Office of the House of Lords but parishes sometimes kept their own copy. The lists are not easy to read, but by no means impossible with some study.

i) Tithe award maps. The custom of "tithing", giving one-tenth of one's income to the local priest, had begun in England as far back as the eighth century, but after the Reformation in the sixteenth century noney payments were usually substituted for payments in kind. The effect of land enclosure and the Agrarian Revolution in the eighteenth century was the need to formalize the tithing system into a type of property tax. Therefore, the early nineteenth century saw many parishes being surveyed by Tithe Commissioners, who produced highly detailed Tithe Award maps. showing exactly who owned what and how much they owed as tithe. The scale on the maps is often as large as ten miles to one inch. Accompanying the maps was a description, giving the name of a field or building, its owner, and its occupier (if different). (See also Chapter 9.)

j) Touching for the King's Evil. In 1626 an Act required a patient wishing to be touched by the King to bring a certificate from priest and churchwardens stating he had not been 'touched' before. These certificates named the patient, and his parents or spouse. The custom was discontinued by George I in 1714.

k) Sketch-maps of pew arrangements were often made to settle arguments between rival claimants. Nearness to the altar indicated high social standing; though not of strict genealogical importance, such knowledge is nevertheless an interesting dimension to the family history.

Outside The Church

Unlike churches in the U.S., English churches are usually surrounded by the graveyard, another valuable source of information. However, only a small percentage of Englishmen have had headstones erected, these being the wealthier elements of society, so do not expect 100% success in locating relevant tombstones. It is certainly worth a try, though. High boots or old shoes will be handy, for the ground may be muddy and nettles high.

To increase the legibility of a headstone, a safe and easy method is to take with you a container of shaving cream. Apply the cream liberally to the surface of the stone, then wipe across with a ruler or rag. You will find that the shaving-cream will have entered the crevices where the monument was inscribed, making the writing much more easily visible. The cream can then be completely wiped off, without any damage to the stone.

Transcribe the inscription carefully - guesses are worse than useless. Make some notes describing the exact location of the stone in relation to, say, the main entrance of the church or a lych-gate or tree. If time permits, make a sketch-map of the location of each stone recorded.

You may wish to photograph the stone as a permanent record. A 35mm camera with adjustable focus and variable shutter speeds is best, using a slow black and white film. Color film has an estimated life of only fifty years and should not be used if you want your negatives to last. Use a flash if the light is poor.

Have the camera parallel to the stone, do not shoot from a standing position. Most importantly, practice before your trip (in varying lighting conditions), in your local cemetery. Eliminate the chance of error on "the big day" when you find the headstone of your umpteenth great-grandfather!

<u>Inside The Church</u>

Take some time to explore the interior of the church. In particular, look for the following:

-monumental brasses. About 3,000 churches in England have at least one brass, which range in date from the thirteenth to the eighteenth centuries. Before the advent of the parish register, brasses recorded pictorially and with inscriptions the lives of the more prosperous members of the community - merchants, aldermen, knights, and gentry. You will find interesting depictions of contemporary costume, and the number of wives and children of the deceased may be shown in picture form. Brasses can often be rubbed, with the permission of the parish priest, but the proper cobbler's wax and paper must be used. It is increasingly the trend for churches to provide hobbyists with replicas of their brasses, to prevent further wear on the originals.

-tombstone effigies, possibly with heraldic devices to identify the deceased. Many are medieval, most are not later than the seventeenth century. Again, there will be little or nothing that may extend your lineage, but what would be more fascinating than gazing on the face of an ancestor dead for so many hundreds of years?

-memorial tablets, similar to tombstones but often with greater biographical detail, can be found decorating the walls.

-rolls of honour, usually commemorating soldiers from the Boer War (1899–1902), World War I and World War II. These give the soldier's full name, rank and regiment, and sometimes the battle where the man met his death. This can certainly be a lead to documentary evidence at the P.R.O.

-parish or local history leaflets. It is impossible to trace your family history without some understanding of national and local events which shaped their lives, and a parish history can fill in many details for you. An excellent example of a longer work is the history of St. Godwald's Parish, Aston Fields, Worcestershire, by Janet Grierson and published by the parish. It shows how inextricably the life of the church was tied into that of the community and shows the evolution of the parish from a chapelry of Stoke Prior to an independent parish with the coming of the railway. Even briefer histories can be most illuminating.

DATES IMPORTANT IN DEVELOPMENT OF THE PARISH

1538 – Thomas Cromwell ordered that parish registers be kept on paper.

1558 – Accession of Elizabeth I. More registers survive from this date.

1559 – Act of Uniformity begins punishment of Roman Catholics and non-conformists.

1598 – Elizabeth I's church synod orders that registers be copied on vellum, from 1538, but many priests copy only from 1558.

1601 – Poor Law enacted – parishes become responsible for the maintenance of paupers.

1649 – 1660 – Interregnum under Cromwell. Most registers not kept.

1662 – Poor Law "Settlement" Act. Paupers must have settlement certificates if they wish to move.

1753 – Lord Hardwicke's Marriage Act registers now kept in pre-printed books, with separate banns books.

1812 – Rose's Act: parish registers to be kept in three separate books.

1834 – New Poor Law ends the responsibility and power of the vestry.

1836 – Great Tithe Act leads to drawing up of Tithe Award maps.

1888 – Local Government Acts end the parish's civic responsibility totally.

CHAPTER 9

MAPS AND THE GENEALOGIST

Why does the genealogist need to concern himself with maps and geography? In the case of English genealogy, there are many important reasons why he should do so. Firstly, the face of England has changed so rapidly over the past two hundred and fifty years that places which were once thriving centers of industry may now be mere hamlets, or contrary-wise, the hamlet which saw the birth of your ancestor may now be a teeming metropolis. Parish and county boundaries have changed, often several times, and this will affect where you need to seek records. For instance, the county of Rutland totally disappeared in 1974, and earlier, the five pottery towns of Staffordshire became the City of Stoke-on-Trent. My own village of Aston Fields, which is now part of the parish of Finstall, Worcestershire, was originally part of Stoke Prior parish. Maps are important sources for this type of information.

Secondly, there is a wide variety of maps which were drawn up for various purposes and which contain much greater detail than we are used to in modern road atlases and geographical atlases. These include estate maps, tithe apportionment maps and glebe terriers. In many cases, these maps show individual dwellings and name the tenants. I shall be discussing these documents in greater detail later in the chapter.

Thirdly, maps are important for tracing possible migration routes of ancestors. One can readily spot the main roads, turnpikes, railways, rivers and canals which may have been utilized. Possible hindrances such as mountains are immediately obvious. Sensible use of maps in research problems can be a great time-saver.

Features on English Maps

The great age of map-making began in the reign of Elizabeth I with the spread of the knowledge of scientific methods of surveying. Earlier maps tend to represent features pictorially and a uniform system of representing features did not arise until the nineteenth century, but this is what gives older maps some of their charm. Features shown will often (but not always) include:

COUNTY BOUNDARIES: The county has been the unit of local government since the Norman conquest, but its boundaries are no bar to migration.

PARISH BOUNDARIES

HUNDREDS: the hundred was a group of parishes united for civil purposes such as keeping the peace. Now a defunct unit of government, but still active in the seventeenth century.

NATURAL FEATURES: such as hills, lakes, valleys, forests.

MAN-MADE FEATURES: such as canals, railways (in later maps), harbours, mines, roads, wagon-ways, bridle-paths (horse-trails), and turnpikes.

Nineteenth Century Maps

The maps on which all modern maps are based and which is the standard for all of them are the Ordnance Survey series. The Ordnance Survey was, and still is, a government agency and was the first attempt to survey Britain in a standardized way with reliable and consistent maps as a result. The first edition, known as the "Old Series", began publication in 1805 with maps of south-east England and 110 sheets had been completed when the survey finished in 1873. The scale on these maps is one inch to the mile and each one measures 30" x 40". Features shown go as small as individual farms and buildings such as lime kilns, and larger houses are named. Maps prepared later in the series show railways and railway stations.

Fortunately for the genealogist, this series has been reprinted and is available from David & Charles p.l.c., Brunel House, Forde Road, Newton Abbott, Devon TQ12 4YG for I2.95 each sheet plus postage. Major credit cards are accepted.

The Ordnance Survey also produced a set of maps which were 25" to the mile between 1853 and 1893. This set had further editions in 1891-1907 and 1906-1922. For urban areas, a very large-scale set of maps was produced, showing five feet to one mile, so that even objects such as lamp-posts and horse troughs were included. This series dates from 1843 to 1894.

Many commercial publishers jumped on the Ordnance Survey's bandwagon and produced atlases, railway directories, town plans etc. based directly on O.S. One such set has been reproduced by David Gardner, Derek Harland and Frank Smith in *A Genealogical Atlas of England and Wales*, Stevenson's Genealogical Center, Provo, Utah, 1974, (2nd ed.) The scale of the maps is five miles to the inch (which compares with modern road atlases). Thus large features such as hills, rivers and railways are shown, as well as county boundaries. Reproduction is not always of the best and some place-names are difficult to read without a magnifying glass. However, a useful index of parishes with pre-1813 registers is included, along with map-references.

Tithe Maps

From early medieval times, each parishioner had to pay a tithe to the parish priest to contribute to his upkeep. The tithe could take the form of food produced by the villager, or a proportion of the goods he had produced during the year, if he were a craftsman.

This system worked well down to the eighteenth century, when it became more convenient to pay a monetary sum than payment in kind. This was because the villager was by now more likely to be an employee of a farmer than an independent worker of his own plot. The tithe system thus became antiquated and needed reform.

Eventually Parliament caught up with the times and passed the Tithe Act of 1836, by which commissioners were dispatched to almost every parish to draw up a large-scale survey of the parish along with a written key and a valuation of the property for tithe-apportionment purposes. 11,800 parishes were covered, about 79% of the parishes in England and Wales. What happened to the remaining 21%? These parishes had already commuted tithes to monetary payment by prior agreement, usually when the parish lands were enclosed (see below).

Most of the plans were drawn up between 1836 and 1841, and all had been completed by 1851. The scale of the map was usually 6 chains (132 yards) to the inch and so are on a very large scale. Individual houses and barns are clearly shown, as well as rivers and roads, and all fields are numbered. According to J.B. Harley in *Maps for the Local Historian* (National Council of Social Service, London, 1972) only one-sixth of the maps were accepted by the commissioners as first-class maps and the rest are very variable in quality. The researcher would therefore want to compare the tithe map with perhaps a large-scale Ordnance Survey map or enclosure map if one exists for the parish.

Accompanying each map was a written key, for which the format was quite rigid. Each parcel of land numbered on the map and the corresponding number on the key will show: the landowner, the occupier, the name and description of the land or premises, the state of cultivation (arable/pasture etc.), the acreage and rental value.

An example given by John West in *Village Records* (Phillimore, Chichester, 1982, 2nd. edition) comes from Chaddlesley Corbett in Worcestershire:

Owner	Occupier	Number on plan	Name & descript. land & premises	State of cultivation
Piercy	James			
The Rev.	Blakeway	44	Pit Close	Arable
		65	The Nine Acres	Arable
George Henry		66	The Five Acres	Arable
(The Old Glebe)		67	Pew Moor	Arable
	George Durant	35	House and Garden	
	John Broad	35a	Garden	
	Elizabeth Bate	154	Pool Meadow	Pasture
		156	Homestead	
		157	Barn Close	Arable
		158	Three Cornered Field	Arable

Space does not permit reproduction of the acreage and rental columns. The above data would be legal proof that a certain person occupied a particular house at the time of the survey, and the researcher would also be able to garner many facts concerning the family's wealth and social status. Considering that the 1841 national census had such little detail in it, the tithe apportionment documents can be highly significant.

Three copies were made of each survey: the first went to the Tithe Commission in London, and they have a complete set for the whole country. The address to which to write is: Office of the Tithe Redemption Commission, Finsbury Square, London E.C.4. The second copy went to the Diocesan Registrar and many have since found their way to the County Record Office. The third copy was given to the incumbent of the parish and may be still with the parish records, or, more likely, will have been deposited in the C.R.O. Thus many record offices will have two sets of tithe maps.

Enclosure Maps

You may have come across the term 'enclosure' or 'inclosure' in reading about seventeenth and eighteenth century England and wondered exactly what that was. During the Middle Ages, each parish was usually owned by one lord who sub-let his land in return for service from the tenants. The parish would have three very large fields, without hedges, divided into strips. The strips were then allotted to tenants in what was considered to be a fair way. Thus a man might have three strips in the first field, two in the second and five in the third, but none of them might be adjacent. This system worked well until the sixteenth century, when sheep-farming began to predominate. Landlords wanted their fields back to turn into pasture. In many places they were successful in performing these 'private enclosures' despite the opposition of Parliament, who liked things to be the way they always had been.

After the Restoration of Charles II in 1660, enclosure of land became an economic necessity and was no longer frowned upon by the central government. Indeed, Parliament began to take a hand in regulating enclosures: every parish that was to be enclosed had to have a parliamentary commission appointed to oversee the process and a private Enclosure Act had to be passed in Parliament which pertained only to that particular village.

What exactly was the job of the Parliamentary commission? John West describes it thus: "a local committee of substantial men, authorized to Act of Parliament, who employed surveyors to divide and re-allocate the commons and heath-land remaining in the village".(1) They sub-divided the large medieval fields down to the sizes we see nowadays, they often re-routed roads more efficiently through the parish, and also commuted the tithe-value, thus pre-empting the work of the tithe commissioners. For this reason, areas which are rich in enclosure maps are usually weak in tithe maps.(2)

(1) West, John, *Village Records* (Phillimore, London, 1982, 2nd edition) p.137.

(2) Harley, J.B., *Maps for the Local Historian London*, 1972)

There were two parts to the paperwork generated by the Commission: firstly, an enclosure award: a written survey of the parish describing the field boundaries in detail, and summarizing the decisions of the Commissioners. The second part was the enclosure map: large-scale to identify the land in question and give good detail. Unfortunately, not all enclosure awards were accompanied by a map. In Worcestershire, for instance, of 117 Awards, fifty-one have no maps and one parish has a map but no written award. Maps tend to be more common after 1770.

Most enclosures were enacted between 1750 and 1850: over 5,000 parishes were enclosed by act of Parliament during this period. Most of these parishes were in the Midland counties, the North-East (Lincolnshire and Yorkshire), Norfolk and the South. The counties to the South-East and South-West of London, along with Devon and Cornwall, had been enclosed much earlier and for them no written awards survive but estate maps can often be very useful (see below).

By the dawn of the Victorian era, it was decided that it was necessary to pass a general act that would provide for the setting up of all future enclosure commissions and so the General Inclosure Acts of 1836 and 1845 were passed. This brings us to a point of spelling: inclosure is the spelling used by parliament and lawyers; enclosure is the spelling adopted by historians. They both refer to the same idea.

Because enclosure maps were so large-scale, their use to the genealogist can be invaluable. They give boundaries, field names, the use to which those fields were to be put, names of tenants, and so on. Later maps (after 1830) often show the layout prior to enclosure; i.e., the medieval arrangement of the land. There were generally two types of map: that of arable fields and meadows, and that of wastelands. The latter can show how new settlements, such as mining villages, were created. Two copies of the award and map were drawn up, one went to the parish clerk (and thus may have been deposited in the County Record Office) and one copy went to the Clerk of the Peace for the county, and so may also be found at the C.R.O.

How did the enclosure movement change life for your eighteenth and nineteenth century ancestors? The renowned historian W.G. Hoskins commented: "..the transformation of the landscape was ... remarkably swift. A villager who had played in the open fields as a boy, or watched sheep in the common pastures, would have lived to see the modern landscape of his parish completed and matured, the roads all made, the hedgerow trees full grown, and new farmhouses built out in the fields where none had ever been before. Everything was different: hardly a landmark of the old parish would have remained...." (Emmison, F.G., *Archives and Local History*, London: Methuen, 1966.p.62

Estate Maps

-Development. Estate maps were unknown in England until the advent of geometrical methods of surveying around 1550. This led to the establishment of professional surveying which initially was used to supplement written surveys of land, in the case of a disputed boundary, for instance. There were many reasons why written surveys had to be undertaken: after the dissolution of the monasteries under

Henry VIII in the 1530's, the land was re-distributed to Henry's favorites, but under Mary Tudor many feared confiscation by the Crown and wanted to add a touch of legality to their ownership by drawing up a survey. Similarly, after the Commonwealth was declared in 1649, many Royalists forfeited their lands to Parliamentarians, only to regain them in 1660 or strike a deal with the new owners. Again, a thorough survey and map added to the legal process. Sometimes owners improved or added to their estates or consolidated their holdings in a parish through enclosure. Again, they wanted this recorded in a permanent way.

The golden age of the local land surveyor was 1750-1850. During that time even areas of the country which had previously been neglected were covered and it is estimated that about 20,000 pre-1850 estate maps exist in County Record Offices and public libraries: this is an average of two per parish! Most show small estates or even single farm holdings, but one in ten covers an entire parish. (Hoskins, W.G., *The Making of the English Landscape*. London: Pelican Books, 1970, p. 179.)

-What the maps show. The scale of estate maps varies, of course, but is generally 3 to 6 chains (66 to 132 yards) per inch. Often one finds a series of maps of an estate included in family papers which date from the sixteenth down to the nineteenth century. They are often highly decorated and show field boundaries, the name and acreage of each field and wood, streams and ponds, greens, unenclosed waste, all dwellings with the names of tenants and/or occupiers. Also shown will be footpaths, wagon-ways, lanes and toll-bars.

The most valuable plans are those accompanied by books of reference, which give more facts about each parcel of land, such as how each parcel was used, its acreage and so on. Field-names given tend to be more accurate than those of the later Enclosure Commissioners.

It should be noted that maps and surveys relate to a manor which may not necessarily mean the whole parish. However, County Record Offices have usually indexed the maps under the parish to which they relate for easy reference. Large collections of estate maps are kept at the British Museum in London, the Bodleian Library in Oxford and at Cambridge University. All these institutions are prepared to photograph particular maps for a relatively inexpensive fee. Maps relating to coal-mining areas may be in the archives of the National Coal Board in London.

Bibliographies of Estate Maps

Emmison, F.G. & G.H. Fowler, eds. *Catalogue of Maps in the Bedford County Muniments*. 1930.

Catalogue of Maps in the Essex Record Office, 1566-1855. (1947; supplements 1952, 1964, 1968.)

A Catalogue of Sussex Estate Maps & Tithe Award Maps. (Sussex Record Society, Vol. LXI, 1962.)

Handlist of Buckinghamshire Estate Maps. Buckinghamshire Record Office, 1963.

Catalogue of the Manuscript Maps; Charts and Plans...in the British Museum. (London, 1844-1861, reprinted 1962) 3 volumes.

Maps and Plans in the Public Record Office I. British Isles, 1410-1860. (London, 1967.)

Glebe Terriers

Although a written survey and not a map, I wish to include a brief description of the glebe terrier, which was a survey of land within a parish to show what was tithable. Most terriers date from 1604 on and generally begin with a detailed inventory of the church's goods (including prayer books, candle-sticks and so on), followed by a survey of the churchyard and the parsonage. Then follows a list of the number of yardlands, ploughlands and oxgangs of the glebe which pertain to that benefice (i.e. living of the incumbent) with minute descriptions of each parcel of land. The terrier concludes with a review of the tithe income of the parson and the customary charges of burials and other services.

W.E. Tate, in his book *The Parish Chest* gives an example of a terrier from Sutton Bonnington, Nottinghamshire, from 1714. As Sutton Bonnington was not enclosed until sixty years later, the terrier is very involved: each meadow and field is divided into parcels of half an acre and the 1714 tenant is named for each parcel in each field. Often the same names occur over and over. An example is the field called 'Meadow Ground':

An acre of lays upon Meadow Gore, my Lord Ferrers on both sides, one half acre lying up at the top of Meadow Gore Lays, my Lord Ferrers on the South, one rood butting to Coal Cart Way, my Lord Ferrers on the East, one half acre butting on the Dockey Hook, John Wheatley lying on the East, one half acre on the Over Latch Pool Mr. Ross on the North, one half acre in the Swathy, the Bull Hook on the South, one half acre against the Meadow Gate lays, John Sarson on the North.... (Tate, W.E., *The Parish Chest.* Chichester: Phillimore, 1983.)

County Maps

County maps can be of great assistance in tracing hamlets and villages which have changed names or disappeared altogether (as many did during the process of enclosure). There were no regional maps before the reign of Elizabeth I, because there were no reliable instruments for surveying.

Between 1574 and 1579 Christopher Saxton surveyed England and Wales and produced a series of esthetically beautiful maps of all the counties. This was before the advent of copyright and many people jumped on the bandwagon, producing plagiarized copies of Saxton's work. In fact, very few even bothered to add details of their own, so it was not until the restoration of Charles II in 1660, when a new method of surveying using triangulation became widely used, that

145

a new series of maps was begun. Oxfordshire was surveyed in 1677, Staffordshire in 1682, Essex in 1678, Middlesex in 1677 and 1680, Hertfordshire in 1676 and Kent in 1680. Again, these maps were often reproduced by other map-makers shamelessly.

The eighteenth century saw a map revolution. Between 1750 and 1800 a more uniform sign code for details was evolved. Previously, rivers, hills and other details were represented pictorially according to the whim of the map-maker. Scale was increased to 1 inch to the mile or even larger,and after 1759 the Society of Antiquarians offered premiums to surveyors who did the best work, and this had the effect of standardizing maps. Private surveyors continued to function well into the nineteenth century, despite the institution of the Ordnance Survey in 1805, but died out, at least in regard to county maps, after the 1830's.

Collections of County Maps may be found at the British Museum, the Bodleian Library in Oxford (the Richard Gough Map Library); Cambridge University Library, The Royal Geographical Society, Lancashire Record Office (The G.E.H. Allen Collection), Guildford Muniment Room, University of Leeds (Brotherton Library), University of Durham Library, and the Library of Congress.

Bibliography

Skelton, R.A. comp. *County Atlases of the British Isles, 1579-1850. A Bibliography*.

(Map Collectors Series, Parts I - IV, 1964-1968).

Rodgers, Elizabeth A. *The Large Scale County Maps of the British Isles, 1596-1850 A Union List*. Oxford, Bodleian Library, 1960.

Philips, P.L. *A List of Geographic Atlases in the Library of Congress*. (6 volumes). Library of Congress.

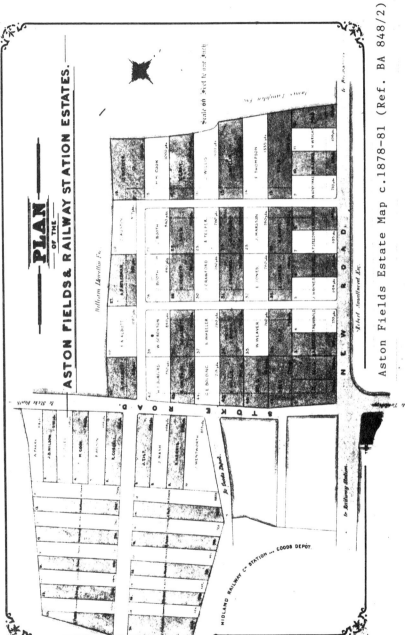

Aston Fields Estate Map c.1878–81 (Ref. BA 848/2)

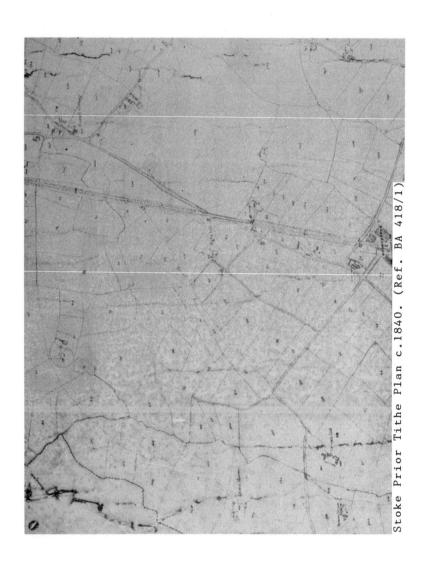

Stoke Prior Tithe Plan c.1840. (Ref. BA 418/1)

CHAPTER 10

PATTERNS OF EMIGRATION AND MIGRATION

Migration of the population can be described as the thorn in the side of the English genealogist. Trying to locate the point of origin of an ancestor's journey can be both time-consuming and frustrating, even if the ancestor in question moved only ten miles. A knowledge of migration patterns, both long and short-range, is essential to the researcher who wishes to conduct his study in a rational way: it will enable him to search first the most likely sources for that time period, geographical location and class of society from which the ancestor came. In this chapter I will first of all examine the patterns of migration from England to the United States (or American Colonies) from the seventeenth to the nineteenth centuries. Later I will discuss patterns of internal migration in England since the sixteenth century and suggest specific sources which may aid the genealogist.

Migration To The American Colonies: 17th and 18th Centuries

Ever since the London Company was granted a charter to colonize Virginia in 1606 by James I, there has been a steady and ever-increasing stream of migration across the Atlantic. Motives for migrating were varied. For some it was purely an economic endeavor, to become farmers or entrepreneurs in the new territory with its fresh opportunities and vast space. This appealed especially to younger sons of gentry, who, because of the law of primogenture, rarely stood to inherit much, but who nevertheless had the verve and drive to make something of themselves.

A second widespread impetus to migrate was the imposition of strict laws on religious dissenters in England. Under James 1 and Charles I, the Church of England became very conservative, almost papist, and would not tolerate the leanings of the Baptists, Congregationalists and Independents. Many left, rather than worship in the Established Church. Politically, these people were rebels, and it was from their ranks that Oliver Cromwell and his party arose to challenge the rule of Charles I in the 1640's. They were the Puritans.

Sometimes people were forced to migrate to serve out a term of service as a bond-servant: very often these were debtors or minor criminals. Often they were people who had to sign the bond in order to pay their passage.

It is worthwhile to examine the origins of each of the thirteen British colonies, because each was founded for a different reason and attracted different types of people.

Virginia

Virginia was founded in 1606 as the London Company, and although the early settlement of Jamestown failed mysteriously, the colony soon became well-known for its tobacco industry. In 1620 its population stood at 4,000; by 1648 this had increased to 15,000. This colony was basically an entrepreneurial enterprise and attracted the wealthy classes, bondsmen, and slaves.

Massachusetts

In contrast to Virginia, Massachusetts was founded by religious exiles, known to history as the Pilgrim Fathers. They sought to found a haven where the rule of God would be supreme – and on their terms. They did not seek toleration for other sects. These people were from the yeoman and lesser gentry and aimed to become self-sufficient farmers.

Connecticut

As a colony, Connecticut shared its roots with Massachusetts and was an off-shoot of it. Its settlers were characterized by religious puritanism and desire for economic opportunity, as in Massachusetts. Connecticut became a separate colony in 1662.

Maryland

Maryland was chartered in 1632 to Lord Baltimore as a haven for Roman Catholic dissenters, who, unlike the Puritans, often came from titled families and could evade the religious laws by bribery. Ironically, however, so many Puritans migrated there that one county was totally Puritan.

New Hampshire

This colony was founded in 1622 out of part of what had been Massachusetts.

Maine

What is now the state of Maine was first settled by the English in 1625 at Pemaquid. It was annexed in 1660 by Massachusetts, which gradually acquired the rest of the area thereafter.

The Carolinas

This area was explored as early as 1584 by Sir Walter Raleigh, but several attempts to establish colonies in the late sixteenth century failed. In 1629 the land south of Virginia was granted to Sir

Robert Heath by Charles I, but he never really made any attempt to colonize, so in 1663, Charles II granted the Carolinas to eight proprietors. They must have been very liberal thinkers, for they hired the philosopher John Locke to draw up a constitution. The Carolinas had proprietary status until 1729, but this was a very turbulent period – the settlers often refusing to submit to the governor and occasionally driving out ones they found obnoxious! The colony was not a financial success, because it was also beset by trouble with the Indians, and in 1728 seven of the proprietors sold out to the King. In 1744 the eighth exchanged his share and the colony came wholly under the Crown, but the colonists continued to be radical trouble-makers who organized a moratorium on taxes between 1765 and 1771. The types of crops grown were principally tobacco and cotton.

Pennsylvania

Another colony for religious dissenters, this time the Society of Friends; the area was chartered to William Penn in 1681 by James II. Laws against dissenters were even stricter at this period than at the time of the Pilgrim Fathers, but I think that James II, a Catholic, was sympathetic to their plight. Anyway, he gave Penn the chance to found a utopia for his people in the New World.

New Jersey

New Jersey was settled originally by the Dutch (1625) and Swedes (1638), but after the Dutch War, the region was granted to James, Duke of York (1664). James (who was later James II), granted primary interest to Lord Berkeley, who in turn sold it to two Quakers in 1674. They sold it to Penn, who called the area West Jersey. In 1682, Carteret sold East Jersey to Penn as well, thus forming a second Quaker colony.

Delaware

Originally settled by the Swedes, this area was acquired by William Penn in 1682 as part of Pennsylvania.

New York

The Dutch began to colonize New York in 1638, attempting to get a handle on the fur trade, but not being really interested in serious colonization. After the West India Company gave up its monopoly in the 1640's (a time of turmoil in England and France), the area experienced a vast influx of Puritans and Huguenots. The colony surrendered to the Duke of York in 1664 after the Dutch War, but it was not until after 1700 that it really began to grow and prosper. Religious toleration was an unusual hallmark of the colony and it also enjoyed a measure of self-government. These people were farmers, mainly in dairying.

Georgia

Georgia was a late-comer, not being colonized until 1732, when Britain was anxious to create a buffer province against the Spanish. The King therefore chartered Georgia to James Oglethorpe, who planned an asylum for debtors released from English gaols and continental religious refugees! The first 120 colonists were chosen for their youth and the skills they possessed, but the colony failed to prosper until the rum trade was allowed in 1742 and the slave trade in 1749. It was therefore principally an economic enterprise.

Some events in England which prompted waves of emigration

Early 17th century: Population level begins to rise dramatically. Lack of extra land to utilize.

1629-1641: Charles I attempts to reign without Parliament, excluding the new middle-class puritans from government. He also sells monopolies and knighthoods and the Archbishop of Canterbury clamps down on puritan practices creeping into the Church.

1642-49: The First Civil War. Ends with the beheading of Charles I. Many royalists flee the country.

1650-51: Second Civil War ends with the defeat of Charles II at the Battle of Worcester. He flees to the continent.

1649-1660: The Commonwealth or Inter-Regnum (between reigns). England is governed by Cromwell and the puritans. Royalists' land are confiscated. The church of England is disestablished.

1660: Charles II is restored. A compromise is worked out with the puritans, but hard-line conservatives press a series of laws restricting the lives of dissenters. Many leave for the sake of better opportunities elsewhere.

1688: James II, a Catholic, is overthrown in favour of his Protestant daughter Mary and her husband, William of Orange. Laws against Catholics enforced more harshly and from time to time 'plots' against the establishment are revealed to maintain anti-Catholic feeling in the country.

1715: James Stewart, the Old Pretender (son of James II) foments an unsuccessful rebellion against the new Hanoverian king, George I. Many Scottish Catholics involved lose their lives or freedom.

1745: The last Jacobite rebellion led by Charles Edward, the Young Pretender fails dismally.

Early 18th century: Consolidation of Protestant power. Beginning of financial institutions such as the Stock Exchange and banks. Evolution of Tory and Whig (Liberal) parties in Parliament. Robert Walpole is first prime minister between 1721 and 1742 – the king is more of a figurehead now.

Late 18th century: Industrial and agricultural revolutions, population explosion, enclosure of the medieval open-fields begins apace.

Emigration 1760-1776

A study of migrants to the colonies in America between 1760 and 1776 has been carried out by Bernard Bailyn in his book *Voyagers to the West* (New York, Knopf, 1986). Analysis of the available records showed that one of the main sources of the emigrant population at the time was the working class of London. It is calculated that London's servant population in 1775 numbered about 90,000, many of them newcomers from the provinces, subject to diseases and poverty and as a rule unattached to family. Employment in most trades was sporadic at best: the silk industry of Spitalfields, for instance, suffered a severe depression after the Seven Years' War in 1756. A government report of 1774 stated that in the provinces 'More than 500 hands in the woolen manufactory in the west of England have embarked for North-America'. These emigrants were mainly from Gloucestershire and Wiltshire, but in the North, the areas around Leeds, Halifax and Huddersfield, and in East Anglia there were similar difficulties. In addition to these skilled workers, farm workers and convicts from the provinces also formed substantial groups of emigrants.

Mr. Bailyn has shown that, with one main exception, most emigrants in this period travelled alone and that these solo travellers were mainly men. The exception was the Yorkshire group, who preferred to travel as family. Out of the sample of 5196 individuals, 2345 (almost half) were from London, although this may not have been their place of birth. Yorkshire contributed 938 people (about 20%) and the Home Counties around London 592 (10%). The Midlands and the West Country had 229 and 253 emigrants respectively, and other areas about 100 each.(1) This kind of information can be utilized by the genealogist who needs to know where an ancestor was most likely to have come from at this period.

During and after the American Revolution, relations with the British government were, inevitably, strained and many Loyalists returned to England rather than remain in a minority situation. Claims for compensation from Loyalists were entertained by the government and papers referring to particular cases are in the Treasury records (T 50, T 79). In the records of the Exchequer and Audit Department (AO 12 and AO 13) one finds claims for pensions resulting from loyalist activities. Accounts of payments of these pensions are also in the papers of the Audit Office (AO 1). Many migrants died in America with goods, land and property in Great Britain, so their wills had to be proved in the Prerogative Court of Canterbury. These, along with the records cited above, are in the Public Record Office in London.(1)

(1) Jane Cox & Timothy Padfield, *Tracing Your Ancestors in the Public Record Office*. (London: Her Majesty's Stationery Office, 1981) p. 65.

After the American Revolution, British emigrants often preferred to go to Canada, which remained a British colony. Numbers of English emigrants to the U.S. tended to make up a smaller and smaller percentage compared with the waves of migrants from Europe. However, they did not cease altogether.

A report published by the House of Commons in 1873 gives the following estimates, which until 1846 include Irish emigrants as well as from the mainland. From 1847 I have included the number of English only in parentheses.

```
1835: 27,000
1836: 38,000
1837: 37,000
1838: 14,000
1839: 34,000
1840: 41,000
1841: 45,000
1842: 64,000
1843: 28,000
1844: 44.000
1845: 59,000
1846: 82,000
1847: 142,000 (28,000)
1848: 188,000 (37,600)
1849: 219,000 (43,800)
1850: 233,000 (46,000)
1851: 267,000 (53,400)
1852: 244,000 (48,800)
1854: 193,000 (38,600)
1855: 103,000 (20,600)
1856: 112,000 (22,000)
1857: 127,000 (25,400)
1858: 60,000 (12,000)
1859: 70,000 (14,000)
1860: 87,000 (17,400)
```

There are several fluctuations in the migration rate during this period. For instance, a severe depression began in 1836 which hit the textile towns of the north particularly hard. They could no longer absorb newcomers from the agricultural regions of southern England, which were also depressed. Prices rose rapidly and many trade groups formed emigration societies to assist members who wished to go abroad. Examples of these societies were the Society of Brush Maskers, and the Potters' Joint Stock Emigration Society. They often announced emigration opportunities in their trade newspapers.

The infamous changes in the Corn Laws of the 1840's caused widespread apprehension amongst farmers and led to a wave of migration. The potato famine which overshadowed the second half of that decade affected not only Ireland but many countries in Europe and England, and the flood of Irish into the mainland caused increased competition for jobs and resources.

The American Civil War of course put an end to migration on a large scale, though this did pick up again in the 1870's and 1880's due

154

to periodic slumps in British industry.

What kind of people were attracted from England in the nine-teenth century? Terry Coleman has analyzed occupations of immi-grants to the U.S. in 1852 using ships' passenger lists. Firstly, he found that the ratio of men to women was now 3:2. The largest occu-pational group was that of the labourers, who formed over 36% of immigrants, followed by farmers (20%) and mechanics (10%). Mer-chants constituted 5% and miners 1%. (About 25% did not state an occupation.) These statistics cover many countries besides England but are certainly interesting as an indicator of the economic needs of the U.S. Very often the stimulus to leave England was the lure of economic opportunities rather than crisis at home. Those possessing useful skills were most attracted and made most welcome. (Terry Coleman, *Going to America*. New York, Pantheon, 1972. p. 299.)

An interesting phenomenon of the early 19th century was the existence of Parish-Aided Emigration. Some parishes in England, rather than have indigent paupers draining their parish coffers, offered to pay the paupers' way to a new home. Passage to South Africa, Canada and Australia were the usual offerings, as these were British colonies. An index exists for names from the Poor Law Records of some counties, namely: Bedfordshire, Berkshire, Cambridgeshire, Cornwall, Devon, Dorset, Hampshire, Norfolk, Somerset and Suffolk. This index is in the keeping of Miss J.M. Chambers, 24, Rookery Walk, Clifton, Shefford, Bedfordshire SG17 5HW, England. Emigration to the U.S. is shown only for the 1830's.

Internal migration in England

England is often thought by outsiders to have been a very static society, both socially and geographically. In fact, nothing could be further from the truth! Historians have shown, by studying parish registers, wills and other primary sources, that movement was actual-ly constant, although short-range as a rule. "It was rare for any family to live in one place for more than three generations" but "all this intense movement was very limited" geographically.(1)

The most mobile segment of the population were male agricul-tural workers between the age of fifteen and marriage, which, inciden-tally, was often delayed to the mid- or late-twenties. This group was hired on an annual basis and the agricultural labourer enjoyed the status of a domestic servant because they 'lived in' on whatever farm they were hired. A fictional illustration of this process occurs in Thomas Hardy's novel *Far from the Madding Crowd* when the shepherd Gabriel Oak looses his own flock of sheep during a storm and so betakes himself to the market town where he waits with other shep-herds seeking work to be hired for a year. Several studies have shown that these labourers moved ten miles or less, unless they were lured to industrial centres such as Birmingham, Sheffield, Manchester, Leeds or Liverpool. Sometimes they were prepared to go as far as London – the capital attracted people from all over the island just as

(1) Peter Laslett and John Harrison, "Clayworth and Cogenhoe" His-torical Essays 1600-1750 presented to David Ogg. ed. H.E. Bell and R.L. Olland (London, 1963) p. 156-18.

it had attracted Dick Whittington. A study of cases brought before the Commissary Court of London between 1580 and 1640 showed that 89% of the deponents were born outside London.(1) In the late seventeenth century the local bishop kept track of men who emigrated from Eccleshall in Staffordshire. Ten out of sixty-eight men who left the parish went to London.

Interestingly, farmers who themselves moved were prepared to go further than their labourers, often as far as 40 miles, but of course farmers tended to stay put as they had their capital invested in their land and would probably move only under extreme circumstances.

The mobility of women is another aspect of migration in England which deserves a special word. Women did not always choose marriage partners from within their own parish: by European standards, the English bride cast her net quite broadly, often going as far afield as 15 miles in search of a husband. However, they rarely went further than 20 miles. The reason is not difficult to understand: England had few good roads, and those passable only in good weather.

Genealogical sources for tracing a mobile ancestor

–The International Genealogical Index (see chapter on libraries). This huge fiche index of parish and other vital records can be of immense use when tracing a rarer surname. Even if the precise ancestor is not located, the IGI can give important pointers as to where to begin one's search in geographical terms. Many surnames are of a local character and analysis of the IGI can determine the county or counties of the origin of that name.

–Marriage Records: There are at least three types of record relating to marriages: the register entry, the banns (which were, after 1753, entered in separate books), and, if the marriage was not by banns, a license or bond. Many parish registers have already been indexed, notably the counties covered by Boyd in his three series. The Pallot Index, which is in the keeping of the Institute of Heraldic and Genealogical Studies, Northgate, Canterbury, covers London parishes from 1780 to 1837, and can be consulted for a fee of L-10 per entry. Many county record and family history societies have begun indexing marriages for their own county. The Federation of Family Societies has published a list of these projects in Jeremy Gibson's *Marriage, Census and other Indexes for Family Historians.* (Third edition, 1988.) This booklet is a very useful guide to have on reference.

Marriage licenses are an oft-neglected source of information as to a person's place of origin. A marriage license was necessary when both bride and groom were from other parishes, or could be obtained to replace the banns if the couple wanted a quiet wedding – particularly common in the case of non-conformists who, despite their religious beliefs, still had to marry in the Established Church. Many marriage licenses are to be found in the county record offices and I refer the reader to Mr. Gibson's admirable booklet cited above, which lists on-going projects to index the licenses.

(1) David Cressey, "Occupations, Migration and Literacy in East London, 1580-1640." Local Population Studies No. 5 (1970) p. 57-58.

Anthony Camp, in an address to the International Society for British Genealogy and Family History, pointed out that the Archbishops of York and Canterbury also granted licenses in cases where the couple were from different ecclesiastical provinces. Canterbury's date from 1534 and are indexed to 1714, but the post-1714 licenses are rarely consulted! They are housed at Lambeth Palace in London but they have been microfilmed by the L.D.S. Church.

-Apprenticeship Records: Apprenticeship was a great advantage to a boy (or girl). It gave him a trade to follow and possibly later entry into a guild, as well as certain advantages under the poor laws: if a boy was apprenticed in a parish, he was entitled to name that parish as his 'settlement' and if he ever became indigent, he could return to it for help. An agreement, known as indentures, was drawn up between the child's parents and the master: these usually mention the child's home parish and his parents' names, the name of the master and other details such as his age. From 1710 to 1811 there was a tax on apprenticeships and they had to be registered centrally. The records are in the Public Record Office, London. An index of apprentices runs from 1710 to 1775 and is at the Society of Genealogists. However, masters taking on apprentices from the parish vestry (that is, the poor), were exempt from the tax and so many apprentices names are excluded. Some county record societies have published indexes or lists of apprentices for various dates in their county.

-Freeman Records: To become a freeman of a city was an honour highly sought after. but admission was strictly limited. The prospective freeman had to carry on a recognized craft or trade there and entry was by sponsorship by a relative (often the father) who was already a freeman himself. The Corporation of London Records Office holds records of many thousands of freemen dating from the Middle Ages, and other cities such as Bath, Norwich, Worcester, and York have similar records. These are an important source of information about the freeman's place of origin.

-Church Court Deposition Books: Church Court Deposition Books were the records of proceedings in various courts under the church's jurisdiction. Peter Clark of Leicester University studied them for an article about migration patterns during the late seventeeth century and he found that deponents, i.e. witnesses, routinely answered questions on their own background before giving evidence. Although clerks of the courts were not uniformly conscientious in their transcriptions, and of course not everyone's ancestor has been involved in a church case, it is worthwhile to make note of. The court records are now in diocesan record offices.

-Probate Records: As noted in an earlier chapter, wills and the probate of them were the prerogative of the ecclesiastical courts until 1858, and both wills and the court documents relating to them can be very fruitful in pointing to the deceased's place of origin. Out of one hundred wills proved in the Consistory court of London in the seventeenth century and later examined by Dr. Peter Spufford, thirteen gave clues as to the deceased's birthplace. Some gave donations to their birth-parish, such as Ann Purslow who left 40 shillings to the poor of the parish of Farndon in Northamptonshire where, she specifically states, she was born. Others do not state this specifically, but may mention relatives there, or merely that they wish to leave money to the parish. It may be a valuable clue to follow!

-Parish Registers: These can sometimes be surprisingly good sources of biographical information, depending on the whims of the parish priest. Often a baptismal entry will name the father of a bastard, but marriage registers and banns books seem to be more likely sources of unofficial entries. Sometimes the parish constables copied the earlier censuses (1801-1831) into the registers as a back-up copy.

-Poor Law Records: There were two types of record that generated locality information. One type related to the finding of bastards' fathers in order that they, not the parish, support their offspring. The mother was usually examined and made to name the father and his abode. The other, more important source are Settlement Papers. Any person who did not own a certain amount of property and wished to move to another parish had to secure a settlement certificate from the parish vestry, which was basically a passport to be presented to the safekeeping of his new parish. If the person ever became a pauper, he could be sent back to his parish of settlement for poor relief. Sometimes a person had difficulty persuading a vestry that he had right of settlement in their parish: this lead to his being 'examined', that is, interrogated, with the purpose of securing evidence for or against the pauper. Detailed autobiographical statements can be found, giving such details as property once owned or apprenticeships undertaken, as well as movement around the country. Settlement certificates can be found bundled together at county record offices, indexed under the name of the parish to which they were handed (not the parish of origin). Examinations will be among the vestry minutes, either at the parish or in the diocesan/county record office.

-The Censuses: Though the first 'useful' census was not taken until 1841, they can still be of help in tracking down an eighteenth-century ancestor's origins, if the general locality is known. Some family history societies have begun census indexes (see Jeremy Gibson op. cit) but there is still much work to be done in this area.

CHAPTER 11

OCCUPATIONAL GAZETTEER

All too often, the failing of the American genealogist research-ing England is that he or she lacks a basic knowledge of the geogra-phy of Britain. It is important to know, for instance, where the major iron foundries were located in the eighteenth century if your ancestor was an ironworker at that period. In many cases, the researcher knows the date of emigration and the ancestor's trade or occupation, but does not know where in England that person came from. By using this gazetteer, you may find useful clues as to where to begin re-search in England.

How To Use The Gazetteer

Occupations are listed alphabetically and in many cases a brief explanation of the industry's history is given. Centres of the industry are listed in alphabetical order, but where a whole county was noted for that industry it is included in FULL CAPS.

The following abbreviations indicate areas which were formerly divisions of Yorkshire:

WR   West Riding
NR   North Riding
ER   East Riding

ALE-MAKING
Alton, Hampshire
Birmingham
Bridport, Dorset
Burton-upon-Trent, Stafforshire
Bury St. Edmunds, Suffolk
Hayle, Cornwall
Henley, Oxfordshire
HEREFORDSHIRE
Houghton-le-Spring, Durham
KENT
Lewes, Sussex
Litton Cheney, Dorset
Masham, Yorkshire (NR)
Newark, Nottinghamshire
Newbury, Berkshire

Norwich, Norfolk
Shepton Mallet, Somerset
Southwick, Hampshire
Spitalfields, London
Stone, Stafforshire
Stow-on-the-Wold, Gloucestershire
Streatley, Berkshire
Tadcaster, Yorkshire (NR)
Tetbury, Gloucestershire
Wakefield, Yorkshire
Wandsworth, London
Winchester, Hampshire
Worcester

BELLS
Bell-founders were usually itinerant, casting bells in pits they dug in fields adjacent to the church, until the industrial revolution.(1)

Chew Stoke, Somerset: 18th century
Loughborough, Leicestershire: 1839 onwards
London

BLANKETS
Witney, Oxfordshire: since the 14th century.

BOBBIN TURNING
The art of making bobbins was an important adjunct to the cotton industry of Northern England.

CUMBERLAND
Finthswaite, Cumberland
Furness, Lancashire and surrounding area

BRASS
Bath, Somerset: 1872–1969
Bristol, Gloucestershire: from the 18th century on
Saltford Mill, Somerset

BRICK-MAKING
Because they lacked their own supply of natural building materials in the south-east of the country, Huntingdonshire and Bedfordshire had a large concentration of brick works.

Ampthill, Bedfordshire
Bardon Mill, Northumbria
Barton-upon-Humber, Lincolnshire
Bridgewater, Somerset
Broadmayne, Dorset
Brompton-by-Sawdon, Yorkshire (NR)
Broxbourne, Hampshire

(1) Brian Bailey, *The Industrial Heritage of Britain*. Ebury Press, London 1982, p. 118.

Cadmore End, Buckinghamshire
Capheaton, Northumberland
Colliers End, Hertfordshire
Crowle, Lincolnshire
Frilsham, Berkshire
Hayling Island, Hampshire
Henley, Berkshire
Kerdiston, Norfolk: 18th century
Maltby, Yorkshire (WR)
Measham, Leicestershire
Mundesley, Norfolk
Napton-on-the-Hill, Warwickshire
Old Fletton, Cambridgeshire
Pucklechurch, Gloucestershire
Riseley, Bedforshire
Slingsby, Yorkshire
Stanley, Yorkshire (WR)
Stewartby, Bedfordshire
Wootton, Bedfordshire
Yaxley, Huntingdonshire (now Cambridgeshire)

BROOM-MAKING
Chesham, Buckinghamshire
Hevingham, Norfolk

CALAMINE
Calamine is a necessary constituent for brass-making and is only found at Shipham, Somerset, where it has been mined since the eighteenth century.

CARPETS
Axminster, Devon
Kidderminster, Worcestershire: from 1735 to present
Wilton, Wiltshire: from the 17th century on

CHAINS
Cradley Heath, Worcestershire: 19th & 20th centuries
Topsham, Devon: 17th to 19th century

CIDER
The main cider regions were, of course, where the best apples were grown: Somerset, the Vale of Evesham in Worcestershire, and Herefordshire.

Attleborough, Norfolk
Banham, Norfolk
Bristol, Gloucestershire
Hereford, Herefordshire
Much Marcle, Herefordshire: 17th century on
Taunton Dene, Somerset
Tuckenhay, Devon: 19th century
Worcester

CHINA-CLAY

William Cookworthy discovered that kaolin was the main ingredient in Chinese porcelain in the eighteenth century and this lead to its being mined in Cornwall and exported to the Midlands.

Lee Moor, Cornwall
Restormel, Cornwall
St. Austell, Cornwall: from 1798 on

CHOCOLATE

The manufacture of chocolate in England is irrevocably associated with the Quaker families of Rowntree and Cadbury, who began operations in the last half of the eighteenth century and attempted to give their workers humane living conditions.

Bournville, Worcestershire
Norwich, Norfolk
York

CLAY PIPES
Broseley, Shropshire

CLOCK-MAKING

With the coming of the Industrial Revolution, clock-making became more wide-spread, but before that time only a few places were noted for the manufacture of clocks. The Clockmakers' Company (Guild) was incorporated in London in 1631.[1]

Askrigg, Yorkshire (NR)
Clerkenwell, London
Warrington, Lancashire: 17th & 18th centuries

CLOTH-MAKING

Cloth-making was the backbone of English industry from the Middle Ages onward. East Anglia (Norfolk and Suffolk) was prominent until around 1750, when it failed to adapt to the new mechanization and went into decline. Other areas prominent in the industry were Yorkshire, which did go with the flow of industrialization, Gloucestershire, and Wiltshire, which also declined after 1750.

Alton, Hampshire
Barcheston, Warwickshire: 16th century on
Beverley, Yorkshire
Bildeston, Suffolk
Cam, Gloucestershire: 1815 onward
Castle Combe, Wiltshire
Chard, Somerset: until 19th century
Clifford Chambers, Warwickshire
Coggleshall, Essex
Crewkerne, Somerset
Croscombe, Somerset

(1) Bailey, op. cit., p. 59.

Frome, Somerset
Glemsford, Somerset
Halifax, Yorkshire
Harlow, Essex
Heptonstall, Yorkshire (WR)
Honley, Yorkshire (WR)
King's Stanley, Gloucestershire
Lavenham, Suffolk: 14th to 16th century
Leeds, Yorkshire: since 14th century
Liversedge, Yorkshire (WR)
Malmesbury, Wiltshire: to 18th century
Pontefract, Yorkshire (WR)
Shrewsbury, Shropshire
Staverton, Wiltshire
Stroud, Gloucestershire
Sudbury, Suffolk
Trowbridge, Wiltshire
Tunstead, Norfolk
Uley, Gloucestershire
Warminster, Wiltshire: to 18th century
Wellingborough, Northamptonshire
Westbury, Wiltshire: 18th & 19th centuries
Wincanton, Somerset: 18th century
Woodchester, Gloucestershire
Worstead, Norfolk

COAL-MINING

The main coal-fields of England are in Gloucestershire, Derbyshire, the West Riding of Yorkshire, Nottinghamshire, Durham, Staffordshire, Leicestershire and Cumberland. Kent coal-fields developed after the Industrial Revolution and others expanded.

Ansley, Warwickshire
Arley, Warwickshire
Aston, Yorkshire (WR)
Audley, Staffordshire
Aughton, Yorkshire (WR)
Bagworth, Leicestershire
Barnsley, Yorkshire (WR)
Bentley, Yorkshire (WR)
Biddulph, Staffordshire
Bolton-upon-Dearne, Yorkshire (WR)
Brampton-en-le-Morthen, Yorkshire (WR)
Brierley, Yorkshire (WR)
Cadeby, Yorkshire (WR)
Calverton, Nottinghamshire
Camerton, Somerset: 18th century
Cannock, Staffordshire
Carlisle, Cumberland
Cheadle, Staffordshire
Chillenden, Kent
Coleorton, Leicestershire: since 15th century
Consett, Durham

Cossall, Nottinghamshire: since 13th century
Cotgrave, Nottinghamshire
Darfield, Yorkshire (WR)
Darton, Yorkshire (WR)
Donington le Heath, Leicestershire: 1290 to present
Dudley, Worcestershire: from the 17th century
Dunham, Nottinghamshire
Durham
Eastwood, Nottinghamshire
Edlington, New; Yorkshire (WR)
Elmsall, North; Yorkshire (WR)
Fairburn, Yorkshire (WR)
Farley, Derbyshire
Featherstone, Yorkshire (WR)
Flagg, Derbyshire
Garworth, Yorkshire (WR)
Hatfield, Yorkshire (WR)
Highley, Shrophshire
Hucknall-Torkard, Nottinghamshire
Huntingdon, Staffordshire
Ibstock, Leicestershire
Kexborough, Yorkshire (WR)
Kirkby-in-Ashfield, Nottinghamshire
Lofthouse, Yorkshire (WR)
Maltby, Yorkshire (WR)
Measham, Leicestershire
Methley, Yorkshire (WR)
Mexborough, Yorkshire (WR)
Monk Bretton, Yorkshire (WR)
Morley, Yorkshire (WR)
Much Wenlock, Shropshire
Newcastle-upon-Tyne, Durham
Normanton, Yorkshire (WR)
Norton Canes, Staffordshire
Ollerton, Nottinghamshire
Orgreave, Yorkshire (WR)
Pontefract, Yorkshire (WR)
Radstock, Somerset: 18th century on
Ripley, Derbyshire
Rowland, Derbyshire
Skelmersdale, Lancashire
Stanhope, Durham
Stanton, Derbyshire
Stavely, Derbyshire
Sutton-in-Ashfield, Nottinghamshire
Taddington, Derbyshire
Teversall, Nottinghamshire
Tilmanstone, Kent
Walsgrave on Sowe, Warwickshire: 16th century onward
Wath upon Dearne, Yorkshire (WR): since 1797
West Bromwich, Staffordshire
Whitwick, Leicestershire
Williamthorpe, Derbyshire

COCKLES
Stiffkey, Norfolk

COPPER
Caradon, cornwall: 19th century
Hartingdon, Derbyshire
Kelston, Somerset
North Molton, Devon
St. Austell, Cornwall
Swinford, Leicestershire
Treborough, Somerset: 19th century

COTTON
   The production of cotton was officially banned until 1774,
because it was seen as a rival to the home industries of wool and
flax, but it was certainly manufactured illegally before that date in
London, Bristol and Liverpool.(1)

Bamford, Derbyshire: since 1770
Barnoldswick, Yorkshire (WR): 19th century
Blackburn, Lancashire: since 14th century
Bradford, Yorkshire
Bredbury, Cheshire
Bristol, Gloucestershire
Cromford, Derbyshire: since 1771
Earby, Yorkshire (WR)
Liverpool, Lancashire
London
Manchester: since 14th century
Papplewick, Nottinghamshire: since 1785
Rochdale, Lancashire
Romiley, Cheshire
Warrington, Lancashire

CRICKET BALLS
Teston, Kent

CUTLERY
Newcastle-upon-Tyne
Sheffield, Yorkshire: since 17th century
Thaxted, Essex: 14th & 15th centuries

FLAX-MILLING
   Flax growing was common throughout the country, though
Somerset, the Lake District and the East Midlands seem to have had
dominance. Leeds in West Yorkshire was the industry's centre in the
19th century, when most smaller concerns went out of business.

(1) Hugh Bodey, *Twenty Centuries of British Industry*.   David and
Charles, London, 1975, p. 154.

Barnsley, Yorkshire (WR)
Knaresborough, Yorkshire
Leeds, Yorkshire
Merriott, Somerset
Netherbury, Dorset

FLINT
Eastern and southern England lie on a chalk belt rich in flint, and Norfolk especially is noted for its flint mines. There, many houses and churches are built of this hardy material.

Boston Spa, Yorkshire (WR)
Brandon, Suffolk
Cheddleton, Staffordshire
Hanley, Staffordshire
Leeds, Yorkshire
Moddershall, Staffordshire

FRAMEWORK KNITTING
Knitting is an ancient art which, until the seventeenth century, was done entirely by hand. The garment produced was usually hosiery, and, of course, it was a cottage industry towards the end of Elizabeth I's reign. A parson, William Lee, invented a machine for knitting stockings which became widely used in London. The independent workers even had their own guild, the Framework Knitters' Company, which rigorously controlled wages and prices. At the beginning of the eighteenth century, the industry moved to Derby, Nottingham and Leicester, where the Framework Knitters' Company had less influence and labour was cheaper. Hosiers owned sometimes hundreds of frames, a few of which would be kept at his shop, but most were hired out to knitters who worked in their cottages. The hosiery industry was slow to benefit from mass–production techniques, which did not become economically viable until almost 1800.(1) Knitters tended to be independent in character and were often non-conformists.(2)

Bonsall, Derbyshire: 19th century
Calverton, Nottinghamshire
Dunton Bassett, Leicestershire: 19th century
Hinkley, Leicestershire
Kegworth, Leicestershire: 19th century
Leicester: since the 18th century
Litton, Derbyshire: 18th century
Loughborough, Leicestershire
Markfield, Leicestershire: 19th century
Nottingham
RUTLAND
Ullesthorpe, Leicestershire
Woodborough, Nottinghamshire.

(1) T.S. Ashton, *The Industrial Revolution, 1760–1830* Oxford University Press, Oxford, 1968, 2nd edition, p. 24.
(2) Bailey, op. cit., p. 106

FURNITURE
High Wycombe, Buckinghamshire

GLASS
Bridgewater, Somerset
Bristol, Gloucestershire
Catcliffe, Yorkshire
Kirk Sandall, Yorkshire (WR)
Newburn, Northumberland
Smethwick, Staffordshire
Stourbridge, Worcestershire
St. Helen's, Lancashire
Wellington, Shropshire: 19th century

GLOVES
Woodstock, Oxfordshire: since Middle Ages
Yeovil, Somerset: since the 18th century

GOLD MINE
Pulloxhill, Bedfordshire: 18th century

GRANITE
Bodiggo, Cornwall
Constantine, Cornwall
Dartmoor, Devon

GRAPHITE
Borrowdale, Westmoreland

GRAVEL-QUARRIES
Branston, Staffordshire
Moreton, Essex
South Cerney, Gloucestershire

GUNPOWDER
Bath, Somerset: 1720-1820
Elterwater, Westmoreland
Faversham, Kent
Two Bridges, Devon

GUNSMITHS
Cradley, Worcestershire
Small Heath, Birmingham

HATS - see also: STRAW-PLAITING
Frampton Cotterell, Gloucestershire London: beaver hats
Manchester: felt hats
Stockport, Lancashire: felt hats

HORSEHAIR-WEAVING
Hevingham, Norfolk: until 1900
Market Drayton, Shropshire

HOSIERY: see FRAMEWORK KNITTING

IRON-WORKS
        Until the turn of the eighteenth century, iron works were dependent on charcoal and therefore on a good supply of timber for their furnaces. The industry was concentrated in the Weald of Sussex and Kent during the 16th and 17th centuries, with some work also taking place in Worcestershire and Staffordshire, but eventually the forests dried up and by 1700 the iron industry had moved elsewhere. Luckily, in 1709 Abraham Darby was able to substitute coke for charcoal at his ironworks in Shropshire, so the production of iron became associated with coal-fields, with nail-making as an important subsidiary. The industry became concentrated in South Staffordshire and North-East Worcestershire, in what is now the Birmingham area.
        After 1783, when the puddling process was perfected, coke could also be used in forges and ironworks sprang up in Staffordshire and South Yorkshire.

Biddulph, Staffordshire
Bilston, Staffordshire
Broseley, Shropshire: 18th century
Cannock, Stafforshire: 15th century on.
Coalbrookdale, Shropshire
Consett, Durham
Dudley, Worcestershire: since 17th century
Heage, Derbyshire: since 1780
Leiston, Suffolk: 19th century
Little Wenlock, Shropshire
Liverton, Yorkshire (NR)
Loftus, Yorkshire (NR)
Lyddington, Rutland
Madeley, Shropshire
Much Wenlock, Shropshire
Oregreave, Yorkshire (WR)
Penrith, Cumberland
Tow Law, Co. Durham
Treborough, Somerset: 19th century
Wombwell, Yorkshire (WR)
Workington, Cumberland

LACE
BEDFORDSHIRE
Honiton, Devon: since 16th century
Nottingham
SOMERSET
Stathern, Leicestershire
Tiverton, Devon

LEAD
Ashford, Derbyshire
Ashover, Derbyshire
Bagillt, Cheshire: 18th & 19th centuries
Bakewell, Derbyshire

Bradwell, Derbyshire
Brassington, Derbyshire
Combe Martin, Devon
Crich, Derbyshire
Hartington, Derbyshire
Killhope, Co. Durham
Monyash, Derbyshire
Sheldon, Derbyshire
Shuckstonfield, Derbyshire
Wheal Betsy, Devon
Winster, Derbyshire: 18th century
Wirksworth, Derbyshire: 1066-1900

LEATHER
For many centuries, Bermondsey in London was the main area for tanners but by the late eighteenth century leather shoes were in more general use and there were tanners everywhere. The main centers of the industry were:

Downton, Wiltshire
Grampound, Cornwall
Hereford
Northampton
RUTLAND
Sawston, Cambridgeshire
Street, Somerset
Walsall, Staffordshire
Winchcombe, Gloucestershire
Worcester
Yeovil, Somerset

LIMESTONE QUARRIES
Alwalton, Huntingdonshire (now Cambridgeshire)
Barrow upon Soar, Leicestershire
Dyserth, Cheshire
South Ferriby, Lincolnshire
Wirksworth, Derbyshire

LINEN-WEAVING - see also FLAX
Alburgh, Norfolk
Barnsley, Yorkshire (WR)

LICORICE
Licorice is a plant, the root of which makes a black sweet confection.

Pontefract, Yorkshire: since 17th century

MALT-HOUSES
Malt-houses were used for converting barley to malt for ale. They were found particularly in Suffolk, Essex and Eastern Hertfordshire.

Bath, Somerset
Boroughbridge, Yorkshire (NR)
Burton-on-Trent, Staffordshire
Diss, Norfolk
Langley, Birmingham
Mansfield, Nottinghamshire
Newark, Nottinghamshire
Oulton Broad, Suffolk
Sleaford, Lincolnshire
Warminster, Wiltshire

MUSSELS
Found in many coastal towns for sale, but Hambleton, Lancashire was famed for them.

NAILS
A spin-off of the iron industry, nail-making is associated especially with the West Midland counties around Birmingham.

Bromsgrove, Worcestershire
Swalwell, Northumberland
Topsham, Devon: 17th to 19th century
Wellington, Shropshire: 19th century
Winlaton, Northumberland

NEEDLES
Redditch, Worcestershire
Studley, Warwickshire

OYSTER-BEDS
Stanswood, Hampshire

PAPER
Bidford-on-Avon, Warwickshire: 17th to 19th centuries
Burnopfield, Co. Durham
Castle Donington, Leicestershire
Chartham, Kent
Cheddleton, Staffordshire
Dartford, Kent
Ditton, Kent
Eppersrone, Nottingham: to 1723
Laverstoke, Hampshire: since 18th century
Ling, Norfolk
Little Eaton, Derbyshire: 19th century
Maidstone, Kent
Neen Savage, Shropshire
Sawston, Cambridgeshire
Tuckenhay, Devon
Watchet, Somerset: since 17th century
Whitchurch, Hampshire: since 18th century
Winchcombe, Gloucestershire
Wookey Hole, Somerset

PARCHMENT
Havant, Hampshire: since 1000 A.D.

PIRACY
Studland, Dorset: 16th century

PORTS
I do not propose to list all of England's ports, most of which are still in operation today and are easily found by reference to a modern atlas. Below are listed ports which are now inland due to silting, are canal ports, or inland ports on rivers.

Axmouth, Devon: to 14th century
Bridgewater, Somerset: medieval
Combwich, Somerset
Frodsham, Cheshire
Gloucester
Landulph, Cornwall: 15th century
Preston, Lancashire
Shardlow, Derbyshire: 18th century canal port
Sharpness, Gloucestershire
Skidbrooke, Lincolnshire
Topsham, Devon
Treknow, Cornwall
Upton-on-Severn, Worcestershire: to 19th century
Wainileet, Lincolnshire
Watchet, Somerset
Weston, Cheshire: on Manchester Ship Canal
Worcester

POTTERIES
Barlaston, Staffordshire: Wedgwood
Barnstaple, Devon
Bovey Tracey, Devon
Burslem, Staffordshire*
Church Gresley, Derbyshire
Clifton, Westmoreland
Coalport, Shropshire
Corbridge, Northumberland
Fenton, Staffordshire
Fulham, London
Hanley, Staffordshire*
Jackfield, Shropshire
Longton, Staffordshire*
Lowesby, Leicestersire: 19th century
Newhaven, Sussex
Potters Marston, Leicestershire
Shalcombe, Isle of Wight
Stanton near Newhall, Derbyshire
Swinton, Yorkshire (NR)
Tamerton Foliot, Devon
Tunstall, Staffordshire *
Wattisfield, Suffolk

Worcester
* These towns form the Five Pottery Towns, now the city of Stoke-on-Trent.

RAILWAYS

Railways were a phenomenon of the nineteenth century. Though most main lines were completed by 1830, the decade 1840–1850 saw a furor of building activity. By 1900 over 21,000 miles of track had been laid down, and tunnels, bridges and sidings had transformed the English landscape. Inevitably, certain junctions thrived solely on the railway business of building and repairing locomotives and carriages.

Birmingham
Bromsgrove, Worcestershire
Carlisle, Cumberland
Crewe, Cheshire
Darlington, Co. Durham: since 1825
Leeds, Yorkshire
Lincoln, Lincolnshire
London
March, Cambridgeshire: mid-19th century
Newcastle-on-Tyne, Co. Durham
Norwich, Norfolk
Rugby, Warwickshire
Stockton-on-Tees, Co. Durham: since 1825
Sunderland, Co. Durham
Swindon, Wiltshire
Wolverton, Buckinghamshire

ROPE

Rope-making must have been a fairly ubiquitous craft but two places were noted as rope-making centres: Kendal, Westmoreland and Royton, Lancashire.

RUSH MATS
Oakley, Bedfordshire
Pavenham, Bedfordshire

SALT

Salt production was essential to life because of its preservative qualities, and several places were being worked in Roman times, notably Droitwich in Worcestershire. Several other towns have been producing salt since the time of William the Conqueror, though a few had to wait for the advent of industrial technology.

Allonby, Cumberland
Droitwich, Worcestershire
Eggbuckland, Devon: medieval
Iscoed, Cheshire: medieval
Lymington, Hampshire
Maldon, Essex
Marston, Cheshire
Middlewich, Cheshire: since 1066

Nantwich, Cheshire: 1066-1856
Northwich, Cheshire: since 1066
Salcombe Regis, Devon
Seaview, Isle of Wight
Stoke Prior, Worcestershire: 19th century
Tamerton Foliot, Devon
Wharton, Cheshire: 19th century

SCYTHE-MAKING
Abbeydale, Yorkshire: since 1777
Belbroughton, Worcestershire
Sticklepath, Devon

SHIP-BUILDING
Ship-building has been carried out at many coastal towns and river towns on a small scale, but I list here the major centres of the industry since Tudor times.

Chatham, Kent: 1560-20th century
Devonport, Devon
Harwich, Essex: until late 18th century
Middlesborough, Co. Durham
Newcastle-on-Tyne, Co. Durham
Portland, Dorset
Stockton-on-Tees, Co. Durham
Topsham, Devon: since 17th century

SHOES
Desborough, Northamtonshire
Earls Barton, Northamtonshire
Kettering, Northamptonshire
Leicester: since 18th century
Longstone, Derbyshire
Northampton
Raunds, Northamptonshire
Rushden, Northamptonshire
Wellingborough, Northamptonshire

SILK
The art of silk-production came to England with the refugee Huguenots when they settled in Spitalfields, London in the late eighteenth century. It was a cottage industry until 1717 when the first silk mill was built in Derby and production became concentrated in the textile areas of the north.

Blockley, Worcestershire
Bocking, Essex: from 1798
Bradford, Yorkshire (WR)
Braintree, Essex: from 1798
Burton-in-Lonsdale, Yorkshire (WR)
Derby
Derwent, Derbyshire
Glemsford, Suffolk: early 19th century

Lothersdale, Yorkshire (WR)
Macclesiield, Cheshire: 17th century cottage industry
Merton, Surrey: 17th century
Pebmarsh, Essex
SOMERSET: cottage industry
Spitalfields, London
Whitchurch, Hampshire

SILVER
Combe Martin, Devon

SLATE
Coniston, Lancashire
Constantine, Cornwall
Delabole, Cornwall
Elterwater, Lancashire
SOMERSET
Swithland Wood, Leicestershire: 12th to 19th centuries
Treknow, Cornwall

SMUGGLING
Dymchurch, Kent
Niton, Isle of Wight
Sixpenny Mandley, Dorset

SPAS
Spas were places where springs of mineral waters bubbled to the surface which were thought to be efficacious in the cure of a number of ailment. Some have been in use since Roman times, notably Bath and Droitwich Spa, but others really came into being during the Regency period of the late eighteenth century.

Bath, Somerset
Buxton, Derbyshire
Cheltenham, Gloucestershire
Droitwich, Worcestershire
Ilkley, Yorkhsire (WR)
Leamington, Warwickshire
Lower Swell, Gloucestershire
Malvern, Worcestershire
Matlock, Derbyshire

STEEL
As an industry dependant on iron and coal, steel-making tends to be found alongside those industries. In the early eighteenth century it was an expensive process and steel was used for cutlery, razors, swords, guns and so on. In the early 1740's a Sheffield clockmaker invented a process which produced more uniform steel of a better quality but it was almost 1800 before knowledge of this process had an impact on the steel industry.

Corby, Northamptonshire
Hamsterley, Co. Durham: late 18th century

Newcastle-on-Tyne, Co. Durham
Sheffield, Yorkshire
Wolverhampton, Staffordshire

STONE-QUARRIES
Barnock, Northamptonshire: to 18th century
Bathampton, Somerset
Beer, Nr. Seaton, Devon
Bradwell, Derbyshire
Brassington, Derbyhshire
Chilmark, Wiltshire
Ditton Priors, Shropshire
Doulting, Somerset
Enderby, Leicestereshire
Halling, Kent
Hamdon Hill, Somerset
Hartshill, Warwickshire
Headington, Oxford: since medieval times
Ketton, Rutland
Polyphant, Cornwall: since 1066
Portland, Dorset Consett, Durham
Purbeck, Dorset
Shap, Westmoreland
Tadcaster, Yorkshire (WR)
Taynton, Oxford
Wilsford, Lincolnshire

STRAW-PLAITING
        Straw-plaiting was introduced to England by James I.   He
established French families in Luton Hoo, who brought the craft with
them, and Luton became the main production centre for straw hats.   It
was a cottage industry in which girls could earn as much as a guinea
a week, a substantial sum in those days.   The industry flourished in
the eighteenth century but almost died out by the end of the nineteenth
century. Its main centres were Caddington and Studham in Bedfordshire.

TAPESTRY
        A tapestry factory was established in Mortlake, Surrey in 1619.

TIN
        The only deposits of tin in England are found in the south-west
counties of Devon and Cornwall. From medieval times, tinners were
independent workers and even had their own courts.   They brought in
their tin to be weighed and sold at one of four stannary towns: Ashburton, Tavistock, Chagford, Plymton.   Underground mining began after
the invention of the steam-engine which enabled water to be pumped
out of the mines, and tinners lost their independence and became
employees of large mining operations. The industry collapsed when
tin (and copper) were discovered in Africa in the late nineteenth century.

Ashburton, Devon
Botallack, Cornwall
Cambourne, Cornwall
Chagford, Devon
Mary Tavy, Devon
Pendeen, Cornwall
Pentewan, Cornwall
Perranzabuloe, Cornwall
Peter Tavy, Devon
Plympton, Devon
Redruth, Cornwall
Tavistock, Devon
Trescowe, Cornwall

TOBACCO
Feckenham, Worcestershire: 18th century
Kendal, Westmoreland
Morden, Surrey: 18th century snuff mills
Sheffield, Yorkshire
Winchcombe, Gloucestershire

TULIPS
LINCOLNSHIRE
Pinchbeck, Lincolnshire

WADD MINING – see GRAPHITE

WIRE-DRAWING
Barnsley, Yorkshire: 18th century

WOOL
Until the Industrial Revolution in the mid–eighteenth century, the woolen industry was the backbone of the English economy, so much so that it was heavily protected against all competitors. Even burial shrouds had to be made of wool by law! The main sheep-raising areas were Gloucestershire and the Cotswolds, Leicestershire, and Yorkshire, but the Cotswold industry failed to adapt to the new technologies of the eighteenth century and decline was rapid – many migrated to the Yorkshire textile towns.(1)

Alresford, Hampshire: to 14th century
Batley, Yorkshire (WR)
Beverley, Yorkshire
Bradford-on-Avon, Wiltshire
Buckfastleigh, Devon
Buckingnam: to 1500
Burford, Oxfordshire
Burton-in-Lonsdale, Yorkshire (WR)
Chipping Camden, Gloucestershire: medieval
Cirencester, Gloucestershire: to 19th century

(1) Bailey, op. cit. p. 103.

Dilton Marsh, Wiltshire
Halifax, Yorkshire
Helmshore, Lancashire
Islay Walton, Leicestershire
King's Stanley, Gloucestershire
Leeds, Yorkshire
Leominster, Herefordshire: to 19th century
Malmesbury, Wiltshire
Minchinhampton, Gloucestershire
Nailsworth, Gloucestershire
Northleach, Gloucestershire
Otley, Yorkshire (WR)
Otterburn, Yorkshire (NR)
Painswick, Gloucestershire
Ruddington, Nottinghamshire
Shrewsbury, Shropshire
Sowerby Bridge, Yorkshire (WR)
Stamford, Lincolnshire
Stroud, Gloucestershire
Styal, Cheshire
Tetbury, Gloucestershire: to 1800
Trowbridge, Wiltshire
Uffculme, Devon
Uley, Gloucestershire
Uppermill, Lancashire
Wakefield, Yorkshire
Wellington, Somerset
Winchcombe, Gloucestershire
Wotton-under-Edge, Gloucestershire: 17th-19th centuries

CHAPTER 12

SOLVING SOME COMMON GENEALOGICAL PROBLEMS

This chapter will explore some of the more common and frustrating problems which you may encounter doing your research trip. It will suggest some solutions and hope that these will lead you to create your own answers, or spot your mistakes.

Unable To Locate A Subject's Birth Certificate

-check that your source of information for place is correct. If in doubt, go to the census nearest to that date and check for a street address. Remember, too, that Registration Districts were changed in 1852.

-check diverse spellings of both Christian and surnames. Did the subject have two forenames originally? They may have been juxtaposed, so be careful.

-child may have been registered with a totally different Christian name. My great-grandmother was always known as Annie Elizabeth. I completely failed to locate her birth certificate, though I did find her baptismal record. Some time later a great-aunt told me she had been registered as Harriet for some unknown reason, and so had had great difficulty proving, for social security reasons, her age!

-child may have been register with a different surname
   a) if illegitimate
   b) to hide illegitimacy
   c) if later adopted

Illegitimacy led to a great deal of lying to the authorities. The father of author Barbara Pym stated on his marriage certificate that he was the son of Thomas Pym, farmer, deceased.
   He was actually Thomas' grandson: his birth certificate showed he was the son of Phoebe Pym, a servant. No father's name was given on the certificate.

-registration was not compulsory until 1875 and many births were simply never registered.

-human error - did you read the indexes correctly or did you tire and miss some entries?

-cross-check with the I.G.I. and parish records.

-if you still cannot locate the child's entry, settle for that of a brother or sister. The same basic information will be given.

Unable To Locate A Marriage Certificate

Marriage records can be difficult and tedious to locate at St. Catherine's House if you are searching a common name, or if your information is incomplete; e.g., missing the bride's first and maiden name. There are, however, other reasons for failure.

-are the names of the parties correct? Check various spellings and any aliases; e.g., name by a previous marriage, or adoption.

-could they have married elsewhere? Check adjacent parishes and nearby large cities. My grandmother married in a Birmingham church though she lived in the parish of Clent.

-check other years. People have often falsified statements orally and in family bibles to hide a 'shot-gun wedding'.

-are you sure a wedding ever took place? Even if its intent was recorded in banns books or a license issued, this does not mean for certain that it happened.

-human error - did you read carefully enough?

-human error - was the marriage wrongly indexed? Try to imagine the possibilities.

-censuses - check where the first child was born. This could provide a valuable clue to the place and time of the marriage.

Unable To Locate A Death Certificate

-start at the latest possible date. This can be established from the censuses, or at least ninety years after the birth date. Work backwards, always bearing in mind the person's age.

-if the subject was widowed, she nay have remarried and died under a different name. Check the marriage indexes.

-did the person possibly die abroad or in military service? St. Catherine's has separate registers for deaths at sea and abroad. The War Office has a list of deaths during World War I, and earlier Armed Services records are in the Public Record Office.

-check at the Principal Probate Registry for a will. This would help pinpoint a date and place of death.

–human error – have you read the indexes carefully enough.

–human error – the information on death certificates can only be as good as the informant. This may not have been a close relative; errors in spellings and facts can ensue.

–alternative sources of information include burial registers, undertakers' records, obituaries, and monumental inscriptions.

Mother's Maiden Name Not Known

Try to locate a marriage certificate or record:

a) check the IGI in London; this is housed in Exhibition Road and the Society of Genealogists.

b) check the Pallot Index. This covers the years 1780-1837 and is especially strong for the London marriages (101 of 103 ancient parishes have been covered); forty English counties are also included. The Pallot Index is housed at the Institute of Genealogical and Heraldic Studies in Canterbury. (See Appendix D.) There is a fee for each search.

c) check Boyd's Marriage Index, either at the L.D.S. Library or the Society of Genealogists.

–did the subject or her husband or siblings leave a will? Check at the Principal Probate Registry. A will can give clues to her family's name and location.

–did the subject's children have any unusual middle names?

–check for the existence of a passport and re-check any family papers for clues you may have missed.

Failure To Find An Individual In The Census

The source of your address information, a certificate, newspaper clipping, etc., will very likely be out of date by the next census. You can:

–search a city directory of a date near to the census date.

–search the electoral rolls.

–if a small town, search its census records and those of adjacent towns. Be diligent, it can be very time consuming.

–human errors – on your part or that of the census-enumerator?

–check IGI, Boyd's, or the Pallot Index.

-could the person have lived in another household; for example, as a servant or visitor?

-a good knowledge of local and socioeconomic history might give clues as to the direction of migration. Wars, for example, have often had a profound effect on migration patterns. (See Chapter 10.)

When you come across an apparently insurmountable problem, do not feel defeated. Spread the facts out, sort them, analyze, and make a plan to get around the problem. Your answer may be buried deep in an index or a roll of microfilm, but if you do not look, you will never find it.

You Wish To Search One Of The Censuses 1891-1901

It is possible to obtain details of specific individuals named on censuses not yet released for general use. You must write to the Registrar General at St. Catherine's House, Kingsway, London W.I., enclosing L-15. You must state your purpose and that the subject is either dead or assents to the search, and you must supply the exact address of the subject. (This can be obtained from a registrar's certificate, burial, or baptismal record, or electoral rolls at the C.R.O.)

CHAPTER 13

THE FAMILY HISTORY SOCIETY:
TO JOIN OR NOT TO JOIN?

England is very fortunate to be served by over sixty local family history and genealogical societies. Hardly any part of the country is without a group to which you can turn for help, and some more populous counties can boast several societies. The oldest, the Society of Genealogists, is based in London with worldwide membership and has a long and scholarly history. For many years the Society was run on the lines of a gentleman's club, but with the burgeoning interest in genealogy since the 1960s, it has dusted off its image, opened itself up and has even moved from its venerable but cramped quarters in Kensington to a more spacious and utilitarian building in the East End of London. Membership applications must be supported by two sponsors, preferably members themselves, or by professional persons of your acquaintance. The cost is $43 for the first year, $28 per annum thereafter. If you do not wish to join the Society but would like to subscribe to *The Genealogist's Magazine* (quarterly), you may do so at a cost of $20 per annum.

Locally-based societies are a great deal smaller than the Society of Genealogists' annual membership fees range from $10 to $15 for overseas members. The emphasis among these groups is family history, a broader-based subject than genealogy, but with genealogical research as its firm foundation.

What do you get for you money? Newsletters, interest and publication lists, and more.

All societies issue newsletters and journals, quarterly. The Norfolk and Norwich Genealogical Society's quarterly, *The Norfolk Ancestor* is a sixteen-page journal, with a professional appearance. Members are also sent a hard-cover annual work, such as tax returns or parish records. The Birmingham and Midland Society for Genealogy and Heraldry publishes *The Midland Ancestor* quarterly, a forty-page journal with regular columns such as "Bookworm" and "Census Strays", as well as articles from members. Most newsletters and journals carry a query column, in which members place ads (free or for a small fee) to help find missing ancestors.

Another useful tool published by many groups is a members' interest list. Members submit lists of surnames in which they are interested, and the reader can scan the list and write to members with whom he or she has a common interest. It would be very useful to establish communication with such people well before a planned visit to England, not only to enlist their aid but to establish a working relationship which could reach fruition during the visit.

According to the size of the society, it will have a smaller or larger publications list. These could include a local genealogical records guide, parish register transcripts, census indexes, monument inscriptions, maps, plus publications of national societies.

These publications are generally unavailable except through the society and as they are in relatively small editions, they become rare and worth their weight in gold.

For the person visiting England, there is access to genealogical society libraries. The size and quality of the collection will vary tremendously, depending on the society. One library I visited was in the chairman's cellar and had a very higgledy-piggledy aspect: there was a card catalogue, and even a section of the IGI, but the chairman was the only person able to locate material. Fortunately, he was obliging and helpful. Another society library I used was housed in the basement of an educational institution, was well organized, and had on duty a volunteer to help members find what they needed.

Some larger societies have established postal lending libraries. This can be expensive but may be worth inquiring about. Generally, the lending library catalog is much shorter than the regular library's catalog.

The Birmingham and Midland Society goes a step further in helping new members by assigning each a correspondence secretary to whom the new member can write with any questions or problems. This is an innovation which should be applauded and imitated.

The overseas member can benefit enormously through entitlement to the Federation of Family History Societies Accommodation Register. Only F.H.S. members may buy a copy, which lists other members in most counties willing to offer bed and breakfast. Not only do you "sleep cheap" (and probably in cozy comfort), but you also get to 'talk shop' and quite possibly benefit from your hosts'local knowledge. The advantages are obvious. Your copy may be obtained for $2.25 surface mail or $2.8S airmail from Mrs. C. Walcot, 1 Strode Manor Farm Cottages, Netherbury, Bridport, Dorset DTG 5NG. Quote your society and membership number.

Remember that English genealogical and family history societies were not established as pedigree societies, such as the Daughters of the American Revolution. They are manifestations of a keen interest in local history and a desire for self-knowledge.

NOTE: A complete list of Family History Societies with addresses is given in Appendix C.

EPILOGUE

Tracing your genealogy and family history is a fascinating past-time and I hope that the reader will find the guidance in this book both informative and encouraging. The fabric of history has been woven by millions of individuals and their lives deserve to be recorded. Many left evidence of their movements and actions in censuses, parish registers, vestry minutes, and polls, even if they themselves were illiterate. It is our task to unearth this evidence and place it in logical sequence.

It is my hope that the section on archaic script and language will not disconcert but will leave you with a feeling of accomplishment at mastering virtually a new language.

The hints for traveling genealogists have been a result of my own experiences and I sincerely hope that they aid in planning and implementing a successful research trip. Enjoy your visit to the old country - may it be fruitful and happy!

BIBLIOGRAPHY

Burke, A.M. *Key To The Ancient Parish Reg-isters.* London, 1908.

Cox, Jane and Padfield, Timothy. *Tracing Your Ancestors In The Public Record Office.* London: Her Majesty's Stationery Office, 1981.

Emmison, F.G. *Archives And Local History.* London: Methuen, 1966.

Emmison, F.G. *How To Read Local Archives 1550-1700.* London: Historical Association, 1967.

Gardner, D.E. et al. *Genealogical Research In England And Wales.* Salt Lake City, UT: Book-craft, 1956-1959.

Grieve, Hilda. *Examples Of English Handwriting 1150-1750.* Essex Record Office, 1966.

West, John. *Village Records.* London: Phillimore, 1962, 1982.

Tate, W.E. *The Parish Chest.* Cambridge University Press, 1960.

APPENDIX A

WHAT TO TAKE TO ENGLAND

This appendix is designed as a checklist for the reader's convenience.

Genealogical Supplies

Pedigree charts
Family group sheets
Research index forms
Will forms
Census forms, 1841-1881
Birth, marriage, death registration search forms
Marriage registration search records
Baptismal register - search records
Records of previous relevant research
An adjustable focus 35mm camera
Black and white film (print or transparency)
Colour film
Pencils with erasers
Pencil sbarpener
Legal pads

Clothing & Accessories

All year round

    Sturdy walking shoes
    Light plastic foldaway raincoat
    Light jackets or cardigans
    Old jeans
    Old shirt or sweater
    Knee-high rainboots or slipovers
    Umbrella

Winter

    Heavy coat (waterproof)
    Warm or thermal underwear
    Gloves

Scarf
Woolly hat
Heavy wool sweaters
Heavyweight pants
Snow-type boots

Spring and Autumn

Lighter sweaters
Gloves
Headscarf or cap
Light raincoat
Shoes

Sumner

Dresses
Cotton skirts
Short-sleeved blouses/shirts
Light-weight pants
Sandals
Shoes

Personal Items

Passport
International Driver's license (available from American Automobile Association)
Britrail pass issued by British Rail (see Chapter 3)
Coach Pass
Credit cards: Visa, Mastercard, American Express, Diner's Club
Travelers checks in pounds sterling
Maps: road map, small scale maps
Itinerary
List of addresses of accomodations
List of appointments booked, with addresses
Flight tickets

Note About Maps

Good road maps of Great Britain are available in most bookstores at a reasonable price, but they do tend to become outdated extremely quickly. For the genealogist, small-scale maps of areas of interest (Ordnance Survey Maps) are available from Her Majesty's Stationary Office, 49 High Holborn, London. VC1V 6HB. These maps show small details such as farmhouses and trails.

APPENDIX B

DENOMINATIONAL REPOSITORIES

Nonconformists in general:

Dr. William's Library, 14, Gordon Square, London WC1H 0AG; tel: 01 387 1310

Specific nonconformist denominations:

United Reformed Church History Society, 86, Tavistock Place, London WC1; tel: 01 837 7661

Congregational Library, Memorial Hall, Farringdon Street, London EC4; tel: 01 236 2223

Baptist Union Library, 4, Southampton Row, London WC1; tel: 01 405 9803

Society of Friends Library, Friends House, Euston Road, London NW1; tel: 01 387 3601

Methodist Archives, Division of Property, Central Buildings, Oldham Street, Manchester M1 1JQ

Roman Catholicism

Catholic Record Society, 114, Mount Street, London W1Y 6AH
Jewish Records

Jewish Museum, Woburn House, Upper Woburn Place, London WC1; tel 01 387 3081/2

APPENDIX C

MEMBERS OF THE FEDERATION
OF FAMILY HISTORY SOCIETIES
IN GREAT BRITAIN AND THE UNITED STATES

Society of Genealogists
Mr. A. J. Camp, 14, Charterhouse Buildings, Goswell Road,
London EC1M 7BA

Institute of Heraldic and Genealogical Studies
Miss S. Fincher, Northgate, Canterbury, Kent

Avon see Bristol and Avon

Bedfordshire FHS
Mr. C. West, 17, Lombard St, Lidlington, Bedford MK43 0RP

Berkshire FHS
Mr. J. Gurnett, 34, Hawkesbury Drive, Fords Farm, Calcot,
Reading, Berkshire RG3 5ZR

Birmingham & Midland Society for Genealogy & Heraldry
Mrs. J. Watkins, 92 Dimmingsdale Bank, Birmingham, West
Midlands B32 1ST

Bristol and Avon FHS
Mrs. K. Kearsey, 135, Cotham Brown, Bristol BS6 6AD

Buckinghamshire FHS
Mrs. E. McLaughlin, 18 Rudds Lane, Haddenham, Aylesbury,
Bucks.

Cambridgeshire FHS
Mrs. P. Close, 56 The Street, Kirtling, Newmarket,
Cambridgeshire CB8 9PB

193

FHS of Cheshire
Mrs. D. Foxcroft, 5 Gordon Ave., Bromborough, Wirral, Merseyside

Cleveland FHS
Mr. A. Sampson, 1, Oxgang Close, Redcar TS10 4ND

Cornwall FHS
Mr. M. Martin, Chimneypots, Sunny Corner, Cusgarne, Truro, Cornwall TR4 8SE

Cumbria FHS
Mrs. M. Russell, 32 Granada Road, Denton, Manchester M34 2LJ

Derbyshire FHS
Mrs. P. Marples, 15, Elmhurst Road, Forest Town, Mansfield, Nottinghamshire NG19 0EV

Devon FHS
Miss V. Bluett, 63, Old Laira Road, Laira, Plymouth, Devon PL3 5BL

Doncaster FHS
Miss E. Whitehouse, 7 Sherburn Close, Skellow, Doncaster, S. Yorkshire DN 6 8LG

Dorset see Somerset & Dorset

Durham see Northumberland & Durham

Essex FHS
Mr. C. Lewis, 48, Walton Road, Frinton-on-Sea, Essex CO13 0AG

Folkestone & District
Mrs. M. Criddle, 22, Church Road, Cheriton, Folkestone, Kent

Gloucestershire FHS
Mr. J. Vaughan, 1, Roxton Drive, The Reddings, Cheltenham, Glos. GL51 6SQ

Hampshire Genealogical Society
Mrs. J. Hobbs, 12, Ashling House, Chidham Walk, Havant, Hants. PO9 1DY

Herefordshire FHS
Mrs. V. Hadley, 255, Whitecross Road, Hereford HR4 0LT

Hertfordshire F&PHS
Mrs. J. Laidlaw, 155, Jessop Road, Stevenage, Herts.

Kent FHS
Mrs. H. Lewis, 17, Abbots Place, Canterbury, Kent CT1 2AH

North West Kent FHS
Miss J. M. Biggs, 39, Nightingale Road, Petts Wood, Orping-
ton, Kent BR5 1BH

Lancashire Family History and Heraldry Society
Mr. R. Hampson, 7, Margaret Street, Oldham, Lancs. OL2
8RP

Leicestershire FHS
Miss S. Brown, 25, Homecroft Drive, Packington, Ashby de la
Zouche, Leics.

Society for Lincolnshire History & Arch. (Family History
Section)
Mrs. E Robson, 135 Baldertongate, Newark, Notts. NG24 1RY

Liverpool & District FHS
Mr. H. Culling, 11, Lisburn Lane, Tuebrook, Liverpool

East of London FHS
Mr. A. Polybank, Flat 2, 193-7 Mile End Road, London E1
4AA

Isle of Man FHS
Miss P. Killip, 9, Sandringham Drive, Onchan, IOM

Manchester & Lancashire FHS
Mr. E. Crosby, 32, Bournlea Avenue, Burnage, Manchester
M19 1AF

Central Middlesex FHS
Mrs E. V. Pirie, 44, Dorchester Avenue, North Harrow, Middlesex HA2 7AU

North Middlesex FHS
Miss J. Lewis, 15, Milton Road, Walthamstow, London E17

West Middlesex FHS
Mrs. M. Morton, 92, Avondale Ave, Staines, Middlesex TW18 2NF

Norfolk & Norwich GS
Miss C. Hood, 293, Dereham Road, Norwich NR2 3TH

Northamtonshire FHS
Miss L. Wesley, 56, Gloucester Crescent, Delapre, Northampton NN4 9PR

Northumberland & Durham FHS
Mr. J. K. Brown, 33, South Bend, Brunton Park, Newcastle-on-Tyne, NE3 5TR

Nottinghamshire FHS
Miss S. M. Leeds, 35, Kingswood Road, West Bridgford, Nottingham NG2 7HT

Oxfordshire FHS
Mrs. V. Lee, Speedwell, North Moreton, Oxon. OX11 9BG

Peterborough & District FHS
Mrs. C. Newman, 106, London Road, Peterborough, Cambs PE2 9BY

Sheffield & District FHS
Mrs. E. Furey, 58, Stumperlowe Crescent Road, Sheffield, S10 3PR

Shropshire FHS
Mrs. G. Lewis, 15, Wesley Drive, Oakengates, Telford, Shropshire TF2 0DZ

Somerset & Dorset FHS
Mr. T. P. Farmer, BruLands, Marston Road, Sherborne, Dorset DT9 4BL

Staffordshire see Birmingham

Suffolk Genealogy Society
Mrs. K. Bardwell, 2, Fern Avenue, North Oulton Broad, Lowestoft, Suffolk

East Surrey FHS
Mrs. M. Brackpool, 370, Chipstead Valley Road, Coulsdon, Surrey CR3 3BF

West Surrey FHS
Mrs. M. Taylor, 60, Ashley Road, Farnborough, Hants. GU14 7HB

Sussex FHS
Mrs. B. Mottershead, 44 The Green, Southwick, Sussex, BN4 4FR

Waltham Forest FHS
Mrs. J. Thompson, 49 Tavistock Avenue, Walthamstow, London E17 6HR

Warwickshire see Birmingham

Wiltshire FHS
Mrs. M. R. Moore, 17, Blakeney Avenue, Nythe, Swindon, Wilts. SN3 3NE

Windsor, Slough & District FHS
Mrs. J. Catlin, 2, Faircroft, Slough SL2 1HJ, Bucks.

Woolwich & District FHS
Ms. S. Highley, 4, Church Road, Bexleyheath, Kent

Worcestershire see Birmingham

Yorks. Arch. Society (Family and Pop. Studies Section)
Mrs. B. Shimwell, 24, Holt Park Road, Adel, Leeds LS16 7QS

East Yorks. FHS
Mr. R. E. Walgate, 9 Stepney Grove, Scarborough, North Yorks. YO12 5DF

York FHS
Mrs. F. Foster, 1, Ouse Lea, Shipton Road, York YO3 6SA

****

International Society for British Genealogy and Family History
POB 20425, Cleveland OH 44120

National Genealogical Society
4527 17th St N., Arlington VA 22207-2363

Chicago Genealogical Society
POB 1160, Chicago IL 60690

Florida Genealogical Society
POB 18624, Tampa FL 33679

International Genealogy Fellowship of Rotarians
5721 Antietam Dr., Sarasota FL 33581

Ventura County Genealogical Society
POB DN, Ventura CA 93002

Houston Genealogical Forum
POB 271469, Houston TX 77277-1469

Jefferson County Genealogical Society
POB 174, Oskaloosa KS 66066

English Interest Group, Minnesota Genealogical Society
9009 Northwood Circle, New Hope MN 55427

Santa Barbara County Genealogical Society
POB 1174, Goleta CA 93116

Genealogical Association of Sacramento
1230 42nd Ave., Sacramento CA 95822

Utah Genealogical Society
POB 1144, Salt Lake City UT 84110

Seattle Genealogical Society
POB 549, Seattle WA 98111

APPENDIX D

REGIONAL TOURIST BOARDS OF ENGLAND

London
British Tourist Authority Information Center, 64 St. James's Street, London SW1; tel: 01-499-9325

London Tourist Board, 26 Grosvenor Gardens, London SW1; tel: 01-730 0791

NOTE: For personal callers only, the L.T.B. has bureaux on Platform 15 at Victoria Station, Harrods Fourth Floor, Selfridges Ground Floor and Heathrow Central Underground Station.

South East England Tourist Board
Chevoit House, 4-6 Monson Road, Tunbridge Wells, Kent; tel: 0892 40766

Southern Tourist Board
Old Town Hall, Leigh Road, Eastleigh, Hampshire; tel: 0703 616027

Isle of Wight Tourist Board
21 High Street, Newport, Isle of Wight; tel: 0983 524343 or 525141

West Country Tourist Board
Trinity Court, 37 Southernhay East, Exeter, Devon; tel: 0392 76351

West Midlands
Heart of England Tourist Board, POB 15, Worcester; tel: 0905 29511

South Midlands
Thames and Chilterns Tourist Board, POB 10, 8 The Market
Place, Abingdon, Oxon.; tel: 0235 22711

East Anglia Tourist Board
14 Museum Street, Ipswich, Suffolk; tel: 0473 214211

East Midlands Tourist Board
Exchequergate, Lincoln; tel: 0522 31521

Lancashire, Cheshire & Peak District
North West Tourist Board, The Last Drop Village, Bromley
Cross, Bolton, Lancashire; tel: 0204 591511

Yorkshire & Humberside Tourist Board
312 Tadcaster Road, York, North Yorkshire; tel: 0904 707961

Isle of Man Tourist Board
13 Victoria Street, Douglas, Isle of Man; tel: 0624 4323

Cumbria, Northumbria & Durham
Northumbria Tourist Board, 9 Osborne Terrace, Newcastle-
upon-Tyne; tel: 0632 817744

British Tourist Authority Offices in the USA
680 5th Ave., New York NY 10019; tel: (212) 581-4700

612 S Flower St., Los Angeles CA 90017; tel: (213) 623 8196

John Hancock Center, 875 N. Michigan Ave. #3320, Chicago
IL 60611; tel: (312)-787- 0490

These offices can supply general information, maps,
etc.

APPENDIX E

AMERICAN/ENGLISH VOCABULARY LIST

AMERICAN	ENGLISH
baggageroom	left luggage office
band-aid	elastoplast/plaster
bathtub	bath
billfold	wallet
broil	grill
call collect	reverse charges
carnival	fair
check (restaurant)	bill
chips	crisps
closet	wardrobe
dessert	pudding/sweet
divided hwy	dual carriageway
down town	city centre
druggist	chemist
elevator	lift
fall	autumn
faucet	tap
freeway	motorway
French fries	chips
garbage can	dustbin
directory assistance	directory enquiries
janitor	caretaker
lawyer	solicitor
legal holiday	bank holiday
liquor	spirits
long distance	trunk call
lost & found	lost property
mailbox	pillar box
make reservation	book
movie theater	cinema

news dealer	newsagent
odometer	mileometer
one way ticket	single ticket
outlet/socket	power point
pantie hose	tights
parking lot	car park
pass (vehicle)	overtake
pavement	road
period	full-stop
pullman	sleeping-car
purse/pocket book	handbag
raincoat	mac/macintosh
restroom	cloakroom/toilet or lavatory
round trip ticket	return ticket
salesclerk	shop-assistant
schedule	timetable
sidewalk	pavement
stand in line	queue
stoplight	traffic light
two weeks	fortnight
windshield	windscreen
wire	telegram
with or without milk/cream	black or white?
yard	garden
zero	nought
zip code	postal code

APPENDIX F

MEDIEVAL LATIN WORD LIST

abatio	annulment
abavia/us	2nd great-grandmother/ father
abortivus	prematurely born
accasatus	resident tenant
acuarius	needlemaker
addico	I promise
adolescens	young man
adoperatio	working; application
adoptivus	adopted
adprimas	first of all
adultus	young boy
aedilis	architect
aetas	age
aetatis	aged
agellarius	husbandman
agenda	mass for the dead
agnomentum	surname
agricola	farmer
aldermannus	ealdorman, nobleman
alius	the other (of 2)
alleluia clausum	Septuagissima Sunday
alutarius	both (of this parish)
amicus	kinsman
amita	aunt on father's side
amita magna	grandfather's sister
androchia	dairymaid
anella	old woman
anime	masses for the dead
Animarum commemoratio	All Soul's Day (Nov. 2)
anno domini	in the year of our Lord

annonymus/a	stillborn child
Annuntiatio	the Annunciatio (March 25)
apothecarius	pharmacist
apprenticius	apprentice
approbatio testamenti	probate of testament
archiator	doctor
arcularius	carpenter
argentum	cash
armentarius	herdsman
asarcha	Lent
Assumptio	Feast of the Assumption (Aug. 15)
Assumptio a Salvatoris Day	Ascension Day
atava	grandmother
aucarius	gooseherd
aurifaber	goldsmith
avia	grandmother
avuncula	aunt
ava/us	grandmother/father
avunculus magnus/major	great-uncle
baccalaureus	bachelor
ballistrarius	gunsmith
baptizatio	baptism
barcarius	shipmaker
bastardus	bastard
beda	prayer
belmannus	bell-ringer
bercarius	shepherd, tanner
bidens	sheep
bigamia	2nd marriage
bijuges (pl.)	candelaria
bolstera	bolster
bondus	head of household
boverius	oxherd
bovicula	heifer
boviculus	bullock
bostio	plough-boy
bramum	well, pit
Brandones	1st Sunday in Lent
braciator	brewer
bubularius	oxherd
bubulcus	oxherd, ploughman
buscarius	butcher
butularius	butter

buttarius	cooper
buistarius	box-maker
chivalerus	knight
cabo	stallion
caelebs	see celebs
caligator	hosier
camera	room, chamber
campana	bell, clock
campanitor	bell-ringer
campus	field
campester	peasant
Candelaria	Candlemas (February 2nd)
candelifex	chandler
capa	cape, hooded cloak
carbo	coal
carbonarius	coal-miner
carecarius	carter, ploughman
caretta	cart
carnificium	shambles, meat market
carnlevaria	Shrove Tuesday
carnisbrevium	beginning of Lent
carrucator	ploughman
casale	village
caskettum	casket
cassatio	nullification
catabulum	pigsty
catallum & capitale	chattel, moveable goods
Cathedra, Festum Sancti Petri in,	St. Peter's Chair (Feb. 22)
causarius	hatmaker
celebs	single or widowed
cellarium	store-room
cellarius	butler
cimiterius	mason
(dies) cene ad mandatum	Maundy Thursday
cerefactor	chandler
cervisiarius	ale-house keeper
Charisma	Whit Sunday
chirothecator	glover
chirugus	surgeon
Circumcisio Domini	The Circumcision (Jan. 1)
cista	coffin
cistarius	box-maker
cistator	treasurer
Clausio Pasche	Sunday after Easter
Clausio Pentecostes	Trinity Sunday

claustrarius	locksmith
coffinarius	basket-maker
cognatus	cousin, kinsman
comes	earl, count
commater	godmother
compater	godfather
Conceptio Beati Virginis	Feast of the Conception (December 8)
conjug:	married
connutrucius	foster-brother
contractio	marriage contract
Conversatio Sancti Pauli	Conversion of St. Paul (Jan. 25)
convicina	neighbor
coppa	hen
coquina	kitchen furniture
cordifer	rope-maker
cordonarius	leather-maker
(festum dies) corpus Christi	Thursday after Trinity
cotuca	tunic
cotarius	cottager
crastinum	tomorrow
croftum	plot of land
crumenarius	pursemaker
cudarus	forester
cutellarius	cutler
cum	by, with
coupa	cup, bowl
cupbordum	cupboard
cutissima	curtain
custor	sacristan
d.s.p.	died without issue
d.v.m.	died while mother living
d.v.p.	died while father living
dayaria	dairy
decada	ten
decennarius	tithing-man
decima	tithing
(festum) Decollationis Sancti Johanni Baptisti	Beheading of St. John (Aug 29)
deducator ferarum	gamekeeper
defensiva	fence
denarius	penny
derelicta	widow
desponsatio	betrothal, marriage
didymus	twin

dies Dominica	Sunday
dies Soles	Sunday
dies Lune	Monday
dies Martis	Tuesday
dies Mercurii	Wednesday
dies Wodenis	Wednesday
dies Jovis	Thursday
dies Veneris	Friday
dies Veneris Bonus/Sancta	Good Friday
dies Sabbati (-nus)	Saturday
dies Saturni	Saturday
digamus	twice married
disjugata	unmarried woman
dispunctuo	settle accounts
deviso	bequeath
doga	wainscot
domesticalia	household goods
domus	house
domus brasinea	brew-house
domus carbonum	coal-house
domus cervisiana	ale-house
domus feni	barn
domus porcorum	pigsty
domus vaccarum	cow-shed
domificator	carpenter, builder
dos	dower, endowment
drapa	cloth
draperus	draper
dressura	serving-board
ducena	twelve
dum	when, since
eductio carruce	Plough Monday (1st after Epiphany)
eloco	give in marriage
emptum	purchase
engia (pl)	mortgage
enopola	taverner
entalliator	stone-carver
ephestris	surcoat
ephipparius	saddler
Epiphania Domini	Epiphany (Jan 6)
equus	horse
eques	knight
ergo	therefore
ericetum	heath, moor
eruptio	spring of water

escaria	sideboard
escarium	manger
et	and
(festum) exaltionis Sancti Crucis	Holy Cross Day (Sept. 14)
excusor	printer
executor testamenti	executor of will
exheredatus	disinherited
exlex	outlaw
expensa	storeroom
extravagus	vagrant
faber cupri	coopersmith
faber ferrarius	blacksmith
faber lignarius	joiner
faber scriniarius	cabinet-maker
fabrica	forge
falcata	measure of a meadow
famulia	household
fantulus/fantula	little boy or girl
fenestra	window
fena	hay-fields
ferdingus	farthing (1/4 penny)
feria	festival, weekday
feria prima	Sunday
feria secunda etc.	Monday
ferma	farm
ferocia	quilt, mattress
ferreum	horse-shoe
ferrifaber	iron-smith
fidatio	betrothal
fidejussor	godparent
filius	son
filius in lege	son-in-law
filius naturalis	bastard
filiaster	stepson, son-in-law
filiastra	step-daughter
filiola/us	god-daughter/son
fiscalia	taxes
flecciator	fletcher
florinus	gold coin
focarium	hearth
fons	well
foramen	window-pane
fossor	digger, miner

fotherator	furrier
frater	brother
frater in lege	brother-in-law
fratruelusa/us	niece/nephew
frethum	hedge
fritha	woodland, pasture
frumentum	wheat
frunitor	tanner
fugarius	drover
fullaticus	fuller
furlongus	furlong (1/8 mile)
Galilea	porch of church
galitarius	shoemaker
ganata	bowl
garba	sheaf (of corn)
garcifer	servant
gardinum	garden, orchard
gardinarius	gardener
gavella	family holding
geldum	tax
gemelli	twins
gilda	guild
(terra) glebalis	glebe-land
grabatum	skirt
gramen	pasturage
grammaticulus	schoolboy
grana	grain
granarium	granary
grangia decimalis	tithe-barn
grotus	groat (coin)
habedassarius	haberdasher
hebdomada	week
heres	heir
histrio	player, minstrel
homo	man
hordeum	barley
horilogium	clock
horrea	barn
hortus	garden
hortulanus	gardener
hospitium	household
hostillarius	inn-keeper
humatus	buried
hundredum	hundred (division of county)
husbandus	husbandman

hypante	Candlemas (Feb. 2)
ignotus	illegitimate
imbrevio	to record in writing
impendo	give, spend
impraegnata	pregnant before marriage
imprimis	in the first place
inconjugatus	unwed
indigentia (pl)	necessaries
infrascriptus	written below
inhumatio	burial
(festum) innocentium	Holy Innocents (Dec. 28)
insinuo	register a will
intratio	entry (into a building)
ire (eo)	go
itaquod	on condition that
iter	path
item	next (on list), also
jakkum	sleeveless tunic
jejunium guadragesimale	Lent
(caput) jejuni	Ash Wednesday
judex	judge
juramentus exhibitum fuit	certificate (of burial in wool)
jus	right, due
juvencula	girl
juvenis	young man
juxta	according to
laboratio	ploughing
laboro ad	work at
laicus	layman
lana	wool or wool-tax
lanatus	"buried in wool"
lanifex	clothier
landa	untilled land
lapis	stone (weight)
lararium	closet
lardaria	larder
largitas	width
latro	thief
lautumus	mason
lectus	bed-clothes, bed
legatio	legacy
lego in manus	bequeath
laetare	third Sunday of Lent
liber	book, freeman
libra	pound (weight or money)

lignarius	joiner
lignum	wood
ligniscissor	woodcutter
linea	linen cloth or garment
macellaria	meat-market
macellarius	butcher
macerio	mason
magister	master (of school or trade)
major	adult
mala	rent, mail
malarium	orchard
malluvium	wash-basin
maunda	hamper
mare	sea
maria	lake
marium	moor, marsh
maritagium	marriage
maritellus	husband
mater	mother
mater meretrix	illegitimate mother
matrimonium	dowry
mauseolum	coffin, tomb
medicus	physician
mensa	food, table
meta	boundary
methodus	road
migratio ad Christum/Dominum miles	die knight
mille	thousand
mobile	movable goods
modius	a peck (measure
molendinum	mill
molendinum venti	windmill
molitarius corlii	leather-worker
morganaticus	morganatic (marriage)
multrix	milk-maid
mulier	wife
multardus	shepherd
munimen	enclosure
murena	marsh
murus	wall
napiria	table linen
natalicium	birthday, Saint's day
natalicium Dominicum	Christmas
nativitas	birthplace
nativitatis Domini	Christmas

nativitas beate Marie	Birth of the Blessed Mary (Sept. 8)
nepos	nephew
neptis	niece
netrix	spinster
nomen proprium	baptismal name
novercarius (testamentum)	stepfather
noncupative facto	oral will
nubo	give in marriage
nubo me	wed
obiit	died
obiit sine prole	died without issue
opus	work
orphanus	orphan
ovis	sheep
ovianus	shepherd
pactum	contract, lease
pagus	village
pajettus	page, servant
pallium	funeral shroud
(Dominica) in palmis	Palm Sunday
palus	marsh, fence
pandoxatorium	ale-house
panis	bread
palna	roof-timber storey of house
pannus	cloth, garment
paraphernalia	married woman's property
(dies) paracevensis	Good Friday
parentalia	family, kin
parochia	parish, parish church
Pascha	Easter Sunday
Pascha Album	Low Sunday
Pascha Minus	Palm Sunday
dies Lune Paschalis	Easter Monday
pascua & pastura	pasture
patella	bowl, pan
pater	father
pater in lege	father-in-law
patrinus	godfater
patruus magnus	great-uncle
pauso	rest, die
peciata	peck (measure)
pecunia	money
pelvis	basin
penarium	cupboard

pendilium	curtain
Pentecoste	Pentecost
penulator	furrier
per	by, on (day of the week)
peregrinus	pilgrim
perempticius	apprentice
(dies Luna) perjurata	second Monday after Easter
persinctus	boundary
persolutio	payment in full
pestilentia	the Plague
pictor	painter
pilleus	cap
pincernarius	butler
piscenarius	fishmonger
platula	plate
plus	more
polis	city
polata	pole (measure of land)
pomarium	orchard
pondus	weight, pound
porcarius	swineherd
porcus	pig
posteritas	descendants
purcingtus	boundary
preco	watchman
precontractus	precontract (of marriage)
pregnatus	pregnant
prehibitus	aforesaid
prememoratus	previously mentioned
presbyter	old man, priest
prevolentia	antecedent will
prida	mortgage
primogenitor	first-born
prevignus	stepson
pro	because of, for
proava/us	great-grandmother/father
procreamen	offspring
proles	offspring
proles spuria	illegitimate offspring
propinquitas	kinsfolk
provincia	shire, county
pucella & puella	girl
puer	boy
puerpera	mother
Purificans	Candlemas (February 2)

quadragesima	Lent
(Dominica) quadragesime	first Sunday in Lent
quadravus	great-great-grandfather
quadriga	wagon
quasimodo geniti	Low Sunday
quondam	formerly
quoniam	since, because
Ramispalme	Palm Sunday
relicta	widow
(dies Dominica) reliquiarium	Relic Sunday (first after July 7)
resurrectio Dominica	Easter Sunday
roparius	rope-maker
rusticus	peasant
(dies) Sabbatinus	Saturday
(dies) Sabbatainus sanctus	Holy Saturday
sacerdos	priest
sarrator	sawyer
shamellum	shambles, meat market
shira	shire
scholarius	scholar
scilicet	namely
scotus de capite	poll-tax
sculptor lapidum	mason
scyphus	cup
se	him
seculum	worldly affairs
sepiens	hay-maker
Septuagesima	Septuagesima Sunday
sepultura	buried
sericum	silk
servitor & serviens	servant
sestertius	shilling
silvacedus	woodcutter
simplex	of low rank
sobrina/us	cousin on mother's side
socius	fellow
solemnia nuptiarum	to celebrate a marriage
solidum	undivided property
solidus	shilling
soror	sister
sororius	sister's husband
spera	sideboard
spondea rotans	trundle bed
sponsalia	banns of marriage
sponsus/a	spouse

statim	at once
stuprata	pregnant out of wedlock
sudarium	napkin
suarium	shroud
sus	swine
sutor caligarius	hosier
sutor chirothecarius	glover
sutor vestarius	tailor
suus	own
taberna	tavern, inn
tabernio	inn-keeper
tabula	board, shutter
tabula mansalis	table
tallia	tally
tannator	tanner
tantellus	cousin
tector	thatcher
tenementum	house
testamentum	will, bequest
textator	weaver
tia	maternal aunt
traditio & tradux	inheritance
transfiguratio Domini	Transfiguration (August 6)
tumba	tomb
tunica	coat
ulna	ell (measure of length)
ulterior	additional
unicus/a	unmarried man/woman
uxor	Mrs., wife
vedovus	widower
viciatus	bastard
vidua	widow
vincula Sancti Petri	Saint Peter's Chains (Aug. 1)
warda	guardianship
xped	christened

INDEX

Allen County Public Library, 25–28 map 29

Alphabet, general 53 lower-case letters 41 upper-case letters 40

American/English vocabulary list, 201 202

Ancient documents, abbreviations and contractions 38 39 archaic terms 38 exercises in reading and interpreting 49–51 handwriting 39–42 Latin reading and interpreting 42–49 spelling 37 38

British Library, location and holdings, and maps 128–130

Calendar date changes, 42

Census, use in finding immigrant ancestor 3 4

City Record Offices, locations and holdings 73–113

Counties in England, after 1974 (map) 15 prior to 1974 (map) 14

County Record Offices, locations and holdings 73–113

County archive research network, 73 74

Customs records, use in finding an immigrant ancestor 4

Denominational repositories, 191

Diocesan Record Offices, locations and holdings 73–113

Documentation hints, 2 3

Ecclesiastical jurisdictions within each county until 1858, 59–65

Emigration and migration, genealogical sources to trace a mobile ancestor 156–158 patterns 149–148

Emigration to the American colonies, seventeenth and eighteenth centuries 149–155

England, climate 34 35 clothing and accessories for the trip 189–190 currency 35 eating out 33 34 electrical gadgets 35 Family History Society membership 183 184 genealogical supplies for the trip 189 manners and customs 34 map features 139 140 maps for the trip 190 private transport 31 32 public transport 32 33 telephones 35 tourist boards in England and the U.S. 199–200

English genealogical resources in U.S. libraries 17–28

English records at the Allen County Public Library 26–28

English records at the LDS Church 18 19

English records at the Newberry Library 25

Family History Centers, branch libraries of the LDS Church 22 23

Family group sheet, chart 11

Federation of Family History Societies in Great Britain and the U.S., members 193–198

Genealogical Library of the Church of Latter-Day Saints (LDS Church), 17–23

Genealogical problem solving hints, no birth certificate 179 180 no census record 181 182 no death certificate 180 181 no maiden name given 181 no marriage certificate 180

Geography of England, 5

217

Handwriting, 39–42 numerals 52

International Genealogical Index (IGI) 19–21 23

LDS Church, 17–23 branch library location and holdings 131

Latin word list, medieval 203–215

Maps, Aston Fields estate map c1878–81 147 county 145 146 enclosure 142 143 estate 143 144 glebe terriers 145 nineteenth century 140 Stoke Prior tithe map c1840 148 tithe 140–142 use of 139–146

Naturalization records, use in finding an immigrant ancestor 4

Newberry Library, 23–25

Occupational gazetteer, 159–177

Parish church, dates important to its development 137 use of gravestones 135 136 use of memorials housed inside church 136 137 use of 133–135

Peculiars, 58 59

Pedigree chart, 12

Primary sources, 2

Principle Probate Registry, location and holdings, and map 126–128

Probate record terms, 65 66

Public Record Office, location and holdings 68–72 116 117 map (Chancery Lane) 114 map (Kew) 54

Record Office holdings, 55–58 66–68

Record Offices and libraries, 55–72

Research basics, 1–3

Research index, chart 13

Research objectives planning for trip to England, 5

Saint Catherine's House, locations and holdings 116 117 map 118

Secondary sources, 2

Ships' passenger lists, use in finding an immigrant ancestor 4

Society of Genealogists, location and holdings 120–126 map 119

Trip preparations, general 7–10

Wills, locations 59